THE CARING GOD

THECARINGGOD
PERSPECTIVES ON PROVIDENCE

Edited by
CARL S. MEYER and HERBERT T. MAYER

Publishing House
St. Louis   London

Concordia Publishing House, St. Louis, Missouri
Concordia Publishing House Ltd., London, E. C. 1
Copyright © 1973 Concordia Publishing House

Library of Congress Catalog Card No. 72-91151
ISBN 0-570-03228-8

MANUFACTURED IN THE UNITED STATES OF AMERICA

Contents

Dedicated to
LUDWIG FUERBRINGER

Contributors

MARTIN H. SCHARLEMANN, graduate professor of exegetical theology at Concordia Seminary, St. Louis, Mo., and first non-Roman Catholic theologian to study at the Pontifical Institute in Rome, also occupies the rank of Brigadier Chaplain in the Air Force Reserves and is the author of numerous articles, studies, and books, including *Toward Tomorrow* (1960), *Proclaiming the Parables* (1962), *Healing and Redemption* (1965), and *The Church's Social Responsibility* (1970).

RICHARD BAEPLER is dean of Christ College and professor of history at Valparaiso University, Valparaiso, Ind. Dr. Baepler studied in Hamburg and Erlangen, Germany, and received his PhD. from the Divinity School of the University of Chicago in 1964. He has been editorially associated with *Dialog* and has served as head of the department of theology of Valparaiso University.

CURTIS E. HUBER is professor of philosophy at Pacific Lutheran University, Tacoma, Wash. Dr. Huber did graduate work at Valparaiso and Harvard Universities and received his PhD. at the University of Wisconsin. He previously taught systematic theology at Concordia Theological Seminary, Springfield, Ill.

RALPH C. UNDERWAGER, professor of psychology at St. Olaf College, Northfield, Minn., is a certified clinical psychologist on the staff of Youth Research Center and director of the psychology department of Nicollet Clinic in Minneapolis. He is one of the authors of *A Study of Generations* (Augsburg, 1972).

DAVID S. SCHULLER, associate director of the American Association of Theological Schools, Dayton, Ohio, has had a varied background in the areas of homiletics, pastoral theology, welfare, and the social responsibility and urban problems of the church. Dr. Schuller served for two years as director of urban seminars for the National

9

Council of Churches. He is the author of numerous books and articles, including the following: *The Church's Ministry to Youth in Trouble* (1959), *Contemporary Social Problems* (1960), *The New Urban Society* (1966), *Emerging Shapes of the Church* (1967), and *Power Structures and the Church* (1969),

CARL S. MEYER † graduate professor of historical theology at Concordia Seminary, St. Louis, Mo. Dr. Meyer (PhD, University of Chicago, 1954) was a member of various historical societies and director of the Foundation for Reformation Research in St. Louis. He is the author of *Elizabeth I and the Religious Settlement of 1559* (1960), *Log Cabin to Luther Tower* (1965), and *Moving Frontiers* (1964), and has edited several books specifically dealing with Lutheran church history. (Dr. Meyer died Dec. 17, 1972, at the age of 65 as this book was being readied for printing.)

WARREN RUBEL, professor of literature at Valparaiso University, Valparaiso, Ind., has been especially active and productive in art and literature as writer and critic.

JOHN C. GIENAPP is assistant professor of natural science at Concordia Senior College, Fort Wayne, Ind.

HERBERT T. MAYER, chairman of the department of historical theology at Concordia Seminary, St. Louis, Mo., since 1964, is also the managing editor of the *Concordia Theological Monthly* and the author of *Interpreting the Holy Scriptures* (1967) and *The Books of the New Testament* (1969).

Foreword

The title of this book is dependent on one of the ancient collects of the church. The collect invokes God, "whose providence never fails in its ordering" or "whose never-failing providence ordereth all things both in heaven and earth." The petitioner acknowledges that man and the world of nature, the universe and the corps of angelic beings, the demonic, the celestial, and the human are ordered by the Omnipotent. He does not raise the question of the origin of evil or of its cause.

The relationship between the providence of God and man's freedom of action must also be raised. God orders all things; the protection of His providence is admitted; the course of this world is ordered by His governance. Is all this a surrender into the hands of God? It can be maintained that man's independence and individualism scarcely allow him to make such a total surrender. His intelligence, his dominance over the forces of nature and the beasts of the field, his know-how in technology and advances in the physical sciences seem to rule out a dependence on God, at least partially if not totally. The story of the rise and fall of nations, peoples, civilizations, and cultures testifies to a relentless procession of time with reoccurring patterns, and it speaks about meaning in history, it seems, or possibly about a glorious consummation not easily discernible.

Considerations of this kind impelled the authors of the various chapters here presented to probe more deeply into the meaning of providence for the Western man of the last third of the 20th century. Some will contend that modern man is not interested in the question of providence; he needs to be convinced first of all of the existence of God. The writers know that the deniers of God's existence constitute one group, a group not concerned about providence. However, there are those who believe that God exists. Nevertheless, if they ponder the question at all, they are not greatly concerned about the meaning of providence for their own lives. They are fatalists or crass determinists; some pay intense attention to horoscopes, predictions based on reading the stars. Can these people be told about the meaning of providence for our age? If so, the question of "God's never-failing providence" needs to be explored from various angles.

The study here presented, therefore, does not deal only with Biblical and theological answers to the question. It is designed to present explorations into other fields of human knowledge, for instance, the social sciences, the behavioral sciences, natural science, the arts and literature, history, and philosophy.

The authority of the Scriptures properly requires that the introductory chapter should present an interpretation of the teachings of Scripture about providence. That the author builds his presentation into the framework of the activities associated individually with each of the three Persons of the Trinity is in harmony with the presuppositions inherent to the Trinitarian belief which he and his co-contributors profess. The concept of a God who creates, redeems, and sanctifies in His providential activities is one that is readily ascertainable from the Scriptures.

The formulation of Biblical teachings into systems of theology has been the preoccupation of many of the greatest Christian thinkers. Augustine, Aquinas, Luther, and Calvin stand out as giants among them. Each one has considerable to say about providence. Augustine's *City of God* dominated the thought of many centuries and is still heard in the 20th. Thomist theology has been elevated into a dominant role by Leo XIII. Perhaps no theologian after Augustine has so profoundly influenced the doctrine of God's sovereignty as John Calvin. In the various editions of his *Institutes of the Christian Religion* Calvin was not consistent in placing the doctrine of providence under "creation," but he was entirely consistent in his belief in providence. He defined providence "not that by which God idly observes from heaven what takes place on earth, but that by which as keeper of the keys, he governs all things." He speaks of God attending "to the regulation of individual events," proceeding according to His set plans. Calvin rules out chance, fortune, and all Stoic and popular variations of these terms.

The contention is sometimes made that the doctrine of providence is not Lutheran: this needs to be faced. An inspection of the indices—better a close reading—of Luther's works can dispel the contention. He says, for instance, that "we would experience . . . afflictions daily if it were not for God's providence." Again he says: "Thus in this passage we observe the providence of God according to whose counsel the ungodly are punished but the good are preserved." The hidden God to Luther is providential. God shows His people His backside, and only after His promises have been fulfilled does He show His face. The classical Lutheran dogmaticians, Martin Chemnitz, John Gerhard, and John Andrew Quenstedt, knew and employed the term. Lutherans have good precedents for using the word. The concept, it must be admitted, is found more frequently in Lutheran theology than the actual term. The Lutheran Confessions speak of God's foreknowledge and predestination, but the doctrine of providence *per se* is foreign to them.

The expression "divine providence" is less frequent in the writings of 20th-century theologians than in those of the Reformation or before. The immanence of God, His transcendence, His absoluteness, the I-Thou relationship are a few of the approaches used by modern systematicians and religious philosophers. An evaluation of these positions, not in a polemical manner, no less than the question of the relationships between the Christian religion and world religions implies an answer to the problem of God's purpose for mankind. Those who would resolve all doubts by reference to God's love in Christ, the message of redeeming and renewing love, can thereby find the meaning of human existence. Ultimately the problem of providence is answered in the suffering, cross, and resurrection of the Christ. The assignments made in this area for a more comprehensive survey of the problem are missing in this volume. The writers for personal reasons could not complete their assignments. Their frustrations in one sense are an actualization of the problem that modern theologians face when confronted with the term.

Philosophers, too, have used the term while contending with the concept. As they speculate about the nature of God, the nature of man, man's freedom and responsibility, the prevalence of "things hurtful" they cannot escape the problems which man's questionings raise. Obviously a multiplicity of answers is given by a multiplicity of philosophers and would-be philosophers. Perhaps there is no one answer that philosophy can or, for that matter, should give. Because

13

Providence gave man the ability to reason, He (it may be supposed) does not wish man to exclude all reasoning in his contemplation of his own affairs and those of his fellowmen. Man will ask about his purpose on earth, the meaning of life and of history, the significance of natural phenomena, cause and effect relationships. Thinking men in their quest for life's purposes will ask about the role of providence.

The behavioral sciences can also be expected to pose their questions. The relationship of psychology to theology is one that has been debated by both psychologists and theologians with, it seems, a measure of misgiving by each group. The working assumptions of the psychologist have called forth the critique of theologians, partly because the theologians have not understood the diverse modes of speech among the psychologists and vice versa. Paul Tillich worked into his theological system principles deliberately drawn from depth psychology. Reinhold Niebuhr, too, saw a correlation between the Freudian view of man and Pauline anthropology. However, Tillich and Niebuhr may be exceptions rather than examples in this respect for other theologians. The various schools of psychology are as divergent as the various theologies. The suggestion posed in our presentation by a Lutheran theologian, who is also a trained clinical psychologist, uses the traditional Lutheran Law-Gospel dichotomy and relates it to the internal-external and closed-open dichotomies in their total relationships to providence.

The social scientists, too, are asked for an answer to the meaning of providence for modern man. Sociology has a "reluctant participation" in the endeavor. An examination of the role of religion in sociology, problems of theodicy, transcendence in an age of secularity, and alternatives for modern man to providence document the reluctance to a greater degree than the participation. That approach accents the need for such an examination. The structures in society are agencies of a provident Deity whose dealing with groups are ordered and regulated as are His dealings with individuals. Human relationships in community are of significance for the theologian no less than for the sociologist. A less reluctant participation in larger theological questions may be the sociologist's answer to challenges which the increasing complexities of society, the problems of urban communities, the conflict of races, and the needs of minority groups pose.

Historians, too, know the question, for they study the records of philosophers and theologians, social scientists, writers of literature, and natural scientists, not merely the deeds of kings and the conquests of generals. War may make rattling good history and peace poor reading, as Thomas Hardy observed; it may be condemned as "that great dust-heap" by Augustine Burrell. But another Augustine —the fourth-century bishop of Hippo—used history to answer the wailing storms of whys raised by the fall of Rome in A. D. 410. Historians found his teaching useful. When the doctrine of providence gave place to the idea of progress, it could not be said (to invert George Eliot's aphorism) that the happiest nations, like the happiest women, have no history, for progress spelled happiness. The pessimism that accompanied the doubts and disbelief in progress echoed the pessimism of those who had sacrificed belief in providence to a belief in progress. Francis Bacon claimed that histories make men wise, and others said that "history is philosophy teaching by example" (perhaps Dionysius of Harlicarnassus said it first). But modern man, if he recognizes the relevance of history, is not always ready to grant such claims, still less ready to see the hand of God (or even His finger) in the courses of nations and in the affairs of peoples. A survey of the approaches that some historians in the past four centuries have taken to the belief in providence, the idea of progress, the problem of causation, the deterministic approach, chance, and change has therefore been attempted.

Yet it was Aristotle who said that "poetry is something more philosophic and of greater import than history." Has the man of letters and poetry, the novelist or dramatist something to say to moderns about a belief in providence? The artist takes modern man on a journey of awareness, asking him to know himself. He points up man's relation to nature and technology. With the philosopher, as poet or painter, he asks the ultimate question, sometimes not pausing for an answer. No modern novelist would indulge in an excursus on "the equal dealings of Providence demonstrated with regard to the happy and miserable here below," such as Oliver Goldsmith wrote in the 23d chapter of *The Vicar of Wakefield*. Few modern men or women would read it, unless mayhap it were an assignment in a literature class which they could not escape. Not all modern literature and art is void of meaning, and among the great

15

writers, for instance, such as Leo Tolstoy, there are those who do not disdain references to providence.

But the modern era is the age of science. Do John Ray and William Paley speak with a louder voice than Charles Darwin and Aldous Huxley? No. Evolutionary biology seems to have dispensed with a belief in providence. Some soft whisperings about providentialism instead of the doctrine of providence may be heard. The probes into outer space, missions to the moon, the disclosure of the secrets of the atom seem to prosper without reference to providence. Science more than literature, history, sociology, psychology, or philosophy seems to have made the belief of former times passé.

However, the foreword of this book is not intended as a summary or a defense, simply as an introduction. The team of contributors believe that they have made an attempt to answer questions that have troubled many Christians over the centuries. Their attempt is addressed to intelligent thinkers within and without the church. They do not intend to enter into controversies with anyone; they ask merely to be heard.

The Research Committee of the Commission of Literature of The Lutheran Church — Missouri Synod made this study possible by a generous grant. The grant from the Research Committee enabled the Editorial Committee to call together a colloquium in November 1968 on "What is the meaning of 'providence' for the present age?" On the basis of a paper prepared by Herbert T. Mayer and questions and discussion-briefs drawn up by various individuals, the group met not only in plenary sessions but also in subgroups. Twenty-three men participated in this colloquium, giving shape and unity to the project.

Two years later most of the authors met together again with several advisors to discuss the preliminary drafts of the papers that had been prepared. Mutual criticism helped greatly to strengthen the content of the papers and their unity and reduced to a minimum overlap that might occur.

Throughout, the Editorial Committee worked in close harmony with the contributors. We acknowledge with gratitude the help given by Prof. Lorman Petersen of Concordia Theological Seminary, Springfield, Ill.

Each author is responsible for the content and viewpoint of his own chapter. Collaboration in the volume does not mean that the other authors or the editors fully endorsed the position any one or all the contributors have taken. However, the two colloquia provided an excellent opportunity for the exchange of ideas and the basis for the variety of the approaches used to the problem.

The study was sponsored by the School for Graduate Studies of Concordia Seminary, St. Louis. In 1922 Ludwig Fuerbringer was chosen by the faculty of that institution to become Dean of the "Post Graduate Department." In commemoration of the inauguration of graduate studies at Concordia 50 years ago this study was launched. Graduate studies in theology must probe deeply into contemporary problems and examine them from the various areas of interest that engage modern man. This composite effort is one such attempt.

CARL S. MEYER †

Divine Providence: Biblical Perspectives

Martin H. Scharlemann

Greek philosophers called it *pronoia* (forethought). They thought
of this term as signifying purposeful direction in the control and
shaping of the *kosmos*. They were sure that the universe had a rational structure and that it was being guided by some kind of
cosmic Reason, whose operating principles could be determined by
the proper application of man's intellectual faculties. Man's *logos*
related to the universal Logos. These men believed, moreover, that
the laws regulating life in a city-state ought to articulate the intent
of that nonpersonal divinity that pervaded the whole world and
guided it toward its destiny.

The Roman Stoics took over the concept of *pronoia* and turned it
into the Latin *providentia* (foresight) as they set about the task of
developing a detailed doctrine of divine providence for their Roman
readers. Their logic was so sound and the ethical principles they
espoused were so noble that Philo, an Alexandrian Jew, did them the
honor of writing an essay on the subject in which he submerged the
distinctive accents of the Old Testament in the kind of thought and
argumentation contained in Seneca's *De Providentia*. Considering
the degree to which Philo's treatment of the Old Testament influenced the thinking of the church fathers, it should not come as a
surprise to note that early Christian teaching was influenced by
Stoic reflections on the subject of divine providence, with their
accent on the disciplinary value of adversity and misfortune.

Although the Scriptures contain no book or chapter that deals
explicitly with the subject of divine providence in a discursive
manner, they do have their own special way of testifying to God's
care for what He created. In doing so they tend to use *ad hoc* words,
expressing in concrete situations His mighty acts toward the world,
toward mankind, and especially toward His people. By way of illus-
tration we point to such statements as the following: God makes

springs gush forth in the valleys (Ps. 104:10), He gives food to all flesh (Ps. 136:25), and He stretches forth His hand against a man's enemies (Ps. 138:7). None of these passages from the Psalms uses the technical term *pronoia*, nor does one find it in any of the canonical books. The Hebrew *pequddā* at Job 10:12 approximates it; yet at this point the Greek text uses *episkopē* rather than *pronoia* in describing God as preserving man's spirit.

Remembering the pronounced Hellenistic outlook of the apocryphal Wisdom of Solomon, one might expect its author to employ the old Greek *pronoia*; he does. It occurs in the verb form at 6:7, and as a noun in 14:3 and 17:2. The root verb, with the preposition *dia*, occurs at Judith 9:5 to make the point that God designs whatever is yet to come. Such a pronounced Hellenistic view of existence is not found in the New Testament. Although the word *pronoia* is found there, the reference in each case is to human forethought or care.[1] The nonuse by New Testament writers of the term *pronoia* as applied to divine providence is a reminder that these men did not find this Stoic term adequate to define the witness that God gave to His providence in Jesus Christ and in His Word.

God reveals Himself in the Scriptures as the One who "declares the end from the beginning" (Is. 46:10). He is a personal being. He upholds and governs the universe He created and its peoples, involving Himself in the course and in the outcome of history through the intervention of His mighty acts, especially by sending His Son to become incarnate. The major stress of the Bible is on God's decision to carry out what is in keeping with His own good pleasure. His foreknowledge *(prognosis)* is depicted not so much as prescience but rather as an act of choice on His part. The term used is derived from the Hebrew understanding of knowing as choosing. (Cf. Ps. 1:6)

Decision-making is a distinctively personal activity, presupposing the ability of willing. God's knowledge of things to come is implied in the term *prognosis* (1 Peter 1:1-2), His planning is suggested by the verbal form of *prothesis* (Eph. 1:9), and His act of selection is alluded to in the verb *proorizein* (Eph. 1:5). All these depict God as One who relates to what He has created on a personal rather than on an abstract basis, as was true of the Logos of Greek

---

[1] The verb occurs at Rom. 12:17, 2 Cor. 8:21, and 1 Tim. 5:8; the noun is found at Acts 24:2 and Rom. 13:14.

philosophy. The God of Biblical revelation is not a notion but a name, as Rabbi Abraham Heschel reminds us. "A notion describes; a name evokes. A notion is attained through generalization; a name is learned through acquaintance. A notion is conceived; a name is called."[2] The God who is named chooses "things that are not to bring to nothing things that are" (1 Cor. 1:28). This God is not the deity of the philosopher but the God of Abraham, Isaac, and Jacob, as Pascal once observed.

The God of Scripture presents Himself as triune. Each of the three Persons in the Godhead has His own part to perform in governing, sustaining, and directing the entire universe toward its appointed end. The subject of providence may properly be dealt with, therefore, in the light of the distinctive involvement of each of the divine Persons. To the Father the Creeds ascribe the work of creation; to the Son the work of man's redemption; and to the Holy Spirit the work of sanctification.

I. Providence and Creation

Most ancient Greeks were persuaded that the universe was a place of order. They called the world their *kosmos*. Yet their gods were not conceived to be creators of matter. Their divinities were, at best, engineers who shaped matter to make the world an orderly place. This *kosmos* was made to cohere by universal Reason. The latter pervaded everything and so became part of the universe. In a real sense, therefore, the world and existence constituted a closed system.

The Scriptures are unambiguous in their insistence that God created the world. The *kosmos* is His handiwork, with a beginning and an end, as determined by the Creator Himself, He who controls it as a separate entity. It was made by Him and for Him. In a formula that the apostle Paul may have taken from the Stoics, he put it like this: "From Him and through Him and to Him are all things." (Rom. 11:36)

The Biblical witness to God as Creator insists that the primary principles of order and direction are not to be found within the cosmic system itself. They flow instead from the will of Him who commands the morning and causes the dawn to know its place (Job

---

[2] Abraham Heschel, "The Jewish Notion of God and Christian Renewal" in *Theology of Renewal* (Quebec: Palm Publishers, 1968), p. 105.

21

38:12). "Every morning," as G. K. Chesterton once wrote, "God says to the sun, 'Get up.' " [3] The sun is His creation and, like everything else, was made to do His will.

Solomon made this point in his opening remarks at the dedication of the first temple. This edifice had been erected, he proclaimed, as the dwelling place of that God who had "set the sun in the heavens" (1 Kings 8:12). The Phoenician architects had designed this building so that at the spring equinox the rising sun would shine through the gates of the temple as far back as the Holy of Holies. This might have suggested to some that here was another sanctuary erected to honor the sun. To obviate such a conclusion, Solomon declared his temple to have been built in honor of that God who had made the sun, saying: "The Lord has set the sun in the heavens, but has said that He would dwell in thick darkness." (1 Kings 8:12)

In theological terminology God's relationship to the universe as its Creator has been called His *providentia universalis*. This is shorthand for the Biblical doctrine that God not only once created the world but that He sustains it. The Word of His power constantly orders the universe (Heb. 1:3). His Word of power is motivated by His good pleasure. (Rom. 8:28-35)

Apart from the Biblical revelation it would be difficult to conclude that God's good and gracious will is the driving force behind the events of history. Left to their own devices, men argue that the "happenings" of the world occur as the result of sheer caprice, turning the story of mankind into a sequence of just one "fool thing after another." But those servants of the Lord whom He endowed with the "inner ear of prophecy" have given men the lasting assurance that God is not only sovereign but also gracious in sustaining His creation. God is the God of nature and of history. To Him the Scriptures ascribe all wisdom and honor and power and glory, as He notes the sparrow that falls from the housetop and counts even the hairs of our heads. (Matt. 10:29-30)

Job felt the utter pointlessness of existence, but only for a moment. He dared to complain to God about his lot. That is always man's privilege; and the promise has been given that he will be heard. Accordingly Job was introduced into some of the mystery

---

[3] Quoted by Roger Hazelton in *Providence: A Theme with Variations* (London: SCM Press, 1958), p. 14.

attending the ways of God. He was made aware of the fact that the Lord is one who can intervene in the affairs of men to work out His own will amid the unpredictable factors and forces of existence. "No purpose of Thine can be thwarted," Job was led to confess (42:2). He had heard God's mighty Yes to the No of existence. The latter seemed to come from some heartless destiny; but he had discovered as Pascal would later, that men "need only look at the smallest things which surround them in order to see God unveiled." [4]

Behind these masks, as Luther called them, the Lord of history is always at work implementing His good pleasure; hence in the words of the hymn:

> God the Almighty, the great Creator,
> Ruler of sky and land and sea,
> All things ordained, and sooner or later
> They come to pass unfailingly.
> His rule is over rich and poor,
> His promise ever standeth sure. [5]

God asserted His lordship when He spoke to Job out of the whirlwind and invited him to answer questions like these: Do you give the horse his might? Do you clothe his neck with strength? (39:19) Can you lift up your voice to the clouds, that a flood of waters may cover you? (38:34) Is it your wisdom that the hawk soars and spreads his wings toward the south? (39:26)

These are questions that men ought to keep asking themselves in order to realize that they are part of a universe controlled by God's wisdom and power. As the very crown of creation, man stands in solidarity with the total *kosmos*. He was designed to represent God Himself here on earth, exercising dominion "over the fish of the sea and over the birds of the air and over every living thing that moves upon the earth" (Gen. 1:28). Yet man chose to rebel against his Creator, turning love into lust and the responsibility for dominion into the desire for domination. Because of this fall into sin, creation itself has been made subject to what St. Paul calls the "bondage of decay" (Rom. 8:21). Amid all this corruption, however,

---

[4] Blaise Pascal, *The Thoughts of Blaise Pascal* (London: Kegan Paul, Trench & Co., 1885), p. 91.

[5] *The Lutheran Hymnal*, Hymn 26, verse 4.

everything God has made eagerly looks forward to that moment of liberation when it will be set free from its bondage to decay.

The world moves forward to its judgment according to the purpose of God's will. As St. Paul warned the philosophers of Athens, God has "fixed a day on which He will judge the world in righteousness" (Acts 17:31). As the universe had a beginning, so it has an end. Creation, therefore, is not autonomous; it is dependent on God's sustaining power even as man is made for obedience to His gracious will.

The ancients had concluded that men were the playthings of the gods and victims of a fate that was either impersonal or cruel. The Greeks called the latter *moira*. For them Sisyphus became the symbol of life's utter futility. That dimension of life still haunts every man, as witness Santiago in Hemingway's *The Old Man and the Sea*, who catches the biggest fish of his life but finally manages to bring to shore only the bones that have been picked clean by a host of sharks.

This brings up the problem of evil. God takes evil seriously and deals with it in His grace and power. Isaiah quotes Him as saying: "I form light and create darkness. I make weal and create woe" (Is. 45:7). Even wrong may be an instrument in the hand of a God who is not only able but determined to dispose things according to His gracious will. The prophet Amos (3:6) put this truth into the form of a rhetorical question: "Does evil befall a city, unless the Lord has done it?"

Because God is involved somehow in all human actions, He does not stand aloof from the evil actions of the Ishmaelite slaves and the officers of Pharaoh. While the question of the relationship of God to evil is difficult, Scripture affirms several points. First, He sets limits to the power of evil (Job 1 and 2) and, second, He can bring good from evil.

The story of Joseph is told to serve as an abiding reminder that God can turn evil to good. His brothers conspired against him and sold him into slavery. They meant this for evil, yet God turned it into good (Gen. 50:20). Such actions occur by divine concurrence. This means that God at times permits wrong to happen; He does not always suppress it by force, as He could. He limits wrong even as He guides everything else in such a way as to fulfill His purposes.

The prophet Habakkuk was led to see this. After wrestling with God to discover why His people should be oppressed and afflicted, why even nature should fail to provide abundant food, he was moved to say: "Though the fig tree does not blossom, nor fruit be on the vines, the produce of the oil fail and the fields yield no food, the flock be cut off from the fold and there be no herd in the stalls, yet I will rejoice in the Lord, I will joy in the God of my salvation." (Hab. 3:17-18)

To live in history means to make responsible decisions. If God were by sheer power either to suppress or to destroy evil, men would be reduced to living without personal choice and individual accountability. They would cease to be responsible persons. Made in the image of God, man was created to live *coram Deo*. God intended man to reflect His righteousness in life and His dominion over the universe. This involves the act of decision-making, which is the essence of interpersonal relationships.

Man was created a being that makes choices. Given the opportunity of choosing, our primal parents decided to rebel, and that "brought death into the world, and all our woe," to quote Milton in paraphrase of Paul (Rom. 5:12-17). Man's revolt marred the image of God in which he had been shaped. As a fallen being, he is without power to turn to God as his Father, often turning truth into a lie and debasing the glory of God (Rom. 1:23). Every man is his own Adam. Only when man is redirected by God's Spirit does he begin to respond properly toward his Creator. Then he is set free under God.

Man's freedom to choose in temporal matters is a major problem in any discussion of divine providence. Man makes choices at every juncture in his life. How do these relate to God's will and to His overarching plan? History is the arena where this issue becomes acute. For, on the one hand, God is sovereign and omnipotent; on the other, man remains both responsible and accountable. Two things are certain, said John of Damascus, namely, that God wills only what is good, since goodness alone belongs to Him; and that we are responsible for our actions and cannot rightly lay the blame for our evil deeds at the door of Providence. (James 1:12-18) [6]

---

[6] Summarized by Roger Hazelton, p. 69.

The godless man solves this problem by denying that there is a God. The atheist of today, like the fool of the psalm (14:2), generally rejects God as a matter of his own deliberate choice. Many contemporary persons eliminate God from life; for, as Creator, God seems to be a threat to their autonomy.

The presence of evil prompts the godless man to revolt against God. There can be no Creator, he insists; for how could He permit evil to flourish abundantly? This problem troubled the writer of Psalm 73. "When I thought how to understand this," the psalmist reflected, "it seemed to me a wearisome task." However, instead of rejecting God he went into the sanctuary of the Most High. "Then I perceived their end," he was led to confess.

The godless man rejects this understanding. He prefers the myth of God's death. As far as he is concerned, God has no place in his personal life, and so he has complete autonomy. There is no God either to direct or to limit him. The atheist prefers to live in the silence and the absence of God. For, as he believes, man can now proceed to be like God, knowing good and evil and so creating his own world. In this view of things God is in fact no more than man on his way to becoming more human.[7]

This freedom involves struggle, as Goetz, the "buffoon of evil and impostor of good" in Sartre's *The Devil and the Good Lord*, observed. He said, "There's no argument; and I tell you, God is dead. . . . I have this war to fight and I shall fight it." [8] Many a person is sure that this battle has been more than half won. After all, man has come of age.

The Biblical prototype for this arrogance is displayed by Nebuchadnezzar as he walked on the roof of the royal palace at Babylon, defying God's providence and exclaiming: "Is not this great Babylon, which I have built by my mighty power as a royal residence and for the glory of my majesty?" To which a voice from heaven responded: "Your dwelling shall be with the beasts of the field; and you shall be made to eat grass like an ox . . . until you have learned that the Most High rules the kingdom of men." (Dan. 4:29-32)

---

[7] John Courtney Murray, *The Problem of God* (New Haven and London: Yale University Press, 1964), pp. 101 – 2.

[8] Jean-Paul Sartre, *The Devil and the Good Lord* (New York: Alfred A. Knopf, 1960), pp. 143 and 149.

This type of arrogance is evident in the second half of the 20th century, which we might call the time of man's second great temptation. In the first temptation the creature wanted to be like the Creator; in the second, many seem to believe that they themselves have become the Creator. They are encouraged to believe this by their affluence and technological know-how. These, they hope, will help to eliminate evil. Freedom is no longer a matter of ideas but of action. Men must therefore devise their own freedom. They believe that the achievement of liberty will help solve the problem of evil. This creator-man may even will his own death if that will serve to eliminate evil. In this way may becomes the "inventor of himself."

Man cannot fully eliminate evil or scheme to use it for good. Only God has the necessary freedom and power to do so. He can show forebearance toward wrong, because He can direct even that which defies His purposes to serve the vindication of His righteous will. (Rom. 8:31-39)

Autonomous man has posed the problem of God as clearly as the Israelites did at Massah and Meribah: "Is the Lord among us or not?" (Ex. 17:7). The issue is clearly drawn: "Is the myth [of God's existence] in Nietzsche or in the New Testament? Is it in Marx or in Moses? Is it in Sartre of Paris or in Paul of Tarsus?" [9]

Let us suppose the myth is in Nietzsche and in Marx. Then what about man's freedom? Man does indeed have considerable room to make choices. He can select various courses of action in the area of life which the Lutheran Confessions call civic righteousness.[10] This is not the question of man's free will in its technical sense. That capacity he lost in the Fall; he cannot on his own decide to come to God. What, then, about this freedom as it relates to God's own purposes? For, as God's creation, man can make choices in every other area of his life.

Perhaps a somewhat parallel situation will be helpful at this point. Most analogies, to be sure, limp; so does this one. It must be understood, therefore, within its own limitations. The comparison might go as follows: The war plans for American troops designated to hit the French coast on D-day during World War II covered

---

[9] Murray, p. 120.

[10] *Apology of the Augsburg Confession* IV (II), 24.

hundreds of volumes. Every conceivable contingency had been taken into account, and a separate plan was devised for each eventuality. If the men got ashore, one set of plans would be implemented; if they were thrown back, another course of action would follow. In some such way we might conceive of our Creator as having a set of contingency plans for every one of the countless choices an individual may make. He has chosen to put many options before His creatures. If an individual decides one way, a certain set of effects will follow; if the choice runs in another direction, a different series of consequences will be started. Without pressing this analogy too far, Scripture requires that we assert God's sovereignty and man's accountability. Neither God nor man is trapped in an inexorable sequence. This paradox is summarized and illuminated in a passage like Deut. 11:26-32:

> "Behold, I set before you this day a blessing and a curse: the blessing, if you obey the commandments of the Lord your God, which I command you this day, and the curse, if you do not obey the commandments of the Lord your God, but turn aside from the way which I command you this day, to go after other gods which you have not known. . . ." (See also 30:15-20; Joshua 24:14-28; Jer. 21:8; Eccl. 15:17.)

The analogy also points to another aspect of divine providence. It suggests that God is always free either to intervene or not to intervene in the affairs of men. Providence is not just prescience but also rule by decision. God has not left His creation to work out its own destiny, as deism suggests. He is not just the great Uncaused Cause or the Prime Mover. His mighty arm can change things, as is illustrated, for example, by His act of raising up Cyrus to be king of Persia and of having him anointed as a kind of Messianic deliverer of Israel. (Is. 45:1)

The Biblical revelation makes it clear that our *kosmos* is not a closed system. Scripture affirms that life, history, and nature are always under God's control. That is one of the meanings of the miracles Jesus performed. He performed them to remind men that the Father in heaven is in constant attendance among men. Especially meaningful in this context is the account of Jesus stilling the storm. This miracle proclaims that Jesus had at His beck and call those powers with which God originally called the world forth out of chaos and which He constantly employs for His own purposes. (Compare Mark 4:35-51 with Ps. 93:4.) Among Jesus' own people the sea was the symbol of all that opposed God. It was the home of Leviathan and of Tehom (Is. 51:9-10). God had once cut Rahab in pieces and pierced the dragon to liberate His people by and from the Sea of Reeds. So our Lord calmed the waters and stilled the storm to assure His followers that their Master wielded the might of that God who is strong to save from all enemies. This power controls even death, as the story of the raising of the youth of Nain makes clear. (Luke 7:14)

Miracles are a problem for people in our culture. Many tend to view the world and existence as closed. The Scriptures, however, assure us that life is open to a sovereign God who heals and liberates and at times chastises His creatures. He is not "Nature's God," to use Jefferson's phrase; He is the Lord of history.

The Lord is not just an architect or engineer in the sense that the Greek gods were thought to work. He is the *Pantokrator*, whose own Son served as the agent and is even now the goal of creation. That is the point of Col. 1:16: "In Him [Christ] all things were created, in heaven and on earth, visible and invisible, whether thrones or dominions or principalities or authorities — all things were created through Him and for Him."

This God, who is busy putting all things under Jesus Christ, is the Lord of the nations. They, too, are subject to His divine providence. They rise and fall at His bidding; they serve His purposes, each for its own time and within its alloted boundaries (Acts 17:26). The very existence of nations and peoples and tongues is intended to testify to the existence and the power of God. The choice of Jacob over Esau (Rom. 9:13) testifies to God's "purpose of election" in dealing with various nations. The presence of "the Constrainer" to hold back lawlessness provides further witness to God's involvement in the affairs of nations. (2 Thess. 2:6-8)

Nations and other political instruments, as St. Paul reminds us, can serve as "ministers of God for good" (Rom. 13:4). Without them men could not reckon with a calculable future. Nor would the church be able to carry on her work effectively. We are asked, therefore, to pray for government officials so that we may lead a quiet and peaceable life, godly and respectful in every way" (1 Tim. 2:1). We offer such a petition, for example, in the collect for the Seventh Sunday After Trinty, which reads as follows:

"O God, whose never-failing providence ordereth all things both in heaven and on earth, we humbly beseech Thee to put away from us all hurtful things and to give us those things which be profitable for us . . . ."

This collect reminds us of the Scriptural teaching that God is the decision-maker who is Lord of heaven and earth. When providence is viewed in relationship to the doctrine of creation, it is not adequate to say that God is provident in the sense that He summons them not to fall into despair and bitterness. Nor does it mean that He is operative through His providence in the hearts of men, so that they become stronger and can enter more deeply into their humanity. Of course, God works in men through His Spirit, operative through Word and Sacrament. As divine Providence, He is wise and powerful enough to have planned history to the end and to control it.

Since our Lord is the God of history and of the nations, we are able to speak of a *providentia universalis.* The Scriptures remind us, however, that we can also derive assurance from what may be called a *providentia specialis,* namely, God's care of the individual. God has an interest in each individual as part of His work as Creator. Providence in its special sense may also be related to the whole matter of redemption; and that is the subject of the Second Article. Hence we turn to the thought of divine providence as it is expressed in God's work of undoing the consequences of man's fall.

II. Providence and Redemption

Salvation is the consequence of a decision reached in eternity. Before history began, God had chosen to seek His glory among men in a community of redeemed people. Therefore He chose Abraham as the progenitor of a nation, which He Himself called out to be a kingdom of priests and His own possession. (Ex. 19:5-6)

The selection of Israel as God's special instrument of salvation was an act of pure grace. There was nothing in that people itself to commend it to the Lord. The basic text for this truth is Deut. 7:7-8, which reads:

"It was not because you were more in number than any other people that the Lord set His love upon you and chose you, for you were the fewest of all peoples; but it is because the Lord loves you, and is keeping the oath which He swore to your fathers, that the Lord has brought you out with a mighty hand and redeemed you . . . ."

Israel became the people of God's presence, chosen to do His will. God arranged a covenant with this people, and a tent of meeting was erected as the place where God offered His grace and where He was to be worshiped. Through this people the knowledge of God was to be brought to all nations. So much did God care not only for Israel but also for other peoples and tongues that He chose to reveal Himself as their Lord.

The selection of one nation as God's own has been called "the scandal of particularity." Yet that is how God exhibited His holiness, His power, and His mercy. Israel responded by saying:

"A wandering Aramean was my father; and he went down into Egypt and sojourned there, few in number; and there he became a nation, great, mighty, and populous. And the Egyptians treated us harshly and afflicted us and laid upon us hard bondage. Then we cried to the Lord the God of our fathers, and the Lord heard our voice and saw our affliction, our toil, and our oppression; and the Lord brought us out of Egypt with a mighty hand and an outstretched arm, with great terror, with signs and wonders; and He brought us into this place and gave us this land, a land flowing with milk and honey." (Deut. 26:5-9)

Despite Yahweh's mercy, Israel sinned and came under His judgment. The Book of Judges provides evidence of this. Enemy nations invaded the Promised Land and destroyed its crops and its cities. Israel's oppressors taunted God's people with such embarrassing questions as: "Where, then, is your God?" This became a continuing problem in Israel's history. The psalmist had every reason to complain: "Why should the nations say, 'Where is their God?'" (79:10). The priests of Joel's time uttered the same lamentation. (Joel 2:17)

God's people of old had to learn that wrath and judgment play a vital role in the providence of the holy God. The prophets of doom kept warning Israel that it could not escape punishment for its many transgressions. They called the people to repentance, but largely in vain.

In Jerusalem many people were confident that the presence of God's temple guaranteed their security. They had little intention of changing their ways. Oppression grew and injustice increased in the face of Jeremiah's cry: "Do not trust in these deceptive words: 'This is the temple of the Lord, the temple of the Lord, the temple of the Lord' " (7:4). In due time the sanctuary on Zion was laid waste; both Israel and Judah were carried off into captivity. Of the northern tribes we hear no more. They disappeared in the ebb and flow of history. Judah was permitted by God's grace to return.

The faithful Jews continued to wrestle with the problem of God's care. Their Lord seemed to be absent and unconcerned. But instead of rejecting Yahweh as their God and adopting the cult of a foreign god, many repented, believing that their prophets had spoken the Word of God in truth. They fell back on the promises God had made and saw in them the possibilities of new life. The people believed the prophet's assurance that as a mother could not forget her sucking child, so the Lord would not forget them (Is. 49:15-16). The Lord assured His distressed people that He would uphold them with His victorious right hand (Is. 41:10) amid all the vicissitudes of a history that is unkind to the conquered.

Deliverance seemed far away to the Jews in distant Babylon; and yet in that foreign land God's people learned that God can bring strength out of weakness and restoration out of suffering. The mysterious figure of the Suffering Servant was offered as one in whose hand the will of the Lord would prosper (Is. 53:10). Having been despised and rejected by men, He would be given a portion with the great. (53:12)

In the providence of God, Israel had been brought to utter humiliation, but that was not to be His last word on the subject. Israel was called to a new future that was set forth in terms of the Suffering Servant. His progress is not marked by conquest and glory, but by quiet labor, infinite patience, and suffering. His suffering was both exemplary and vicarious. Glory lay beyond that ignominy and agony which was to be part of His mission.

Here the prophet, as John Bright reminds us, was given the privilege of gazing into the very mystery of the Godhead. Through Isaiah's message Israel was to learn that the victory of God's servant was not to be procured by force or spectacular power but by sacrificial labor. This is a word profound enough to reach down into the depths of all suffering. It offers new hope for those who experience that brokenness of existence which comes not from having sinned but for having done God's will. Here was a strong summons to the people of Israel to see their future in a new light. Victory was to be achieved through the vicarious sacrifice of a Servant yet to come. Suffering was to be transfigured by a cross. No longer is rejection and pain to be sheer futile and pointless agony. It is to be an instrument of redemption. In this way the blessing of Abraham will come to the nations of the world.[11]

In the fullness of time that Servant came. After His death and resurrection Candace's minister puzzled over the words of Isaiah about this Servant. Philip opened his mouth, we read, and told him the good news of Jesus (Acts 8:35). Then he realized that the true Israel had come and that the temple on Mount Zion, which he had visited, had been superseded by the incarnate Word. (John 1:14)

Jesus Himself had talked about rebuilding God's temple. To that end He gathered around Him the faithful in Israel to constitute a new Israel. This new people, the church, St. Paul called the temple of the living God (2 Cor. 6:16). Within that living temple God is at work in Word and Sacrament. The world surrounding the church resembles somewhat the scaffolding used to build the ark of Noah (2 Peter 2:4-10). When it has served God's purpose as the arena of His saving work among men, it will be replaced by the new heavens and the new earth in which righteousness dwells. (2 Peter 3:10-13)

Like Israel of old, the church is called for service to its Lord. The church as the new Israel lives with a double heartbeat. These might be called *ekklesia* and *diaspora*, respectively. As *ekklesia* the new Israel assembles around Word and Sacrament to receive strength and assurance that the Lord is indeed among them in His grace and judgment. With His presence each goes into his *diaspora* to serve his fellowmen wherever they may live and work.

Church and world are not the same. The Gospel does not happen everywhere, as advocates of the "Blondelian Shift" insist.[12] There are no "secular equivalents" to the proclamation of the Gospel and

---

[11] John Bright, *The Kingdom of God* (New York: Abingdon Press, 1953), p. 149—53.

[12] Named in honor of Maurice Blondel, who formally suggested that God works in His grace out in the world more than in church.

the administration of the sacraments. The full dimensions of God's providence, therefore, are not known by men in general, graced as they may be. God still chooses to make the secret of His reconciling purposes known through the preaching of His Word and the celebration of His sacraments.

The Gospel reminds each one that he, in his individual self, is the person for whom God sent His Son as the Suffering Servant. The doctrine of providence, therefore, as Albert Outler correctly states, is not to be thought of as being the equivalent of some "cosmic Linus' blanket." [13] It provides the certainty that God cares so much for each person, burdened as he may be with the problems of existence, that He was willing in Jesus Christ to share the agonies of life and absorb the violence of men in order to redeem them all. God's governance of the world, then, is not that of a meddling director or of an absentee landlord but rather of one involved with mankind so deeply that in His Son He experienced all brokenness to heal it and all forsakenness to disperse it. We are glad, therefore, to pray "that the course of this world may be so peaceably ordered by Thy governance that Thy Church may joyfully serve Thee in all godly quietness." [14]

The Gnostics of the early Christian centuries set out to disengage the divine from the hurly-burly of everyday life. They said it was unworthy of God to be committed to matter, since the latter was thought to be utterly evil. They failed to understand how a perfect Creator could be held responsible for a world and an existence so frustrating as that of man's life in the body and on this planet. By way of anticipation, St. Paul answered them in writing to the Colossians that the Creator is also the Redeemer, and the Redeemer is also man's Maker. Creation and its Creator are not sundered from each other. The former is the object of God's work of restoration.

On that conviction, Dietrich Bonhoeffer could write from prison: "Who am I? They mock me, these lonely questions of mine. Whoever I am, Thou knowest, O God, I am Thine." [15] He knew that in Christ God had given notice that no one lived outside divine providence.

---

[13] *Who Trusts in God* (New York: Oxford University Press, 1968), p. 131.

[14] From the Collect for the Fourth Sunday After Trinity.

[15] *Letters and Papers from Prison* (London: SCM Press, 1953), p. 165.

In Christ Bonhoeffer faced death by hanging and looked hopefully toward the future. Bonhoeffer did not believe that the world is the result of a process, as Pierre Teilhard de Chardin describes it.[16] The world is not just a huge developmental movement into the future, driven by the twin principles of increasing complexity and growing awareness. Nor is man the product of cosmic forces throwing off new forms of life and finally fashioning man as the most complex of all creatures and that being who is most aware of himself. Man cannot contribute much toward the attainment of some point of perfection known as *Omega*. The most significant of all historical events took place in the past, when Jesus Christ was crucified and raised again. As the end approaches, evil seems to increase as a continuing consequence of man's revolt against his Maker.

Whenever our Lord spoke of the last days, He described them as so full of tribulation that God in His mercy would shorten them for the sake of the elect (Matt. 24:22; Mark 13:20). That is part of His providence, for He is a God of grace, wisdom, and power. Accordingly He has put us all on notice that it is precisely amid fear and distress that we are to look up and take courage. Anguish of nations is a sign of the end. It is one of the indications that "your redemption is drawing near" (Luke 21:28). Such terror heralds the day when God will punish His enemies.

For the present, God's children live in expectation of the Parousia. In the meantime they see only in "a mirror dimly" (1 Cor. 13: 12). Only occasionally and in a fragmentary fashion do men get a glimpse of the conquest of evil. Most of God's providential ways are hidden. We accept the Biblical testimony that those who refuse to see God's merciful providence place themselves under judgment. They themselves fall under the condemnation of that divine wrath from which there is escape only in accepting as the Lord of glory Him whom "the rulers of this age" (1 Cor. 2:8) sent to a cross because they did not understand "the secret and hidden wisdom of God." (1 Cor. 2:6-10)

In this wisdom God not only watches over His creation and redeems mankind, but He also calls men together in community to experience a foretaste of the perfect reconciliation that is the

---

[16] Especially in *The Phenomenon of Man.*

heritage of all believers. This last process can be included under the term "sanctification." That divine activity also relates to providence. It is a subject we must now consider.

III. Providence and Sanctification

The Holy Spirit has the very specific task (*providentia specialissima*) of working out God's eternal plan, especially as this involves individuals in their relationship to God and to His people, the church.[17] The Holy Spirit calls men by the Gospel and keeps them in that one true faith which the whole Christian church confesses everywhere and at all times.

St. Paul exhorts his readers to live in such a way as to be worthy of this calling. He asks them to practice lowliness, meekness, patience, and forbearance in love and an eagerness to maintain the unity of the Spirit in the bond of peace (Eph. 4:1-3). This apostolic request quite obviously confronts the Christian with the problem of his vocation in a given culture and economic system. The question came up in Corinth, especially for those who belonged to the slave classes. These men and women had, of course, heard of the new freedom which the Gospel always offers. They wondered how this applied to their status. The apostle laid down the general principle that each one ought to remain in his position and not try to escape his responsibilities (1 Cor. 7:17-24), even if the master was unjust (1 Peter 2:18-25). He affirmed that the Gospel did not prohibit slaves from seeking their freedom legitimately, but it was more important for them to understand that a slave called by the Gospel was in fact a freedman in the Lord.

The question of vocation has become crucial in contemporary society. Many Western nations no longer live in an economy of scarcity but enjoy a great abundance of things. This affluence helps to create the revolutionary ferment of our day. Technocracy, in the opinion of many, is an enemy of basic human values. A counterculture has grown up in our society in revolt against what it believes to be the dehumanizing forces of the contemporary industrial order. By rejecting the "systems approach" to human life as degrading, this counterculture imitates, somewhat feebly, to be sure, the life

---

[17] See, for example, 1 Peter 1:2.

goals of those who believe the good news that Jesus Christ has over-come dehumanizing principalities and powers. Likely there would be little interest in humanizing life if the Gospel had never been sounded out in the world.

One aspect of this dehumanization has been singled out by Langdon Gilkey, who has made the suggestion that today's tech-nology plays a role equivalent to that of fate in ancient society.[18] He argues that the powers of science and the expertise of technology have, in a very real sense, brought on man's bondage as fate did in the ancient world. Therefore faith and religious commitment are highly necessary. This is indeed a legitimate concern for Christians as they think of their responsibilities toward society and toward their own vocations in terms of God's providential care for them.

Take the man on the auto-assembly line — and there are many of them! Cars move by each work-station at the rate of 50 to 65 an hour. Each man has about a minute to do his particular "thing." The line never ends; more cars keep coming. The system never takes into ac-count the fact that sometimes people get tired. Life on such a line is totally impersonal. Foremen point with their fingers to assign men to their jobs or to call on them to do other things. The one bond that unites these workers is the never-ending physical agony of it all.

How does a Christian relate this kind of job to what the Scrip-tures teach on the subject of divine providence? Here his faith offers him the reminder that the individual's significance is not definitively determined by either industrial management or labor bosses. In fact, the very indignities he experiences may well increase his awareness of the ugliness inherent in any human situation. That painful awareness may enable him to hear God's answer to other children of His who complained about their lot in life. (Is. 45:12-13)

In the story of Christian piety, Brother Lawrence stands out as a shining example of the possibilities for glorifying God by means of the most menial tasks. If we can imagine him working on an as-sembly line, we can suppose that he would have used his position as a *kairos*, that is, an opportune moment for exhibiting a kind of personal warmth and interest in his fellow workers. He would con-

---

[18] Langdon Gilkey, *Religion and the Scientific Future* (New York: Harper & Row, 1970), passim.

siderably alleviate the situation and even warm the heart of his foreman. And what is more, we can suppose he would avail himself of every device for improving conditions so that men might have a better chance to remain human. He might well join a labor union, because he would understand this as a method of applying organized power to the task of ameliorating working conditions. He would not make the kind of neat distinction between soul and body which might allow him to say, "As a Christian I need to be concerned only with the soul-life of my fellow workers; the problems of their physical welfare are someone else's responsibility."

The providence of God is concerned with man's physical welfare as much as with his spiritual well-being, because man was created an entity. The Scriptures affirm that God cares for the whole man, for God made man in his entirety and proposes to keep man in his body, soul, and spirit to the end (1 Thess. 5:23). Says the psalmist: "Thou knowest me right well; my frame was not hidden from Thee when I was being made in secret, intricately wrought in the depths of the earth." (139:14-15)

In sanctifying the individual Christian working on the assembly line, the Holy Spirit will lay it on the heart of such a person to remember that he is responsible for "redeeming the time, because the days are evil" (Eph. 5:16). The present is the time for service. This is one way of taking up the full armor of God and contesting those principalities and powers which set out to distort and destroy what God creates and offers.

A worker may well decide to redeem the time by making his fellow church members aware of the ugly factors that he and others must face each day. Being God's people, his congregation and his denomination may be persuaded to reflect on man's inhumanity to man and then, as servants of a righteous God, undertake pronouncements and tasks that will counter the dehumanizing forces which exist.

The followers of the Lord have been given the assignment not only to proclaim the kingdom of God but to drive out demons. Few things are more demonic in contemporary life than those structures in the economic, social, and political sphere which debase human beings, reducing them to working units or even less. The Lord came to undo such "world rulers of this present darkness" (Eph. 6:12), and

Christians live not only to make known His victory but to implement it in the face of all evil (James 2:14-17). That is one way in which sanctification by the Spirit becomes effective in testifying to providence.

The time to put such guidance to work is always now. This requires special emphasis in our day, for our age is obsessed with the future. At times the present does not seem to matter. In the life of the church this stance toward the present is called the theology of hope. Its basic thesis is that God works for tomorrow. It holds, moreover, that sanctification is a movement from God's Spirit which makes the individual restive and ill at ease with the present.

This theological interpretation of time is used to justify the need for revolutionary change. The Biblical notion of Messianism is introduced to make the point that the Scriptures stand for an open future.[19] The risen Christ is made the symbol of a better future. Men ought, therefore, to apply their creative powers to undoing the economic, social, and political structures that oppress them. The church must organize "guerilla units," Richard Shaull suggested to the Conference on Church and Society sponsored by the World Council of Churches in 1966.[20]

The theological motivation for this kind of action includes the belief that the exodus of Israel from Egypt provides an abiding model for revolutionary activity undertaken on behalf of the future.[21] Such concentration on the future is obviously related to the fact that we all live with the Einsteinian rather than the Copernican view of the universe. Everything seems to be racing pell-mell into the future. Only in the future will we know what truth is. It does not come to us from above but from ahead, it is said.

As a result the Biblical accent on the present as the moment of opportunity has been obscured. There has been a growing neglect of the insight that every minute is a providential time unit. Time itself is God's creation. The Biblical writers not only locate events chrono-

---

[19] For example, in Bruce O. Boston's "How Are Revelation and Revolution Related?" *Theology Today*, 26 (Feb. 1969), 142—55.

[20] Richard Schaull, *On Church and Society* (World Council of Churches, 1967), p. 25.

[21] As, for instance, in J. M. Lochmann's "Oekumenische Theologie der Revolution," *Evangelische Theologie*, 27 (1967), 631—46.

logically but also give interpretations of them. The fact that God preserves what He has created does not mean the fragmentization or abrogation of the present. It argues instead for its utilization. The proper choice a man makes in the present makes history more than a process. Every *now* is some kind of *kairos*.[22] Roger Hazelton once put it like this:

> Because all human happenings are conditioned by God's creating power, subject to His constant judgment, upheld by His patient wisdom, and cherished in His redeeming purpose, they form together a living fabric of memory and hope, of decision and of destiny, into which God has entered and with which he is mightily and everlastingly engaged.[23]

Men do not achieve their own *kairoi*. God in His gracious providence offers them. They always stand in continuity with all those previous moments in which God chose to act mightily. When, therefore, we celebrate the Lord's supper in His remembrance, that present moment is filled with abiding significance for us. God reminds us of what He has done in the past and of what He has promised to do in the future. The present moment combines the past and the future.

There is much truth, to be sure, in the following observation by Thomas Mann:

> Time has no divisions to mark its passage. There is never a thunderstorm or blare of trumpets to announce the beginning of a new month or year. Even when a new century begins it is only we mortals who ring bells and fire off pistols.[24]

Yet there is much more to say for St. Augustine's insight that the present is not only the moment of experience; it is also that of remembering the past and of living in anticipation of the future. He applied his view of the nature of the present to saying a psalm. This is how he said it:

> I am about to repeat a psalm that I know. Before I begin, my expectation alone reaches over the whole: but so soon as I shall have

---

[22] See John March, *The Fullness of Time* (London: Nisbet, 1952), p. 20.

[23] Hazelton, p. 129.

[24] *The Magic Mountain* (New York: Alfred A. Knopf, 1967), Chap. 5.

once begun, how much so ever of it shall take off into the past, over so much also my memory reaches: thus the life of this action of mine is extended both ways: into my memory, so far as concerns that part which I have already repeated, and into my expectation in respect of what I am about to repeat now.[25]

Many moments of life contain their tragic elements. These threaten a person with frustration and the feeling of nothingness. The psalmist felt this threat of extinction, and so he asked that the flood not sweep over him or that the deep not swallow him or the pit not close its mouth over him (69:15). Jesus entered the lowest depths of tragedy so directly and overwhelmingly that He felt constrained to cry, "My God, My God, why hast Thou forsaken Me?" (Matt. 27:46). He went down into the pit for us, and though the floods overwhelmed Him, they did not destroy Him. Now His followers need not experience the same despair. They know that in spite of tragedies their lives are in God's providential care. In His providence God often utilizes the tragic to bring about greater trust and confidence in His ways by His children.

No human being deserves any good thing from God, and yet He "makes His sun rise on the evil and on the good, and sends rain on the just and on the unjust" (Matt. 5:45). So great is His generosity. Every tragedy is a reminder that God in His grace normally sheathes the sword of His wrath to exhibit His care for His people. He also maintains those conditions which make it possible for His work of redemption in the church to be carried forward.

Furthermore, the Lord once uttered a hard word when some individuals in His audience called attention to the tragedy of the Galileans who were murdered by Pilate in cold blood and also that of the 18 people who were killed when the tower of Siloam collapsed. His questioners hinted that these people might have been more sinful than others. Jesus replied: "I tell you, No; but unless you repent you will all likewise perish." (Luke 13:5)

In his own person St. Paul felt some of life's tragedy. He suffered from what he called "a thorn in the flesh." It caused him wretchedness and embarrassment. Yet when he asked that God remove it, he received the reply: "My grace is sufficient for you, for

---

[25] *Confessions*, Book XI, Chap. 28, sec. 38.

41

My power is made perfect in weakness" (2 Cor. 12:9). There was no more to say.

God's children, led by the Spirit, learn to face tragedy and hope, knowing that its ultimate resolution is found in Easter as the sequel to Good Friday. In Baptism men are taken back into the agony of the Lord's crucifixion so that they might live with Him in newness of life (Rom. 6:3-10). The cross provides contact with the tragic side of life to transform it by giving it a context and meaning. Charles Kingsley's prayer is instructive at this point: "Teach us by Thy cross that, however ill the world may go, the Father so loves us that He spared not Thee." [26]

Prayer is part of the relationship to God's providence that His children enjoy. John Chrysostom once observed that "he who prays has his hand on the rudder of the world." [27] Prayer does change things. Praying does not consist only of accommodating one's will to the purposes of God; it reaches out to find and implement God's good pleasure. It can, in fact, open up new courses of action. King Hezekiah's experience of having 15 years added to his life in response to his prayer is an abiding reminder that God can and does introduce something new in response to man's request. (2 Kings 20:2-6)

However, there is no magic in prayer. Men relate to God on a person-to-person basis. The nature of this relationship is exhibited in the lonely darkness of Gethsemane as the incarnate Lord Himself prayed, "My Father, if it be possible, let this cup pass from Me; nevertheless, not as I will, but as Thou wilt" (Matt. 26:39). The words were spoken in anguish and in the hope that there might be some alternative to the cross. However, sin could be atoned for only by death, death on a cross by the second Adam. (Rom. 5:12-21)

Christians have learned from Christ's example to bow to God's will. Jesus' experience was not recorded by the evangelists to teach that it is useless to pray. We read of this prayer to learn that God's vision (providentia) begins before time and contemplates the end from that vantage point. His Spirit has been given to His children to assure them of His special care and to encourage them to trust in Him as Christ did.

---

[26] Quoted by Hazelton, p. 153.

[27] Ibid., p. 181.

God's Unsearchable Ways

The end which God had in mind from eternity, and which He had foreshadowed by His mighty acts in the Old Testament, was revealed with the coming of His Son and especially with His death and resurrection. Thereby God's children of old were the clue to history and to their own destiny. Our victorious Christ is not just some vague symbol of good for the universe. He is its redeemer. He invites men to walk humbly with God, certain that God's help is always contrapuntal to their need. The Holy Spirit, therefore, is known as the Paraclete. He constantly brings the mystery of God's providence to our minds to call us to trust and faith.

No discussion of providence will solve this mystery of God's ways with His creation. In the final analysis the providential will of God is largely hidden from men. St. Paul confronted the riddle of God's action in hardening Pharaoh's heart while He liberated Israel. Instead of seeing it as an insoluble problem, he chose to enter the mystery; he was shown the principle of God's "purpose of election" (Rom. 9:11). He found that he could take exception to that operating principle only by becoming as presumptuous as clay asking its molder, "Why have you made me thus?"

That is the point to which the whole presentation on divine providence has brought us in reflecting on the specific accents of the Biblical revelation in this matter as these relate to the participation of the individual Persons of the Godhead in the work of sustaining and directing the world and all that is in it. Few problems have received full solution; but some of the dimensions of the divine mystery have been indicated. God does not wish to stop all thinking on this subject, yet to the mystery that will always remain there is no more adequate response than the words of the apostle Paul:

"O the depth of the riches and wisdom and knowledge of God! How unsearchable are His judgments and how inscrutable His ways!" (Rom. 11:33)

Providence in Christian Thought

Richard Baepler

Plato, used by many Christian thinkers, set down life in a rational and providentially ordered universe. His distinction between being and becoming allowed him to identify an ultimate Good with an ultimate Mind whose intelligibility pervaded the world, even though the world was merely the realm of change. Platonic dualism explained evil either by denying its reality or by assigning its cause to inferior agents permitted for some reason or another by "providence," not destined for eternity. Providence *(pronoia)* was related to the ultimate rationality which lay beyond the realm of becoming, in which a man could participate by virtue of his own mind's innate capacity for discovering and contemplating the supreme Good in the realm of unchanging ideas. To the extent that life and policy was rational, it shared in the providential ordering of the world, which would prevail no matter how unkindly history would deal with an individual or a nation.

Another form of Greek philosophy that eventually influenced Christian thought was the philosophy of the Stoa; it differed from Platonism by rejecting dualism, insisting that reality is one. Key Stoic concepts such as destiny, fate, necessity, and law merged into the notion of an inexorable reason *(logos)* which moves through and unifies reality. This absolute determinism was in turn joined to the notion of providence with its suggestion of beneficence, moving all reality toward its consummation *(telos)*. Such an optimistic monism had to account for physical pain and social inequalities. The Stoics developed several theories to explain evil. They ranged from the disciplinary or moral value of evil to finding it essential in the nature of things for the production of good. Not all these theories agreed with each other, nor were all the thinkers consistent with themselves. An especially grave problem for the deterministic Stoics was that of human freedom. Their most generally accepted solution was to teach an uneasy coexistence between the absolute determinism of nature and history on its way to fulfillment and the free will of man. Man could choose to live according to nature (reason) or accept the unhappy consequences of failure. For many Stoics freedom was to will for oneself the will of necessity, already decreed by fate.

The stern demands of strict Stoicism limited its appeal to a few. Many more preferred an eclectic philosophy that mixed Stoic and Platonic elements. But the spirit of Stoicism flourished in Rome. Its invitation to endure in this world rather than seek for a "beyond" was especially congenial to the Roman spirit, preoccupied by the exercise of power, the rise of empire, and the attending historical events. In Rome history, philosophy, and art were enlisted to explain and justify Roman destiny and rule. In his *Hortensius* the great eclectic, Cicero, brings philosophical doctrines such as providence, freedom, and immortality to the service of the commonwealth. Virgil's *Aeneid* presents the hidden meaning of history as culminating in the establishment of Eternal Rome, the providence of fate having now showered civilization with the benefits of the Augustan age.

Within this eclectic philosophical world Christian theology came into being, based on Scripture held to be a revelation from God and proclaiming that the principalities and powers, including fate, had indeed been conquered by Christ.

In contrast to this Greco-Roman philosophy, the Hebrew conception of God was strongly shaped by remembrance of persons and redemptive events through which a personal, righteous God had acted in their people's long history. They also had an expectation of a future new world. In the Hebrew writings there is a strong sense of mysterious divine purpose in human life, full of conflict and freedom. The great prophets accompany the life of the people with a constant interpretation of their history from the standpoint of God's righteous judgment and personal care. Though universal notes are sounded, the emphasis is on the destiny of the Hebrew people as bearers of God's righteousness, and the individual or national suffering is drawn into the mysterious purposes of God in combat with the powers of unrighteousness.

This sense of history as the arena of decision and purpose persisted in the Christian movement. It inherited the Hebrew Scripture and renewed the notion of God as a personal Will directing

46

history toward its consummation. God cares for His people and acts on their behalf through Christ and crucial events within the life of the new community of the new Israel. The warm, caring personalism embodied both in the concept of God and in the ideals of the Christian life contrasted with the impersonality of Hellenistic philosophical thought.

As the Christian movement spread into the Hellenistic world, its theology was shaped in large measure by the issues being discussed by the philosophers. Particularly the Alexandrian Christian intellectuals, Clement and Origen, engaged the best pagan minds and worked out approaches to the questions of freedom, evil, providence, and human destiny. Although they are always careful to point out the differences between pagan and Christian thought, they often proposed solutions to these problems which blended elements of Biblical thought and current philosophy. In the West Christian and pagan thought occupies itself with the significance of contemporary happenings. In the first important Christian Latin writer, Tertullian (d. 220), this preoccupation is already clear.

Before Tertullian, Irenaeus, living in Gaul but writing in Greek, sketched out a view of God's economy in history, particularly as it applied to the history of salvation. Tertullian translates Irenaeus' Greek *oikonomia* as *dispositio*, which becomes a key term also in its application to "secular" events in history not intimately associated with salvation history. The word *providentia* appears in his writings but is used most often to apply to the foreknowing activity of the Spirit which enabled seers to predict the future, including events coming to pass in his own century.

The meaning of contemporary events and thus also the meaning of the past occupies Tertullian's thought. Fighting the determinism of the Stoa, he stressed man's freedom and God's freedom, which he finds quite compatible with an inexorable will of God moving through history. While the judgment of God in past and contemporary events is part of general history and of Roman history, Tertullian in his *Apology* takes a positive view of the history of the Roman Empire. He lived at the end of the second century's long period of peace and attributed these prosperous circumstances to God's acting through the Roman Empire, notwithstanding the persecution of the Christians. Rome is, he concedes, about as eternal as anything human, and the spread of Christianity to all parts of the world in the context of the empire is for him a providential arrangement. The end impends for all, however, even though Christians pray for its delay. He commends Christianity to the Romans as a part of their own history. They should turn to the true God in obedience. Against the Roman who thought that natural disaster or famine was due to the displeasure of the gods over the presence of Christians, he turned the polemics of Latin philosophical skepticism against polytheism and produced historical arguments to show that such troubles antedated Christian origins. But the main force of his argument is to interpret contemporary events as fraught with meaning—as God at work confronting man and calling him to obedience.

However favorably disposed toward the Roman Empire some Christian writers might have been, the conversion of Constantine and the subsequent recognition of the church by the state was a new thing, a novel and portentous divine intervention in history. In the East a characteristic enthusiastic Christian response was the reference to Constantine as the 13th apostle. Eusebius of Caesarea (d. ca. 340), court theologian and historian, went far beyond that in applying eschatological imagery to these events. He formulated the idea of a new Christian commonwealth which represented human history at its highest level, just a shade removed from the final restoration of souls to eternal life.

For Latin Christian writers such as Arnobius (d. 330) and Ambrose (d. 397), the creation of the Christian empire is indeed a confirmation of divine providence. Much more reticent about exalting the person of the emperor than Eusebius, they generally resisted extravagant language. Ambrose, for example, exercised a prophetic role in his relationship to the new occupants of the throne. He maintained that the emperor is a servant of God's church.

The Latin world soon would face the ordeal of barbarian wrath and with it a threat to the assumption that God was ordering all things to their good. On Aug. 24, 410, Alaric and his troops stormed into the city of Rome. For the first time in 800 years the city was sacked, sending shock waves around the empire disproportionate to the direct political significance of the event. Pagans blamed Christians for evoking the judgment of the ancient gods. Christians wondered about the seeming impotence of their own God.

Augustine of Hippo (d. 430) gave himself to the double task of apologetics with regard to the pagan claims and the interpretation of the faith to the despairing Christians after the fall of Rome. Although the first chapters of the resulting literary effort, *The City of God*, were rushed into print at once, the work took more than 20 years to complete. It contains a comprehensive discussion of providence in history, complementing the account of providence in his own personal life in his *Confessions*.

Augustine is an enigmatic figure in the church's history. He often appears as a lonely giant in the West, an innovator in theology who was out of step with much of the church. Recent research tends to confirm and explain this judgment. For example, we know of a considerable group of Neoplatonists with whom Augustine was associated. It is generally agreed that his conversion to Christianity was preceded by a philosophical conversion to a form of Platonism which in turn influenced his theological development. The Platonic theory of the education of the soul as it rids itself of the beclouding effects of passion and earthly attachment mingles in Augustine with various Christian themes, and especially expresses itself in his ascetic inclination and thought. This Platonic infusion created a tension in Augustine between the concern for the meaning of events, traditional in the West, and the Platonic tendency toward detachment from the transitory phenomenal world.

His conversion to Christianity involved the basic experience of discovering sin, his own inability to break from sin, and the inrush of God to free him from the power of sin for the love of God. Retrospectively he saw his life as God's continuous pursuit of him. Since God is eternal and immutable, that pursuit (election) is rooted in His very being. The Scriptures now opened to him as if he were reading them for the first time. He was, he says, hearing the Spirit, not the letter.

Now he grasped the correlation between faith and understanding, which gave him the solution to the basic intellectual problems posed by Greek thought, including the relationship of providence to freedom. For Augustine divine foreknowledge and human autonomy are not contradictions. On the contrary, the former is the necessary guarantee of the latter. "The religious mind will therefore choose and profess both, affirming them both in a spirit of faithful devotion." [1] Therefore man is not dominated by accident, fate, or necessity. Also with respect to moral righteousness, grace does not destroy free will but helps it to achieve its purpose. Liberty is precisely the power of using free choice to good ends to become holy. The ability to do or to refrain from evil are proofs of free choice. But the supreme form of liberty is the desire not to do evil but to do good, because the individual has been confirmed in God's grace, a state not fully accessible to us in this life. Thus Christian wisdom allows a man to live and act in this world freely, creatively, with love and hope. He regards events as unique and unpredictable. To him they are not manifestations or interventions of arbitrary, inexorable fate. Although faith may imperfectly understand a given event, all events finally bear witness to the paradoxical work of God in the world.

The will of God is therefore not simply active in a general providential ordering of the world or in guiding it to its appointed goal; it is present and involved in every human act, even in acts of evil. Because evil is the absence of good, God in no way is to be blamed for evil. That blame resides in man, all men. All men therefore stand under condemnation. The fact that some and not others are given the gift to turn to God is a mystery. Most often Augustine insists on being silent before this mystery. At other times, especially in the long course of controversy when all words cannot be properly weighed, he allows himself to be led into the metaphysics of double predestination, interpreting the Biblical passages according to the independent logic of his philosophical thought, giving this doctrine a gloomy and, as some theologians have pointed out, horrible character.

In the philosopher-theologian Boethius we find this logic carried to its conclusion. In his *Consolations of Philosophy* Boethius constructs a doctrine of divine grace and predestination which detaches the soul from the cares of this world in the confidence that all is ordered for man's good — but without once mentioning Christ. This is far from the Augustine who, on the basis of Christ, expects everything from God's promise to care for and intervene in human life. Augustine does not flinch from linking the will of God to every event,

---

[1] *City of God* 5. 9.

even the evil deeds of men. Even the use of the idea of God's permission of evil does not diminish His involvement.[2] "Who can refrain from trembling at those judgments when God does according to his pleasure even in the hearts of the wicked, at the same time rendering to them according to their deeds?"[3]

God's involvement in the historical process is the theme of *The City of God*. Here, too, there is a remarkable linking of divine involvement and human volition. God is leading the race to final judgment and His eternal rest, but this is occurring through a double historical process which He guides. The actors in this process are the citizens of two cities, animated by two strivings, two loves, two futures. Both types of citizens are potentially present in Adam. In Cain and Abel they appear distinct, and Augustine proceeds to trace the history of the world as the conflict between the two communities. The "City of the Earth," Babylon, is built on the struggle for man's glory, moved by self-love and resulting in fratricide of which the history of pagan Rome provided many examples. The "City of God," the new Jerusalem, Israel and Christendom, is built on the love of God, for God's glory. The coming of Christ is crucial in the process. All of history is made to serve the emergence of the City of God, which alone is eternal. Not to be identified fully with the institutional church, this city nevertheless consists empirically of the Christians who are invited now to build a commonwealth in which faith and love would make the old and necessary virtues new jewels in the common life. Augustine is not advocating a Christian empire. He comes to the conclusion that no earthly society can be identified with the City of God, diverging in a striking manner from the view of Eusebius and the hitherto general optimism about the new Christian empire. As Israel was buffeted by history so, he suggested, will earthly society be buffeted, for the pride of man is operative in the Christian empire as well as in the pagan. Peace and prosperity do not follow from the national worship of the true God.

Thus he can also explain to the Christian who has suffered under the hard and violent hand of the barbarian that the meaning of life cannot be found in this world but must be rooted in God's will and

---

[2] *On the Trinity* 3. 4.

[3] *On Grace and Free Will* 20.

destiny for him. When a man's heart rests in God, he can accept suffering and loss together with peace and prosperity in humility and equanimity, not quarreling with God over His policies in the world. Thus suffering is not senseless, but leads the Christian to find the meaning of life in the possession of God and the search for His truth, not in degrees of luck or in the search for prosperity.

Despite Augustine's involvements as bishop and leading citizen in Hippo, and despite his attention to the details of history and its larger meanings, he finally does not offer a specific interpretation of the meaning of the critical contemporary events in imperial history. He neither refutes the pagan nor supports the traditional Christian argument. He pointedly omits such providential interpretations as the simultaneous appearance of Augustus and Christ, which was rapidly becoming a Christian convention. Although able to offer large perspectives by assimilating history to the plan of Eden-Calvary-Final Consummation, he provides little specific guidance for understanding his own times in a particular way.

On this matter Augustine stands quite alone. His student, Orosius, declined to take the lofty attitude of his master and attempted to deal with concrete affairs. He took up the theme of relative happiness in human life, arguing that what was happiness in the good old times for the Romans clearly was not the same for those they conquered. And he suggested that the contemporary barbarian might appear to future historians as a noble initiator of a new and prosperous reign. He continues the tradition of linking Augustus and Christ and argues that the Christian empire has brought greater happiness to earth. Yet he tempers this optimism by noting the dark side of the barbarian incursion and allowing that at the last times the devil will indeed be let loose for one last effort before the final judgment.

In 440 Salvian of Marseilles wrote *On the Governance of God* in response to the complaints of wealthy Christian Gauls who were suffering the unfortunate results of being on the highway of barbarian invasion. He examines many Scriptural accounts of God's judgment and shows his readers how God judges in history and also points out that He is not automatically propitiated by acts of repentance and piety. God's care may indeed be exercised through adversity, though some comfort may be had by distinguishing between present and future judgments of God. From the latter the believer is absolved when he repents, but not necessarily from the former. The general framework of argument is the same which we have noted in Orosius, though with Salvian the rhetorical aim is to move a Christian audience to self-criticism and repentance and away from easily accepting a view of God as sentimentally beneficent.

Finally we refer to Gregory the Great (d. 604), who continues this line of thought and is certain that God is good and will triumph. He is equally certain that he is standing in the very last times. A rash of natural catastrophes confirms this for him. Increased volcanic activity in Sicily is a premonition of hell. The flooding of the Tiber and the ravages of the plague are signs to call people to repentance. All events — whether in nature or history — are part of a grand divine design, and Gregory is prepared to read them as such and to act. His remarkable achievements in Italy and England are done as responses to God's will under the urgent expectation of the End. Civic as well as ecclesiastical duties are undertaken in a kind of emergency ethic.

This ethic becomes the basic medieval pattern of action, for the medieval pope, emperor, or crusader justifies much of his policy by appealing to God's will, His providential design, and the duty of His agents to act accordingly. In this development Augustine's *The City of God* is misread as justification for policies which claim clearly to discern the will of God in history providentially at work on behalf of the "City of God," identified, to no one's surprise, with the civic and ecclesiastical establishment.

In the Middle Ages Thomas Aquinas (d. 1274) is the theologian who, according to Paul Tillich, set in motion the intellectual forces that issue in the secularizing of Western thought. Tillich contrasts Augustine and Thomas in their basic approach to the question of God and reality. For Augustine, God is known immediately in the very act of knowing. The relation between faith and knowledge meant that Augustine began with an understanding of God and proceeded to account for the rest of empirical reality, assimilating empirical data to that understanding. By contrast, Thomas introduced the newly discovered Aristotelian philosophy to theology, which began with empirical data and from that proceeded to prove the existence and reality of God.

With Aristotle came the challenge of Arabic intellectual power, undermining a number of Christian presuppositions. Thomas' effort was aimed at meeting this challenge by taking account of all knowledge and data in order to relate them to the Christian faith. In Aristotle he thought he found the intellectual apparatus to do just that. Thomas was Christian in his deepest convictions and presuppositions and in the end acknowledged that the power of reason had to be supplemented by revelation in order for the full Christian mystery to be exhibited.

A useful way to grasp the thought of Thomas is to consider the basic structure of his *Summa*. The plan of the work presented in the prolog of *Quaestio 2* begins with God, revealing Him as the source and goal of all things. All that is created — that is, all creatures endowed with spirit — come from Him and return to Him. All human effort toward happiness, all human history, is finally understood within that motion of exit and return. So God governs all events in His majestic, mysterious way, through His love drawing free beings to Himself. Should man not respond to this work of God, which encounters him in many ways, it is finally not God who rejects man but man who turns from his own true and highest good. All things are given this potential by God, who creatively interpenetrates all beings as they actualize their potential, each toward its own end and goal. All events and beings are seen from this ultimate standpoint. There is a serenity in Thomas, who seems to write without having doubts and finds a place in his great scheme for all phenomena.

In the course of his discussion on providence, in the *Summa* as well as in other writings, Thomas proceeded in his celebrated manner to analyze all questions related to the issue. Among the main questions with which he dealt are the distinction between arbitrary and ordered providence, the relation of human freedom to God as the cause of all action, the place of animals in providence, and the definition of evil with respect to providence.

With respect to the question of God's action and man's freedom, Thomas maintained the profound Augustinian intention, but endeavored to work it out in Aristotelian terms, specifically through the use of the doctrine of forms. A form is that by which a thing is a distinct entity and by which it can move to its proper end. God's creative power respects the form of each creature, interpenetrating it in such a way that God is continuously active in the action of each

54

form. Man's form involves the capacity to know and choose the good. Thus God acts in man precisely through his free will. The energy of action is love, God's love and man's love. As for Augustine so for Thomas the work of Jesus Christ is central, but we are clearly dealing in the *Summa* with the establishment of a Christian metaphysics. The categories of history recede into the background. Despite the very cerebral and optimistic tone of his argumentation, one cannot escape the impression that Thomas thought in the presence of God, that his world finally and ultimately had the nature of a symphony. Not that chaos was unknown, but God the Creator was steadily at work, originating being even as the sun gave light. The two convictions, that God had the quality of intellect and that the world finally made logical and rational sense, dominated this massive effort.

We should not pass to the turbulent time of the Reformation without remarking on some of the developments which transpire in the centuries following Thomas. The disputes of the High Scholastic period raise many issues. Particularly in Duns Scotus (d. 1308), the nominalist, the interest in empirical phenomena reaches important new levels. Scotus worked analytically to break up the Thomistic synthesis. Thomas had admitted that the human capacity for reason had limitations and therefore needed ecclesiastical or revelational authority to support it or to complete its conclusions. Thus the problem of reason versus revelation becomes a central issue, posing questions not really entertained in the previously regnant Augustinian theology: the relative authority of pope, council, Bible, church.

With Scotus another important element is introduced: the concept of God and man is defined in terms of the supremacy of will. Intellect had dominated the Thomistic notion of God, suggesting at the same time a rationally ordered universe. Will dominates in Scotus' description of God, suggesting that although the world is ordered as God has presently willed it, He could will it otherwise. This shift produced many new debates concerning the interdependence of will and intellect in God and in His relations to the world. Divine and human freedom must be reconsidered in their interrelationship. Can and does God "interfere" with the lawfully ordered universe which He established?

Our interest is perhaps better served by noting the shift in perspective that this nominalist movement brings. Attention is increasingly given to empirical phenomena as the manifestation of that which is willed by God. Stress on the uniqueness of observed phenomena attempts to explain such phenomena by empirical analysis and lends credence to Tillich's interpretation of the general trend of intellectual history and perception of reality. This interpretation sees this trend as a gradual dissociation of God from the world, so that man comes to view God and the world as separate and unrelated entities, a view that leads to the contemporary secularization of thought—a major problem for contemporary theology.

To pass from Thomas and Scotus to Luther is to move into another era. Many of Luther's presuppositions are still those of medieval Christendom. The name of God comes easily to his lips; St. Paul's statement in 1 Corinthians 15 about God being all in all appears frequently in his writing. Yet there is something new. Gone is the serenity of Thomas; in its place is a turbulent soul, examining his own and others' experiences amidst a whirlwind of events and chaos, searching ruthlessly his own inner self, and through this all apprehending his own world and the meaning of the Bible in a fresh, original way.

His scholastic teacher, Gabriel Biel, had summarized the theological task as *ratio, meditatio,* and *lectio.* Nothing so clearly signals the new in Luther as his own contrasting *ratio, meditatio, tentatio.* Luther is indeed a man of *ratio; ratio divina* he called it. Yet the *tentatio (Anfechtung)* points to the most interesting and instructive side of Luther and his theology.

Luther does not call the existence of God into question; more frightening for him is the prospect that God may be the devil or, more commonly, that the God with whom we have to deal is the God who places impossible demands upon man and executes judgment and wrath on men who do not fulfill these demands. Thomas described evil as a lack of good which allows all possible stages and degrees of good to exist. Thus evil is necessary for the perfection of the universe. For Luther the world is a battleground between God and Satan, and only in Christ does it become clear, from revelation and through faith, that God is governing the affairs of man and his world.

Thus God moves mysteriously in the world, acting in paradoxical ways through His masks, the *larvae dei,* in ways which are contradictory to the intellect's expectations about God. We may sample some of Luther's thought in the following passage from *The Bondage of the Will:*

> Therefore, that there might be room for faith, it is necessary that all those things which are believed should be hidden. But they are not hidden more deeply than under the contrary of sight, sense, and experience. Thus, when God makes alive, He does it by killing; when He justifies, He does it by bringing in guilty: when He exalts to heaven, He does it by bringing down to hell. . . . Thus He conceals His eternal mercy and loving-kindness behind His eternal wrath: His righteousness, behind apparent iniquity. This is the highest degree of faith—to believe that He is merciful, who saves so few and damns so many. . . . If, therefore, I could by any means comprehend how that same God can be merciful and just, who carries the appearance of so much wrath and iniquity, there would be no need of faith.[4]

This way of talking about God and faith leads us to the heart of Luther's theology and the source of his language of paradox: the theology of the cross.

Paul Althaus writes:

> The theology of the cross permeates all of Luther's theological thinking. All true theology is "wisdom of the cross." . . . The cross hides God himself. For it reveals not the might but the helplessness of God. God's power appears not directly but paradoxically under helplessness and lowliness. Thus it is that God's grace is hidden under his wrath and that his gifts and benefits are "hidden under the cross," in other words, under "trouble and disaster."[5]

The theology of the cross provides Luther with a new way of apprehending reality. Intellect, ordinary experience, and Scripture combine to impress one with a sense of God brooding in the background of life. This is the God whose providential ways are hidden, the God of predestination, the God who puts to death that which He has made. It is only when faith comes into being and grasps the

---

[4] Martin Luther, *The Bondage of the Will* (Grand Rapids: Wm. B. Eerdmans Publishing Co., 1931), pp. 70–71.

[5] *The Theology of Martin Luther,* trans. Robert C. Schultz (Philadephia: Fortress Press, 1966), p. 30.

revelatory word of the cross of Christ that the new apprehension of reality takes place and the reliable paternal heart of God discloses the final truth of both judgment and grace.

This faith, as Althaus points out,[6] for Luther is not a static thing, but rather a constant, dynamic grasping after this reality. Thus the cross is not simply a historical event from which theologians can draw certain theological conclusions. For Luther faith in Christ is participation in the cross, finally participation in the very suffering of God for the world. Repentance and faith, the daily dying and rising of the Christian man, is a living out of the cross as through the hidden ways of His discipline God strips away the old from man and shapes a new creation. In similar ways love for the neighbor means participation in the cross, the laying down of one's life for a brother. The battle against sin in one's own life and against evil in the world is of a piece with God's struggle against the evil distortion of His world. Thus the first, and possibly the last, answer of the Christian to the problem of evil is the struggle against its presence in all areas of life in the power of God's forgiveness in Christ. In this view God's forgiveness is the destruction of the key aspect of evil: the sentence of death that every man carries.

This theological emphasis in Luther is rooted in St. Paul's writing, but it is also influenced by the monastic theology of mortification and the medieval tradition of meditation on the cross. Luther takes these themes, allows them to control his theological work, and places them in the mainstream of subsequent theology. The theology of the cross gives him new scope for handling the problem of trouble and evil in life, at least in one's personal life. Troubles can be seen as blessings bestowed by the God who kills in order to make alive by driving man to Christ. They become purgative and purifying, and much Christian preaching will work with these themes.

Although Luther has a strong sense of history and a sense of God willing all events to occur, he does not appear to wrestle with the problem of evil as it appears to be most acute to many of our contemporaries. Meaningless catastrophes, the death of innocents, intensified human malice — these problems do not seem central to

---

[6] Ibid., p. 33.

him. And yet it seems he provides some resources for dealing with these phenomena. He is utterly realistic with himself and in looking at the world. His *Anfechtungen* are not unlike the reported experiences of anxiety and meaninglessness in contemporary life. His understanding of God allows enormous mystery, acknowledges an inscrutable will at work which eludes explanation, which indeed forbids any facile attempt to "explain" events which do not make sense. Such a view of God even allows for a lively doctrine of the devil, who is granted great latitude in his evil plans. God wills all, except sin. The logical contradictions inherent in these statements stand unresolved in Luther's thought. Such knowledge of God is beyond man's capacity. Luther prefers the truth of experience and revelation to the logical resolution of these problems. Thus he continues to speak in the language of paradox, and above all speaks of faith as "contrary to the appearances," as light shining in the midst of darkness, and as struggling for expression as it coexists with unbelief and despair. Sufficient and reliable knowledge of God is present in Christ our Brother. Meditation on His life as the way of the cross, in whom God the Father Creator is fully present, is the way to such living knowledge. In a famous passage from his Epiphany sermon of 1526, Luther writes:

> This order must be carefully preserved. We are not to ascend to the study of the divine majesty before we have adequately comprehended this little infant. We are to ascend into heaven by that ladder which is placed before us, using those steps which God prepared and used for this ascent. The Son of God does not want to be seen and found in heaven. Therefore he descended from heaven to this earth and came to us in our flesh. He placed himself in the womb of his mother, in her lap, and on the cross. And this is the ladder which he has placed on the earth and by which we are to ascend to God.[7]

The paternal heart of God thus revealed as that of the bountiful, caring Father encourages Luther to elaborate a remarkable theology of creation expressed, for example, in his explanation of the First Article of the Creed, in which God is pictured as showering His creatures with gifts. Here redemption and creation tend to merge in Luther's thought, and the gift-character of God's world leads to

---

[7] Quoted by Althaus, p. 187, note 19.

trust in His providence and to the doxology of receiving with thanks and praise.

In the writings of John Calvin (d. 1564) the notion of divine providence becomes increasingly prominent, especially as he comes to explore the problem of predestination, which is obviously closely linked to providence. In the definitive edition of the *Institutes* providence is dealt with at great length, following directly his section on creation. Predestination, on the other hand, is treated in the context of redemption and justification.

Calvin stands in the classical Augustinian tradition, quoting frequently from the bishop of Hippo. Most interesting is his strong repudiation of any view of God which separates His creative activity from His active involvement in the world. He rejects any view which suggests that God set the world and its laws into motion and thereupon retired from active governance of His world. He seeks to be faithful to the picture of God in the Bible.

The Bible depicts God as constantly active and powerful in the world, and Calvin wishes to explore this dynamic activity of God in guiding and moving events and in governing nature. He is equally vigorous in opposing what he holds to be a widely prevailing mood: that all things happen fortuitously — good or evil fortune. Calvin wants faith to go even farther. "But who so has learned from the mouth of Christ that all the hairs of his head are numbered (Matth. x. 30), will look farther for the cause, and hold that all events are governed by the secret counsel of God" (I, 16, 4). Nor is Calvin satisfied with a doctrine of general, universal providence rooted in the regular occurence of nature. He insists on a special providence of God for man (as the crown of creation) and for the church in particular as His elect. Faith can indeed make sense of particular events which might otherwise appear to be a fortuitous congery of contingencies or ordinary natural causes. He explores incidents, particularly from the Bible, to illustrate this. He does not hesitate to draw on the scholastic tradition for the necessary distinctions which help to account for the apparent contradictions and problems in this view.

In the final edition of the *Institutes* a strongly pastoral interest prevails as he devotes a whole section (I, 17) to the use of the doctrine of providence. Here Calvin repeatedly stresses that this doctrine is finally intended to lead the faithful to the Word of God for instruction and meditation and to prayer. Felicitous events will evoke thanksgiving, adversity will provoke self-examination and repentance, and a sense of the divine presence in all of life will increase the Christian's sense of dependence on God. Knowing that God is the ultimate cause of all that happens does not relieve man of responsibility, but on the other hand

> when once the light of Divine Providence has illumined the believer's soul, he is relieved and set free, not only from the extreme fear and anxiety which formerly oppressed him, but from all care. For as he justly shudders at the idea of chance, so he can confidently commit himself to God. (I, 17, 11)

Should adversity be wholly inexplicable, the believer finally bows before the sovereign power and might of God. Thus in Calvin, in comparison with Thomas Aquinas, we see a return to an essentially Augustinian view, a serene and powerful evangelical description of the triumphant sovereignty of God, who will finally overcome and prevail in His glory.

The Protestant scholasticism which followed the generation of reformers appropriated much of the heritage of medieval scholasticism in dealing with providence. This doctrine was commonly dealt with in connection with the doctrine of creation and sought to set forth the themes of God's work of preservation, governance, and direction of the world to its goal. Three concepts were prominently used in this connection: *Conservatio* is God's fidelity to His creatures by which they receive daily life from His hand. *Concursus* describes God's accompaniment of our freedom in daily events, reminding again how theologians always insisted on the relative freedom of man in dealing with ordinary events. *Gubernatio* refers to the various ways by which God directs the course of events. *Gubernatio* generally embraced such distinctions as *permissio, impeditio, directio,* and *determinatio.* Under each of these headings various problems from ordinary life and from the Bible are analyzed. Through all these distinctions the effort is made to account for the ways in which God operates in the world. Through the use and application of these distinctions in the analysis of problems drawn from ordinary life and from the Bible the dogmaticians explain God's relations to the world. Among a number of them there is also the effort to give some expression to the Christological emphasis of the Reformation by some suggestion that a most special providence of God is at work in the activity of the Holy Spirit drawing men to Christ and keeping them in Him.

For more than a millennium the providential view of history formulated by Augustine was the common assumption among the thinkers of the West. From time to time theologians or philosophers reinvigorated it, as did Calvin in stressing the presence of God acting in the world and doing this especially for the sake of the church, but few challenged it. The poetry of John Milton can still take it for granted, but by the following generation it has become for many a pious opinion on its way to being, indeed, hotly contested. Jacques Bossuet's *Discours sur l'histoire universelle* in 1681 was a last, brilliant effort to stay the subversion of the Augustianian view already under-way ever since Petrarch removed the label "Dark Ages" from classi-cal pre-Christian times and attached it to the Christian era. Renais-sance humanism had discovered the Greeks and Romans. Christian historians themselves were being attracted to the history of nations as distinguished from the history of the church — the central theme of the Augustinian interpretation — and in time were stressing the importance of the former at the expense of the latter. Before long the conventional periodization of "Before Christ" and *Anno Domini* would become a pious convention and would be effectively sup-plemented by a new designation: the classical, medieval, and modern epochs.

Indeed, although the grand idea of providence in history gradually dissolved in its theological form, it persisted in a number of ways until very recent times. The idea of progress, purposeful progress in history, was one such form. The notion of a preestab-lished harmony, particularly as set forth in liberal economic thought, was another. Historical-philosophical dialectics as found in Hegel and Marx surely traces its ancestry to the venerable doctrine. And it must be added that the doctrine of providence, at least in a deistic mode, survived well into the modern era because a number of theologians were able to accommodate it to these various embodying ideas. For theologians of a century ago in Great Britian and America, for whom the 19th century seemed the century of manifest destiny, the synthesis of liberal theology and various ideas of purposeful progress and evolution kept the notion of providence very much alive. But as these embodying ideas collapsed under the impact of war and the profound eruptions of unpredictable human evil, the notion of providence disappeared as well. The old dark figure of fate seemed in many respects to have regained the field.

How has modern theology dealt with the notion of providence? This issue is bound up with the God question itself, a major difference between the situation of Luther and our own time. Modern theology has had to struggle with the limited empirical horizons that science has set for many of the educated today, horizons which seem to call into question the very notion of revelation itself. The prestige of the empirical, and our difficulty in relating the empirical to that which is beyond the scope of empirical inquiry, dominates among our problems. This is true despite the continued interest in religion and in a poetic approach to reality, and in the revulsion against a materialistic understanding of our world.

The methodological father of modern theology is Friedrich Schleiermacher, who attempted to place the Christian faith on a basis which could not in principle be threatened by the findings of science or made irrelevant by secular ethical-moral systems. Accordingly he argued that science could not oppose religion, and religion had no claim on science since they represented distinct modes of thought dealing with distinctly different levels or areas of life. As religion should not be confused with science, so it should not be confused with a particular system of morality. Rather, religion is found in the area of the universal human experience of dependence in which God directly authenticates His own presence to man in ways which could not be accessible to science.

The most striking thing about the last century and a half is how Schleiermacher in fact set the terms in which theology was done, a fact recognized by all those theologians who have attempted to fight the subjective implications of his thought. Take, for example, a theologian such as Rudolf Bultmann. Accepting the results of the modern scientific picture of the world, Bultmann depicts man as faced with the question of whether or not he is simply a determined object in a closed system or whether he in fact has freedom and finds fulfillment in what for all practical purposes is a system in which death seems inexorably to have the last word. Bultmann argues that the question of self-understanding involved here is not one which science can deal with. While the Word of God cannot and does not alter the laws of the universe, it can and does create a new self-understanding which promises freedom and fulfillment—which leads from bondage to the world to freedom to love my neighbor, trusting in a God who is Himself different from and not contained by the system of the universe. Thus God is hidden to normal sight, but the Word of the cross received in the decision of faith reveals Him indeed to be Father. The controlling distinctions here seem to be those of Schleiermacher, given intellectual structure by the existentialist epistemology of most contemporary theology.

This general methodology strongly influences—one might say controls—the massive Christocentric theology of Karl Barth, the Law-Gospel reading of the Bible by the Lutherans, and the "acts of God" or "history of salvation" theology. (I am not discussing the most recent new departures such as that by Wolfhart Pannenberg, who seems intent on avoiding this problem.) This methodology correlates revelation and inward, personal faith in such a way that no significant statement about God and His activity can be legitimately made which is not involved in an inward, personal relation to Him in faith through Word and Spirit. When such faith arises, "the face of the world changes and I can speak of God as my Savior, my Creator, my Judge" (Gerhardt Ebeling). In a similar way the "history of salvation" theology, which celebrates the "mighty acts of God," seems at first glance to be directly avoiding this subjectivity by pointing to acts of God in history, to the gathering of the people of God, and to the lordship of Christ now and in the future. The same problem of method may be discovered here, however. The "lordship of Christ" means that He reigns in the heart of the believer, scientific evidence not being able to verify or falsify that statement. While there is much reference to Christ as Lord of history, this usually has in mind His reign in the hearts of believers and the fact that one day He will be acknowledged as Lord by all. The question of providence asks how He reigns elsewhere in the world. "The mighty acts of God" is a very slippery concept until statements are made on how God is active in events not within the history of salvation. There is a strong propensity in contemporary theology not to deal with this question.

Even in the theology of Paul Tillich, who always has the apologetic task in mind, the same methodological distinction is made. Theology must be existential. Thus his doctrine of providence (which he opposes to fate in the great classical Augustinian tradition) is an account of how God in His freedom creates free people who are nonetheless driven creatively, together with all history, toward fulfillment. This divine drive is not interference; it is "a quality of every constellation of conditions . . . which 'drives' or 'lures' toward fulfillment." [8] It is the divine answer to the question of prayer which asks God to bring each moment or constellation of events to fulfillment according to His will. Since meaningless evil is present in the world, the doctrine of providence is paradoxical, requiring faith "in spite of," faith that God will direct a man to fulfillment even when his creaturely existence is threatened by meaningless evil. But one man cannot speak for others or for events which do not touch him. Theodicy in this sense is ruled out on methodological grounds.

The theology of Tillich lends itself powerfully to preaching and to apologetic work for people who resonate to the existentialist's analysis of human life. For many others, however, the existential limitations would have to be abandoned and a new effort made to describe God in His realtionship to history in general, to people and things, and to do this in ways rooted in empirical studies of the various structures of human life and experience.

This brief and sketchy critique of contemporary theologians is borrowed from an analysis by David E. Jenkins [9] and another by Langdon B. Gilkey,[10] the latter attempting to account for the virtual disappearance of the concept of providence from theology today. Both point to the severe limitations of the modern mentality under impact of the modern experience. Gilkey notes a number of other matters which should be summed up here. He points out how the accepted view of God has been moralized, probably under the impact of humane Christian teachings. The notion of a God who works good and evil, who does not act under "the rules of the game" as

---

[8] Paul Tillich, *Systematic Theology*, I (Chicago: University of Chicago Press, 1951), 267.

[9] *Guide to the Debate about God* (Philadelphia: Westminster Press, 1966).

[10] "The Concept of Providence in Contemporary Theology," *The Journal of Religion*, XLIII, 3 (July 1963), 171–92.

we understand them outrages modern man and is not acceptable to him. This eliminates the brooding, inscrutable God of the Bible and the classical theologians, before whom Augustine, Luther, and Calvin trembled. Associated with our inability to think of God as involved in every moment of life (because of our habit of thinking of causes as random and immediate) is our view of man as free and independent from divine control or prompting.

Both of these authors point to a needed correction if the notion of providence is to be reinvigorated. They both point to a renewal of natural theology, not in the sense of an original, rational knowledge of God but as an exploration by theology of the structures of human life, the natural and social processes, with a view toward restating the doctrine of God the Creator in terms and categories that are faithful at once to the tradition of the doctrine of providence as well as to our knowledge of the structures and processes of life and history.

Although the doctrine of providence strictly speaking refers to the relationship of God to creatures and events, the Trinitarian tradition exerts a needed pressure not to allow the doctrines of creation, redemption, and sanctification to go their own ways. Both the Reformation and pre-Reformation traditions are instructive on this point. Both traditions face in common the serious challenge of keeping God and the world together in their preaching of the Gospel, daring to talk—however modestly—of the ways of an inscrutable God in our world.

A Philosophical View of Providence

C. E. Huber

In one of his St. Thomas More lectures John Courtney Murray offered a perceptive assay on the delicate balance a Christian must preserve when dealing with the doctrine of God. "In the things of God," he wrote, "it is perilous to misplace either one's agnosticism or one's gnosticism. The risk is the loss of one's God, who is lost both when he ceases to be God, because no longer unknown, and when he ceases to be our God, because not known at all." [1] It is indeed possible to claim too much for our knowledge of God and His ways with men, as it is possible to refuse to say enough. When one considers the fact that the doctrine of God encompasses the full range of elements constituting the Christian faith and that the church's theology has examined that faith for almost two millennia, the suspicion easily arises that the balance between godly ignorance and knowledge has been tipped too far toward the latter. The fact is, however, that the bulk of theology has developed as it has in an effort to preserve the balance.

The organized church, it has been argued, is the only human institution which has perpetually prized economy in thought and has consistently cast a jaundiced eye at every effort to expand the domain of knowledge concerning God. Far from being a sign of anti-intellectualism, this effort has emerged from the depths of the church's faith that God, if He is to be truly God, must finally command the awe and silence of every human heart and that His people must guard themselves against the recurrent pretense of wisdom that dilutes their worship of Him and constricts His love and sovereignty to more manageable and hence controllable proportions. Knowledge is power, and the claim to full knowledge of God is indeed the claim

---

[1] In *The Problem of God* (London: Yale University Press, 1964), p. 64.

to have put God where we would like Him, namely, where we can decide whether He is useful or not. This, of course, is to make Him no God at all. What, therefore, is known of God must not be the knowledge His people have discovered through their investigative efforts, much like pioneers forging a settlement out of a wilderness. The true knowledge of God is gained only when He reveals Himself to us as He chooses and when we accept in humility the grace of the understanding He provides. Thus arises the idea of a *provident* God, whose providence embraces finally even what we may claim to know about it and its workings in human life.

All this is said by way of introduction to the task of the writer: to examine the concept of providence in the light of contemporary philosophy. The introductory remarks are deliberately chosen to serve as a map whereby the reader may locate the intention and scope of this philosophical effort and see it in the greater context of the surrounding faith within which the task takes place. Philosophy makes reason the principal arbiter in human affairs. In modern times this rational commitment has too often been viewed as entailing the negative judgment that anything that is more than what demonstrative reason can grasp is either irrational or superfluous to human knowledge and purpose. This prejudice does not follow *logically* from the philosopher's commitment to rationality, but seemingly this has not disturbed many Western thinkers since the Enlightenment. This situation is strong evidence for the belief that even atheists finally operate in a greater context of faith — or unfaith — than their own philosophies can justify.

We are frank to acknowledge at the outset a commitment to the Christian faith, and within this context we propose to pursue a rational inquiry of the complexities involved in the idea of providence. While it would be proper to discuss this commitment philosophically, that is not the particular issue of our task. Rather, we are concerned to honor God by maintaining the delicate balance between our knowledge and ignorance.

The traditional doctrine of providence encompasses a remarkable array of important issues in philosophical theology. Because of the familiar currency of the language about providence, these distinct issues often become confused or blurred, and they overlap one another to generate serious confusions. For example, one of the earliest confusions to arise in the church's thought was between God's omniscience and His causal agency. God's foreknowledge was taken to entail an exclusive causal determination of all events in human or natural history. But this is on the face of it not a necessary consequence, and it therefore serves as an example of the confusions we must avoid.

As usually understood, the concept of providence expresses the faith of the Christian community in God's sovereign and benevolent care for and governance of the created world in general, and His guidance of the individual events of human and natural history in particular. Specifically, the concept intends to express (1) God's foresight with regard to all events in history in such a way that with respect to Him it cannot be said that any event is purely fortuitous or without a place in His eternal plan and knowledge; (2) God's causal agency or governance in relation to all events; (3) God's benevolent disposition and purpose toward men, which is realized in His causal power and rule over events and in His continuous preservation of the order with which He governs them. The concept of providence thus understood entails and presupposes as basic a concept of God, of the "world" or cosmos, and of His relation(s) to it. These are not only basic to the idea but they are also the substance of the fundamental philosophical issues which the idea spawns. Since our purpose here is to examine providence and not the entire theological panorama, we shall discuss particular problems related to (1) and (2) only so far as they have immediate bearing on (3), inasmuch as providence typically has special reference to a set of relations obtaining between God and the world.

The doctrine of providence in our secular, naturalistic age poses a special problem for modern men. It is a truism of the times that our nagging religious doubt does not result from our ability or inability to find a gracious God, but rather from our inability to find God at all. In philosophical fashion this may be put in the formal mode of speech by saying that "God" is a term for which modern men cannot find a meaning or referent. The various issues raised by the belief that there is a God have usually been debated on a logical and philosophical level not common to ordinary intelligence and with a painful precision which made the whole issue seem rather more academic than crucial for everyday life. There was objective curiosity about the problems, but seemingly no room for genuine existential involvement on the part of the Christian laity in their attempted resolution.

Since God's providence is a species of the more general doctrine of God, we should expect that it, too, is embroiled in the same difficulties and questions. There is one facet of current experience, however, which makes providence a uniquely lively puzzle among ordinary and unsophisticated Christians. For this concept involves not merely a highly articulated and remote set of arguments but also people, their lives, their attitudes, their hopes, and their fears. The concept of a provident God is the idea of God-with-us rather than a bare and abstract God *a se*. The common temperament may find it easy to ignore or avoid the simple atheist. But if God's care or compassion for the human situation is challenged, the invitation to argument is almost impossible to refuse. To ignore it is to ignore an issue which involves the ordinary events of one's own life and their direction at the hand of One who is for us and with us. The peculiar liveliness, then, of doubts concerning providence reflects the fact of our deeply felt stake in the issues.

THE EMPIRICISTIC BIAS

The developments of philosophy in recent times, together with developments in technology and communications, have tended to call into question and often flatly to deny the meaningfulness of talk about God and His relations with the cosmos and men. The rise of the natural sciences since the 17th century accounts in no small part for the corresponding weakening in the confidence that behind the scientifically ordered and explainable appearances there dwells the Almighty One, the Holy One of Israel, Creator and Redeemer, Lord of lords. Philosophers since Hume and Kant have taught us that the cosmos is a closed and self-contained system within which individual events have their causes in other individual events. The causes of all events, they said, can be explained in terms of time- and space-bound categories of thought. The traditional notion of providence might accommodate this view since, so far as it goes, it makes no judgment about the independence of the universe as a whole. But the scientific, naturalistic temper has never been content to rest there.

In the 13th century St. Thomas Aquinas argued that the universe as such demanded an explanation, and he found it in God's creative and providential activity. However, ancient and modern naturalism insists that no meaningful explanation can be fashioned for the universe as a whole, since such an explanation would require extra-empirical, non-spatiotemporal categories of thought which are simply not available to the human mind. Therefore this view holds that we are confined to the strictly observable or predictable finite causes of experience. These allow no appeal to a Provident Mind or Will that transcends the universe. This chief dogma of empiricism enforces a limitation on the historic Christian assertion that God is the Creator and Sustainer of the creaturely world, who orders it according to a benevolent plan. This empirical limitation, therefore, deserves priority in our examination of the issues.

The point of departure for the empiricistic bias is the insistence that human knowledge is possible only in those areas where some kind of sense experience, interpreted rather broadly to include, for example, the data of memory, is available to furnish the reference for true assertions. For example, it has been argued that the assertion "It is raining" is true only when it is in fact raining and otherwise false. Thus, the argument goes, assertions such as "God is good" or even "Stealing is wrong" can be regarded as true or false only if there were some states of affairs to which the assertions referred. Since it was taken for granted that such states of affairs could not be identified in our *sense* experience, it was concluded that such statements could not be proved either true or false. That is, the empiricists concluded, they were not assertions or propositions at all and therefore quite literally without cognitive meaning. Lately it has been argued that such assertions may have other functions than that of describing some state of reality. However, this did not alter the empiricists' view of reality, although it modified their understanding of the concept of a meaningful statement. The empiricists continued to argue that only assertions that could be judged true or false by actual or possible sense experience are meaningful.

This scanty description of what we are calling the empiricistic bias will illustrate the fundamental assumption on which that bias rests. The empiricists assume that "reality" is a term which is properly used to describe only that which is subject to our sensory experience. Where the latter is lacking, there can be no understandable descriptive use of "real" or any meaningful belief about the existence of objects or events which are being talked about. Since it is held that God and His mighty works in history are not entities that can be confirmed or disconfirmed by empirical observations, it is claimed that the assertions which Christians make about God and His acts are neither true nor false. They are without informative or cognitive value and give us no meaningful reason to believe that the real world as a whole or in its parts is in any way related to "God." This bias emphasizes not the *falsehood* of religious propositions about God but their inability to communicate any information about reality. They are, cognitively speaking, *non*-sense.

The persuasiveness of this view depends on the ordinary man's and the not-so-ordinary philosopher's willingness to equate "real things" with observable objects. It is a prejudice as old as man himself. It emerges in the history of thought time and again to disturb the dreamers, the superstitious, the idealists, and the men of faith. Much contemporary philosophy has again exposed the dimensions of the bias and by careful argument has established the falsehood of the empiricistic claim.[2] It will suffice here to give only a sketch of the argument refuting that prejudice and to cite references in which the detailed progress of the arguments can be found.

To think of our experience as made up of tangible things — for much of it is — is quite natural. So our language reflects in its nouns and adjectives the odors and textures, the colors and sounds of an existence crammed with highly overcharged sensory stimulations and far too little silence for the soul to feed on. Material objects are the stuff of a materialistic society. However, the question at issue is whether we are entitled to argue from this fact of experience to the conclusion that *all* experience, and descriptive language about it, concerns itself wholly with the actual date of our perceptual

---

[2] An exacting discussion and set of arguments which support the view that religious statements (called "God-sentences" or "G-sentences" by the author) are verifiable and have cognitive significance is found in Raeburne Heimbeck's *Theology and Meaning* (Standford, 1969). His argument hinges on the empirical entailment of G-sentences and the implications of this for verifiability. The argument suffers, I think, from the problem created by the analogical character of the predicates of G-sentences.

senses. This does not follow any more than it would be legitimate to argue that since every American we have met speaks English all of them must. In more formal terms, the question is whether the states of affairs which must exist for descriptive statements about them to be meaningful and true must themselves be states of affairs perceivable by the senses. However, a great many affairs of concern for human beings are truly (and falsely) described, talked about and believed in, although they cannot be perceived by our senses. And this is because these affairs are of the sort that have nothing to do directly with our senses at all, and not because our senses are not sufficiently developed. Strictly speaking, we cannot perceive the feelings of other people with our five senses, yet we constantly make cognitively meaningful judgments about them. It cannot be denied that there *are* numbers, for if there were not, we could not "do" arithmetic or talk about which number is between 1 and 3. Yet no one expects to pet his lucky number or stand in the Selective Service line waiting for his number to "come up" so he can measure it prior to burying it. In short, it does not follow from the fact that we cannot get hold in some sensory way of the many different sorts of things we talk about (truly and falsely) that they are unreal, nor have we been given a good reason to suppose so. And so it does not follow that because the assertion "God provides the seasons for our good" does not refer in each of its elements to any readily *observable* state of affairs, it cannot refer to any state of affairs whatever. It is only the empiricistic bias that would lead us to this hasty conclusion. I have tried to show why the bias is itself unfounded.

The arguments *for* that bias are subtle, and while we cannot dwell on the nuances of all of them, perhaps one more representative *kind* of the argument will illustrate the ingenious persistence of the bias and its repeated failure. In an article in *Mind* Paul Edwards, the capable philosopher and editor of the prestigious *Encyclopedia of Philosophy*, has argued that the concept of Being-itself in Tillich's

---

For a comprehensive survey of the debate about religious discourse see Frederick Ferre, *Language, Logic and God* (New York, 1961). For a critique of the verifiability criterion of meaning see Carl Hempel, "Problems and Changes in the Empiricist Criterion of Meaning," in L. Linsky, ed., *Semantics and the Philosophy of Language* (Urbana, Ill., 1952). A brief but precise statement of the arguments and counter-arguments is found in Alvin Plantinga's *God and Other Minds* (Ithaca, N. Y., 1967), esp. Chap. 7.

theology (his term for "God") is meaningless.[3] Indeed, he has concluded that the whole of Tillich's theology is meaningless. He argued as follows, and if his argument is valid, most talk about God in any formal theology is invalid.

Edwards noted that most talk about God was anthropomorphic and hence metaphorical. "God is our Father" is a good example. Now, to determine if this kind of speech is correct, he examined how we understand metaphorical language. His general conclusion was that we understand it "because we can specify the content of the assertion in non-metaphorical language, because we can supply the literal equivalent." So when, to use his own example, someone says he will not flee the country because of a scandal but "stay and face the music," we know what he means. He does not mean that he chooses to stay and listen to some music. We know what he means, says Edwards, because the metaphor can be reduced to or "reproduced by one or more sentences all of whose components are used in literal senses." His general conclusion is that "when a sentence contains an irreducible metaphor, it follows at once that the sentence is devoid of cognitive meaning, that it is unintelligible, that it fails to make a genuine assertion."

Now, everything in this argument against religious language (and *for* a naturalistic view of the world) depends of course on what Edwards means by reducing metaphors to sentences whose elements are used in their "literal" senses. It can easily be argued that, in our example, "God is our Father" indeed contains the metaphor "father," but that this is reducible to the literal statement that God is our Creator and Preserver. But Edwards will not countenance this because, as he indicates, this would be a substitution of two metaphors for the original one and would not be a substitution of any literal terms. "Creator" is not used here literally because Christians do not mean that God creates the world as, for example, an artist created a masterpiece. So Edwards, using examples from Tillich's systematic theology, argues that the "literal" sense of a term cannot be applied to God.

What then is the literal sense of a term? Edwards suggests there

---

[3] "Professor Tillich's Confusions," *Mind*, LXXIV, No. 294 (April 1965), pp. 192–214. Pp. 197–206 are reprinted in Ronald Santoni, ed., *Religious Language and the Problem of Religious Knowledge* (Bloomington, Ind., and London, 1968), pp. 146–55.

may be more than one for any given term. Referring to Tillich's view that God is personal in the sense that God is the ground of everything personal, Edwards writes that here the word "ground" is "clearly not used in any of its literal senses." So there may be several literal senses to a given term. But how do we find them? What are they like? What distinguishes the literal sense of "number" from the metaphorical sense of "number"? It is important to note that Edwards does not answer these questions. He hints in various ways that where observation is lacking, the literal senses of terms are also lacking. He says that to lack literal significance is to lack referential meaning. But why cannot "Creator," for example, refer? Because we cannot observe Him? Because, to use Edward's phrase, we cannot "independently identify the features" of the Creator? The only appropriate answer is that we cannot independently identify the features of St. Paul either, but surely we can say, literally and truly, that he was a courageous missionary. We cannot see Saint Paul either, but that does not preclude referring to him as once living.

How does one distinguish the literal sense(s) of "number" from its metaphorical sense? Lacking "sensory observation" or "supersensuous" faculties with which to become acquainted with some prime number, for instance, between 16 and 20, it seems I cannot discover the *difference* between the literal sense of the term "number" and the metaphorical sense. I might *assert* that in the sentence "I've got your number" the term is used metaphorically, but that in the sentence "The number two is even" it is used literally. But how do I *know* the former *is* metaphorical and the latter literal, if I do not know what "literal" means? Edwards argues that "literal sense" means or entails "having reference to sensory objects." That means we are back to the old claim. To suppose that there are no literal senses for terms in mathematics, history, art, physics, or religion merely because these terms have no sensory referents is quite incredible. For, as we have tried to show earlier, it is completely unfounded to identify reality only with what is sensorily perceived. Furthermore, we claim literalness for some uses of "number" and similar terms and "metaphoricality" for other uses of those terms. In many cases, as we have shown, no sensory observation is possible. I conclude that we have no reason to accept Edwards' argument that meaningful speech about God is impossible, or to believe that metaphors applied to God are necessarily irreducible to referential terms.

This reasoning, of course, is hardly a proof against all versions of the argument expressing the empiricistic bias. However, it illustrates the nuances in the perennial effort to relate all descriptive assertions to sensory experience and to identify reality with the sensorily perceivable. No surviving form of that argument has succeeded in that effort. This is recognized by many philosophers who have found it painful to accept that failure.

Let us summarize the course of the argument so far. Since it is acknowledged, however reluctantly, that cognitive language does not require sensory reference, or that at least no proof exists to support this claim, we may continue to think and speak of God and His ways with men without fear of violating our rational endowment. Terms such as "God" and "providence" may indeed refer. Sentences using them may be regarded as true or false, depending on the states of affairs to which reference is made. This may be done because the arguments against this form of speaking (and believing) fail in their goal. Those who wish to contend that God in His providence is indeed occupied in His lively work of forging all things into His gracious plan need not be troubled by doubt arising from the empiricistic bias.

Faith's Problems

However, we must in all candor and with one eye on the elements of faith in the doctrine of providence outlined above acknowledge other problems that come to the fore. It is clear, for example, that Christians wish to speak meaningfully and truly about the divine sustenance by which they live. As we have seen, there is good reason to assume that we can. But then we must as a next step try to understand how we can tell when we do speak the truth about God's love. More technically, we are obliged to identify in some way those states of affairs by which the truth or falsehood of our beliefs may be judged. There appear to be a number of impediments in the way of that attempt. Since, in our understanding of the concept of providence, God is the primary causal agent in human and natural history, the question arises as to how He can be a cause within the structure of existence. The belief in providence surely does not compel us to repudiate natural causes or to relapse into mysticism. Yet when we affirm the power of human intelligence to sort out natural causes at work in the world, the providence of God sometimes seems to vanish behind a cloud of natural laws. Some churchmen limited God's work only to those events whose ordinary causes had not been discovered. Thus He became a "God of the gaps." As science developed, God seemed to occupy less and less of a place in the domain of human explanation. He vanished, in Julian Huxley's phrase, like the "last fading smile of a grinning Cheshire cat." The traditional effort to explain this paradox involves the distinction between primary and secondary causes. But before taking up this issue let us continue the enumeration of other perplexities that arise.

It is well to remember that in our concept of providence God also functions as a cause for the preservation of the cosmos as a whole; He is not merely at work within the particularities of historical events. So the question arises about God's transcendent causal relation to the universe. "He upholds all things by His Word of power," the church confesses (Heb. 1:3). But the "upholds" requires an explication to save it from the crude charge of superfluous dreaming. The question at stake is the degree to which the cosmos may be regarded as autonomous and self-sufficient, independently self-explanatory without God as an author or governor. To this issue we shall also address ourselves. But there are others.

Explicit in the concept of providence is the belief that God realizes a purpose in history, that history itself exhibits His purposive determination, and that His purpose is good. If this belief is to be regarded as true, we must appeal to some kind of evidence in support of it. Further, supposing we have grounds for accepting the efficacy of God's action in history, how can we enjoy a measure of human choice and freedom, which normally connotes the absence of determination by other causes? And finally we confront the problem of the origin of evil. For if we acknowledge that God is Author and provident Lord of creation, we must either attribute the reality of evil to His creative will or deny its reality in life. The church can plausibly do neither of these. Failing one of these solutions, we must find an alternative.

These questions are forced on us by the persistence of our faith and a human need to reconcile our rationally interpreted experience with the demands of faith. The centuries-long struggle of men of faith to answer these questions is a measure of their complexity. Man's attempt to answer these questions has seriously threatened to upset the precarious balance between a godly agnostic and a gnostic spirit. Therefore caution in this brief attempt to answer these questions is not the evidence of impoverished inquiry but of the restraint imposed by the wish to honor God by letting Him be God and readily acknowledging the mystery of His divinity. To claim more than the understanding He grants usurps His glory. To acknowledge less than faith leads us to assert denies the Word by which every living being is saved and called to account.

The context in which these questions are raised is the Biblical witness. Satisfying answers to these inquiries must therefore be placed in the same context. Those who, in another context, antecedently deny the possibility of providence have no theological problem about causation, purpose, or evil. Such persons have an altogether different set of problems, not less serious for all that. Since our context is Biblical, it will be helpful to recount, albeit summarily, the essential character of this context as it concerns our present purpose.

It is not necessary either for faith or for philosophy to believe that human knowledge is confined to the data of sense experience. We should not define experience so narrowly as to preclude the range of nonsensory data that is being discovered today. The precognitive and conscious life of man is just beginning to be understood through research into the central nervous system. Christians have good reason to continue to maintain that their faith is illuminated by experience and illuminates it in turn. Christianity also contends that faith defined as trust and confidence in God, though it arises in and is illuminated by our experience, is not confined to human dimensions alone. As a human enterprise, the church traces the historical ground of its faith to the prophetic and apostolic experience which gave rise to the Biblical witness. No logical or philosophical presuppositions require us to reject the consistent witness of prophets and apostles concerning their experience of God's revelation. Nor do we insist that this witness must conform to contemporary standards of demonstrable fact before we accept it. The Christian religion, and this is true of every grand metaphysical system of thought,

78

rests on unproven and unprovable grounds. The ultimate origin of our faith is found in the gift of God, just as the prophetic and apostolic witness was His gift. The task, then, of Christian theology is not to attempt some kind of sensory certification for the Biblical witness to faith, but rather to understand it rightly. That has largely been the substance of theology since apostolic times. Contemporary Christians are heirs of a long tradition of efforts to unpack the Biblical Word so that God's intended revelation might enrich and beautify the contours of our personal lives and our historical communities.

Understood in this way, the context in which we may venture solutions to our questions without fear of irrelevance or contradiction is the context of the Biblical witness. Its interpretation provides the understanding we seek. Where it does not, any "overbelief" that goes beyond our historical ground fails to secure the justification that this context alone can provide. Such "overbelief" threatens to tilt the balance between knowledge and ignorance dangerously toward idolatry of the intellect. The dictum of Ludwig Wittgenstein may serve to sum up this caution: "Whereof one cannot speak, thereof one must be silent."

With this context in mind we proceed to our first concern about the role of God's work within the natural structures of the universe. Specifically, we ask how we can ascribe causal agency both to God and to some particular event within the causal nexus of events. For our purposes we can combine this consideration with the second problem concerning the relation between God and the cosmos. In the former case the problem involves the possibility of at least two causes for any given natural event, namely, God's provident work of direction and preservation, and the natural or secondary causes identifiable through empirical inquiry. In the second case the problem involves the intelligibility of claiming for God the sole causal role in the preservation and determination of the cosmos itself. These questions can be combined because in both cases the issue is the nature of God's causal power. Evidently we cannot ascribe causal agency to God logically or statistically. Attempts to do so result only in pushing the problem into another area that requires explanation, and then is usually left unexplained. The concepts of cause, chance, and contingency when applied to natural phenomena are well defined for purposes of prediction and control. In their defined senses it is apparent that any univocal ascription of these terms to God is religiously ludicrous.[4] So the question remains: Precisely what state of affairs is being described by the claim that God is the primary cause of the world's continued preservation and direction and of the particular events—even chance events—within history?

The full significance of the discussion about contexts now becomes apparent. For in the context of the Biblical witness and the community which seeks to understand it in faith, God is confessed as one who reveals Himself in the purposive ordering of history. This confession is not arrived at by processes of observation and inductive reasoning. This would put the cart before the horse. Our antecedent trust in God leads us to interpret nature's course as being under His direction and control. Our discoveries of natural order are, as it were, defined and manufactured interpretations of experience. They serve the achievement of human purposes, generally of prediction or control. But assertions about God's purposes in history and His efficacy in realizing them by ordering of particular events are not claims we can fully understand or define. Our definitions would always be relative to human purpose, and we cannot assume an identity between our imperfect purposes and what God wills. Therefore we must acknowledge that the sense in which God is said to be a "cause" is analogous to its common use. However, we have no strictly specifiable reference which would give a thorough understanding of that state of affairs. Silence and mystery surface here as men struggle to understand God's provident will. It does not follow that we understand nothing, and so are asserting nothing. There is as much legitimate mystery about Being in physics as there is in theology. But it is not all mystery, and the mystery we confront when assessing God's ways with men is the sort that evokes worship as well as determined efforts to understand.

The way in which God functions as Cause and Sustainer of his-

---

[4] A precise explication of these terms in their scientific sense and an estimate of their relation to theological issues is provided by William Pollard, *Chance and Providence* (New York, 1958), esp. Chap. 3. The logic of causal arguments and predicates involving God is also examined scrupulously in Plantinga's book *God and Other Minds* cited above.

tory must be something like the parallel human functions, without the imperfection attending the human estate. The analogical meaning of terms such as "cause" has been explicated and defended for some 700 years, and whether that defense is satisfactory cannot be examined here.[5] But it is clear that the incentive to speak of God in these ways emerges from personal confidence in His grace rather than from impersonal investigation. The will to worship Him in all His glory as Creator and Redeemer cannot be thwarted by demands for more knowledge than He has given us. Where details of understanding are lacking in our knowledge of God's ways, we must nonetheless confess our dependence on Him. For the fact remains that we are not under the constraint of reason to deny the meaningfulness of our confidence or confession, as we have seen, but we are under the constraint of faith that gladly worships the mystery of God's providential care.

The concept of God's governance of the world suggests a further observation. It is necessary to admit that this belief, because it is true, entails the denial that the world as such is self-explanatory. Since this is so, we deny that it is a closed system of finite causes fully explicable by human inquiry alone. The autonomy of natural existence and our knowledge about it are therefore directly challenged by this Christian view of providence. Those who have come under the spell of the sufficiency of science may find this hard to accept. But it needs to be pointed out for their benefit that the claim of autonomy for empirical knowledge and nature is an "overbelief" of the naturalistic temper, unjustified by the principles of science and pregnant with damaging consequences to human well-being. It will be worthwhile to see why this is so.

A common criticism of faith's insistence that nature and history are dependent on God as provident Lord is that this belief lacks demonstrative proof and remains superfluous to rational inquiry about naural processes. An intelligent response to this charge will admit the lack of demonstrative proof and point out that the enter-

---

[5] See Eric Mascall, *Existence and Analogy* (London, 1949); also Frederick Copleston, *A History of Philosophy* (London, 1951), Vol. 2, esp. Chaps. 35 and 38. An excellent treatment of the theory held by Thomas Aquinas may be found in Robert Patterson's *The Conception of God in the Philosophy of Aquinas* (London, 1933), Chap. 7. The most exhaustive study of the problem of analogy in Aquinas, and a defense of it, is Reginald Garrigou-Lagrange, *God: His Existence and His Nature* (St. Louis: Herder, 1934).

prise of science lacks that same justification. The scientific method cannot justify the truth of its entire procedure. Any proof drawn from outside that method would not be "scientific," or rationally grounded. It would be a mere prejudice. So both science and providence rest on equally unprovable grounds, however credible both may be. Lack of proof, then, is no reason to reject either one.

The claim that providence is a belief that is superfluous to rational inquiry may be granted. This concession is made with the strict limitation that it is superfluous only to those rational investigations whose purpose is to order our experience for *proximate* understanding and satisfaction. It is allowable to reason as such to ask for *ultimate* explanations about the universe as a whole. Any other view must claim that questions such as, "Why does anything exist?" or, "What purpose does history have?" are meaningless. This is the point of view of the naturalistic temper, well expressed by philosopher Ernst Nagel.[6]

However, it seems evident that since we are in fact referring to the universe, the entire state of affairs, we are asking an intelligible question about the reason for its existence. No *empirical* investigation can answer that question, since there are no empirical data "outside" the universe to account for its existence. Hence science is confined by its purposes to the study of finite data within the experienced world. Only those blinded by the empiricistic bias or the naturalistic temper will be inclined to rest content with the limited conclusions that empirical study yields. This prejudice does not rest on proof that it is meaningless to talk about nonempirical states of affairs, ultimate origins, or designs of the world. It cannot provide any cogent reason for thinking so, whereas there are sound reasons for contending that questions about the cosmos as such are indeed meaningful. Since this is so, it follows that it is not superfluous to rational inquiry to ask for explanations that extend beyond what empirical data can provide. The way is then open to religious answers that are immune from the charge of rational impropriety.

We have been attempting to explain and justify the Christian

---

[6] See Nagel's *Logic Without Metaphysics* (Glencoe, Ill., 1956). An authoritative contemporary statement of the naturalistic temper based on linguistic-analytic considerations is Willard Quine's collection of essays, *Ontological Relativity and Other Essays* (New York and London, 1969).

contention that history and nature are not autonomous in the sense that they are sufficiently self-explanatory. Neither is it meaningless nor superfluous by rational standards to demand answers to certain questions about their origin, nature, and direction. We have shown that the opposite view is based on an unfounded naturalistic bias that claims more for science and meaning than it can support by evident reason. Since this is so, we have justified the claim that belief in God's providence is rationally defensible and meaningful. We have done more. For now we are in a position to appreciate the *quality* of the choices that confront us.

LIFE'S PURPOSE

Some philosophers ask us to think of a world that exists without explanation, a brute fact without reason, oblivious to human need or concern. They tell us that a search for purpose and meaning in human life, our lives and all of human history, is a vain and superfluous quest unworthy of our intelligence and, at the same time, the breeding ground of superstition and nonsense. Bertrand Russell has given powerful philosophical expression to this naturalistic faith in his essay "A Free Man's Worship" (1902). He writes:

> That Man is the product of causes which had no prevision of the end they were achieving; that his origin, his growth, his hopes and fears, his loves and his beliefs, are but the outcome of accidental collocations of atoms; that no fire, no heroism, no intensity of thought and feeling, can preserve an individual life beyond the grave; that all the labours of the ages, all the devotion, all the inspiration, all the noonday brightness of human genius, are destined to extinction in the vast depth of the solar system, and that the whole temple of Man's achievement must inevitably be buried beneath the debris of a universe in ruins — all these things . . . are yet so nearly certain, that no philosophy which rejects them can hope to stand. Only within the scaffolding of these truths, only on the firm foundation of unyielding despair, can the soul's habitation henceforth be safely built.[7]

Russell believed that despite the senselessness of life and the finality of doom which he believed he could make his belief the source of heroic love for his fellowmen:

------

[7] *Mysticism and Logic* (London, 1951), pp. 47–48.

83

To take into the inmost shrine of the soul the irresistible forces
whose puppets we seem to be — Death and change, the irrevocable-
ness of the past, and the powerlessness of man before the blind
hurry of the universe from vanity to vanity — to feel these things
and know them is to conquer them.[8]

Again:

Brief and powerless is Man's life; on him and all his race the slow,
sure doom falls pitiless and dark. Blind to good and evil, reckless
of destruction, omnipotent matter rolls on its relentless way; for
Man, condemned to-day to lose his dearest, tomorrow himself
to pass through the gate of darkness, it remains only to cherish,
ere yet the blow falls.[9]

For Russell the absurdity of life and the mindlessness of the cosmos
were sources of love and compassion for the human condition. Over
the course of some 70 years, two world wars, and a host of lesser
ones, it became clear that men could not maintain that noble result
when nothing but absurdity could be found in life and death. Virtually the full range of modern literature, drama, and the arts shows
that a "faith" in life's fundamental meaninglessness produces only
despair, disillusion, and irresponsible action. For Sartre man is
"a useless passion" and "an unhappy consciousness." Camus ago-
nizes in *The Myth of Sisyphus* about the "unreasonable silence of
the world." And Beckett's lonely soul waits forlornly for Godot, and
waits . . . and waits. It is a sound judgment on human life and destiny
so conceived that we cannot feel "at home" in a universe that is
allegedly the product of chance and probability. Such a world in-
spires neither confidence nor sympathy and offers neither orientation nor meaning to our existence in it.[10]

How different the spirit of those who live by the faith in the
promise, "I am the Light of the world; he who follows Me will not
walk in darkness, but will have the light of life" (John 8:12). The
choice is between despairing over human life seething with the

---

[8] Ibid., p. 55.

[9] Ibid., pp. 56—57.

[10] Karl Löwith gives an incisive characterization of the despair bred by the
sense of an autonomous world in *Nature, History and Existentialism* (Evanston, Ill.,
1966), esp. pp. 24 ff., here paraphrased.

turmoil of absurdity or celebrating the joy revealed by God's providence and grace.

Another issue posed by the concept of providential activity concerns the nature of the evidence for the claim that God realizes a benevolent purpose in His preservation and determination of nature and history. The principal modern objection to this belief is that the nature of the reality to which propositions about God's purposive design allegedly refer does not render to our observation the evidence which would make such propositions either referential or true. Hence, it is argued, such statements are false or altogether meaningless. However, the psalmist says:

> By the word of Yahweh the heavens were made,
> their whole array by the breath of His mouth;
> He collects the ocean waters as though in a wineskin,
> He stores the deeps in cellars.
>
> Let the whole world fear Yahweh,
> let all who live on earth revere Him!
> He spoke, and it was created;
> He commanded, and there it stood.
>
> Yahweh thwarts the plans of nations,
> frustrates the intentions of peoples;
> but Yahweh's plans hold good for ever,
> the intentions of His heart from age to age.
> Happy is the nation whose God is Yahweh,
> the people He has chosen for His heritage.[11]

It is held that such hymns, as well as more ordinary language about God's providence, do not describe a genuine state of affairs. For example, can the Christian assert truly that World War I was a part of God's plan? How do we arrive at the judgment that His purpose in history is providential?

The demand that we must be in a position to verify or falsify judgments about God's providence by appeal to sensory criteria completely misses the character of our assertions. In the absence of any sound reasons for insisting that we must be referring to empirical states of affairs for our confessions of faith to have the requisite meaning or truth, we are at liberty to affirm both the purposive character of natural and human history and the benevolence of God

---

[11] Ps. 33:6-12, Jerusalem Bible.

revealed in that purpose. For judgments about providence are the product of our antecedent faith in and commitment to God, conceived and understood within the heritage of a community of believers who acknowledge the Biblical witness as the arbiter of permissible judgments.

The interpretation we may give to current patterns of history as revelatory of God's judgment or grace, or our estimate of the "message" to be found in some natural catastrophe, or in the apparent orderliness of nature are conditioned not by empirical observation of the events alone. They are also conditioned by the values we have learned in the confessing community of faith and by the yardstick of the Scriptures, which ground that faith in history. Our judgments can claim no more finality or certainty than faith allows. Faith enables the Christian to discern a benevolent purpose in history, even though he may interpret a given event to be a proximate cause of pain or dissatisfaction. The entire interpretive scheme in which providential judgments are made is not determined by relative human standards of convenience or cultural mores. The interpretation is determined by the context of a community's faithful, insistent reliance on the Lord's general promise that among those who love Him all things work together for good.

This stance in the face of disaster, bloodshed, violence, and pain seems foolhardy if the support for its truth is sought in our own short-range goals and relative assessments of good and evil. By such standards natural and human adversity are at times so outrageous as to evoke our most emphatic revulsion and a tendency to total despair. Nothing is more naive than to regard evil as an illusion. Yet by providential plan the community of believers suffers evil, seeing there the hand of their awesome Lord who in "ways past finding out" promises to nourish and redeem them nonetheless. The *faithfulness* of the community, when confronted by disappointment or temptation to usurp God's prerogatives, justifies its claim that it lives under the hand of a benevolent God whose gracious hand weaves the fabric of a purposive life. This justification does not, indeed, allow a satisfying empirical description of the providential reality to which faith clings. But it certifies the appropriateness of the claim.

In the church's historic judgment we come closest to an accurate description of the reality of God's benevolent purpose when all finite satisfactions are emptied from the concept (negative theology). This is done in order to magnify the blessing which the church confesses to be proportionate to God's promise, not in order to deny human significance to the concept of divine benevolence. A true blessing from God must transcend the limits of precise human description. So once again we are reminded of the limitations arising from faith's deposit, which grows out of the Biblical witness and from the finitude of our human experience. Our analogical descriptions of benevolence provide only a vague suggestion of the reality to which they refer. The incentive to worship drives our understanding to the limits of mystery where it at last must rest in the positive contentment that a God of mystery provides.

FREEDOM AND EVIL

The last two issues with which we shall concern ourselves involve the concepts of human free will and the origin of evil. How and why do these concerns arise? Simply stated, our belief that we make choices in our daily behavior *freely* seems to be at odds with our belief, implied by the concept of providence, that God is the primary cause of every occurrent event, including human choices. That He sustains us in our existence while we make choices implies at the least that He cooperates with our choices. We must grant the stronger claim that since the direction of human history is under His benevolent guidance, God is causally operative also with regard to our particular choices. In some sense He determines them. Thus arises the problem of how we can truly think of ourselves as free agents and simultaneously affirm, also truly, that God "determines" our choices. The problem of evil becomes an issue because it is obvious that we make many evil choices, and so it would seem to follow that it can be (truly) said that God is also a cause of moral evil in the world. And further, since there are harmful natural events, God as Creator and Preserver must also apparently be the cause of natural or physical evil.

We must now decide how to approach an answer to these questions. The decision is complicated by the fact that Christians have historically taken at least two quite different approaches, each with something to commend it. On the one hand, theologians and philosophers have sometimes chosen to regard God's causal agency in a sense which is equivalent to our common or even technically defined sense of the term "cause." They have then proceeded to examine whether there is any logical inconsistency in affirming both God's agency in human and natural affairs and our freedom to choose among alternative courses of action. On the other hand, others have preferred to deny any exact equivalence of meaning for the term "cause" when attributed to God and men. The univocity of meaning, as it is called, is denied by these men because they hold that it would be improper to predicate of God any finite sense or limited power implied by usual concept of "cause." Unfortunately we cannot here evaluate these two approaches with the care they deserve. However, there is good reason, I believe, to prefer the second of the two approaches outlined above. Briefly stated it is this.

On the view that causal predicates attributed to God have univocal meaning, it is not self-evident that this entails some contradiction in saying that God determines our actions and that we are free in our choices.[12] Yet, supposing that it were consistent to make such a claim, this does not seem to be the sort of claim with which Christians would be content. For all that would be asserted is that it is not logically impossible for God both to have created us as free moral agents and also to determine our actions. Of course, Christians might be happy to discover that God would not find this logically impossible to do, but their attitude of worship and commitment prompts something far more assertive. God is just not *any* "cause" on all fours with the kind of natural or human agency we commonly identify in experience. He is an ultimate cause, a transcendent agency that defies complete and adequate description. Nothing less than this will satisfy the attitude of worship which a genuine trust and confidence in God evokes. If so, then the assumption that God's causal agency is semantically equivalent to human agency will not harmonize with the attitude of worship that seeks to exalt God in wonder, love, and praise. In this case it will be regarded as irrelevant to argue about what is logically possible for God. So we must prefer

---

[12] A close analysis of the so-called free will defense is found in Plantinga, pp. 131−55.

the second approach and assert that the sense in which God determines the particular acts we freely choose to do is analogous to the ordinary sense of "determines" but in a way which far exceeds our ability accurately to describe.

If we adopt this approach, we have a way of answering our questions that appears to do full justice to the numinous character of our Lord and to the worship appropriate to Him. The impulse to worship that the Christian community has exhibited from its earliest beginnings has driven it to affirm the benevolence of God's providence and to take comfort from it in times of trial and adversity. At the same time it is apparent that Christians have not wished to deny the truth or importance of their own role in effecting the changes in the human condition which God willed. Side by side they have acknowledged His beneficence for all the goods and successes they enjoyed *and* their own role in bringing them about. Christians have not regarded this double posture as presenting any difficulty because both judgments were justified by the faithfulness they exhibited and the human experience of choice. Furthermore, when the natural question arose concerning the responsibility for evil in the world, Christians could not hold God accountable, because the claim that He is the cause of evil could not be justified by the faith of the community. The claim that we, as imperfect sons, are responsible is the testimony of the experience of the believing people of God. The longest recorded argument within the community over this issue is found in the Book of Job. The resolution in this document still finds acceptance among the imperfect children of a provident and gracious God.

The problem of evil cannot, however, be settled quite this summarily. A critic might be persuaded to accept the attitude of worship as sufficient justification for speaking of God as the transcendent determiner of those free choices which we make that result in a positive good. but he might then point out that by the same reasoning, since God is affirmed to be the transcendent cause of every event, He must necessarily be affirmed the transcendent cause of our evil choices as well. Hence, even though the critic accepts what we may call the "superlative" sense of God's causal role, he may still charge that there is an inconsistency in refusing to attribute evil to God in that sense. It will not do, in answer to this objection, merely to hold that the context of the faith justifies this inconsistency. That would be a claim that the Biblical witness and its interpretation in the church justify not only claims that go beyond the (empirically) verifiable but also *irrational* claims.

Problems like these have no doubt been a reason for saying that God does not cause but permits or cooperates in the evil choices we make. However, so far as can be discovered, there are no satisfactory interpretations of "permits" or "cooperates" which eliminate from them a causal implication. Therefore, we are confronted with a problem. We need a logical strategy for asserting that God is indeed the transcendent cause of every event, but not the cause of any evil resulting from human choice or the evil in nature (for example, terminal cancer or hurricanes). The following solution to this problem with some modern elaboration seems to supply us with this strategy.[13]

In a world in which praise and blame are appropriately attributed to human beings, there must be free choice. Without it there would be no sense to rewards and punishments at all. (No one sends computers to prison, though we may sometimes want to!) Thus, when God created persons who were free to choose, He created a moral order in which persons were free to choose evil as well as good. To say then that God is not the (transcendent) cause of evil is to acknowledge that the moral order He created necessarily contains whatever evil is required for there to be a *moral* order at all, that is, a world in which either good or evil is possible to free moral agents. God could not have created evil, but the possibility of evil was essential to His will that men have free choice and not be worthless robots. Thus responsibility for moral evil belongs to men who exercise their choice, whereas the natural order within which men act out their choices lies within God's providence. All this presupposes a good God and one who is powerful enough to create the world and wise enough to order it as He has. But this conception

---

[13] Again the reader is referred to other sources for details. What follows must suffice for these purposes. See Plantinga, esp. Chaps. 5 and 6. A less recent but still cogent study is that of F. R. Tennant, *Philosophical Theology* (Cambridge, 1956), Vol. 2, Chap. 7. On God as the cause of evil see M. Pontifex, *Freedom and Providence* (New York, 1960), Chaps. 4—8. This is Vol. 22 of *The Twentieth Century Encyclopedia of Catholicism.*

of God is the Christian concept and the explanation given is consistent with it.

Concerning natural evils, we cannot be held responsible for them since we cannot choose *not* to allow tidal waves, cancer, and the like.[14] Hence it might be thought that in this case God must be the sole accountable cause for natural evil. If it is held, however, as the context of the faith indeed insists, that Satan and his hosts are efficacious in producing evil, it is possible to attribute natural evil to them as the consequence of their free choices. Although it may be argued (again) that we are asserting more than our observation allows, it does not follow that we are asserting anything meaningless, as we have repeatedly argued, or that belief in the demonic is irrational.[15] And these beliefs enjoy with the others we have considered the assent of the community that holds them in continuity with the Biblical witness, which is the historic ground for their affirmation. They are therefore justified by the context of the faith.

An additional note is in place concerning the scope of natural evils. Our judgments of what is evil in nature are typically conditioned in part by our learned values. For example, when we consider a storm evil because it has wiped out hundreds of human lives or

---

[14] Human accountability for nature's travail is not clearly defined in those Biblical texts associating natural evil with the fall of man. The position taken here excludes human culpability but not a causal role.

[15] Theologians advocating what is called process theology specifically attempt to avoid the entire problem of natural and moral evil by redefining the concept of God so that God's omnipotence does not entail His ability to override the laws of nature or the potentials for good or evil which are latent in natural order. On this view natural evil in decreasing amounts over the long run is a necessary complement to an evolving universe, necessarily *not* intended by God, who is a "fellow sufferer" with us. Since God is also not conceived in this view as having the power to override human will, no problem of divine determinism arises either, and free will is legitimately, though with some limitations due to natural factors, ascribed to men. See John Cobb, *A Christian Natural Theology* (Philadelphia, 1965); Schubert Ogden, *The Reality of God and Other Essays* (New York, 1966); Charles Hartshorne, *A Natural Theology for Our Time* (La Salle, Ill., 1967); *Man's Vision of God* (Hamden, Conn., 1964); *The Divine Relativity* (New Haven, 1948). The limitations placed on God in process theology do not seem consistent with traditional formulations of His omnipotence and sovereignty. But this type of theology does take the naturalistic bias seriously as a threat to theism, unlike many of the continental existentialist theologies which tend generally to ignore that bias altogether and hence risk a measure of irrelevance to contemporary thought. See, for example, Rudolf Bultmann, *Jesus Christ and Mythology* (New York, 1958), esp. Chap. 5. Among American theologians, Paul Tillich is most outspoken against the concept of "God" in the process theology described above. See *Systematic Theology*, Vol. I.

vast possessions, we are likely to think that any storm is equally evil, even though no human loss is involved. Thereby we add an incalculable amount of evil to nature's score. But it is not evident that *all* storms, earthquakes, and other rampages of nature are evil, especially when human well-being is not affected. Similarly it is not evident that all forms of human suffering deserve to be called evil, since some may be reasonably regarded as good even by those who suffer. The intent here is not to deny the reality of evil but to take note of the important fact that we ought not glibly pass judgment on the value of an event. Careful assessment is called for, especially by those who must try to discern in life and nature the good intent of a loving Providence.

I have tried in this discussion to present a general philosophical view of the doctrine of providence which would satisfy both the urging of the Christian will to worship God as Preserver and Provider and also the demands of our rational nature. This has been done also with a keen sense of the Biblical witness and its place in the life of the community of God's people. But beyond the requirements of reason and a godly confidence Christians have the exciting opportunity to grow in their appreciation of God's providence by steeping themselves in the texture and substance of human existence. When this is done, then providence becomes an intimate source of joy and comfort for oneself and others and an experience of God's manifest grace. Then it will be properly understood and become an effective word for our time.

Providence and Psychology

Ralph Underwager

Relating the doctrine of providence and that body of theory, knowledge, and practice comprising psychology requires first an examination of the current state of psychology. The viewpoint taken throughout is that of a clinical psychologist and psychotherapist. Psychology, seen from the position of a clinician, is in a curious condition. There are many strong indicators of health and vitality, but nevertheless there is a sense of discomfort and malaise.

Nineteen states (at the time of this writing) have licensing laws which establish and protect the right of psychologists to do whatever psychologists do and to sell such services to the public. Historically such steps represent the maturing of a body of skills into a profession. Major insurance companies recognize the value and benefit of psychological services by including payment for such services within health and medical coverage. The demand for psychologists continues to exceed supply and job prospects remain relatively healthy. Social status for psychologists is stable and comfortably high. The mark of that regard is seen at the cocktail party when another guest learns that you are a psychologist. The dialog is then likely to run, "Oh, so you're a psychologist! Well, I had this dream . . . ." The psychologist then either plays the game and offers instant analysis or escapes as rapidly as possible to a group that has not yet discovered his profession.

These external signs of vitality are not matched by an internal sense of well-being. A recent president of the American Psychological Association forecast the death of clinical psychology within a few years. Professional journals contain many articles complaining that psychology has no "place" or identity of its own. Medicine has hospitals; the church has worship facilities; the law has courtrooms; psychology has no place in which it belongs outside the university setting.

In addition to these more professional concerns, psychology is engaged in attempts to rid itself of the "medical model" in relating to people. As one of the three "mental health" professions (psychiatry, psychology, and social work) psychology seems troubled when research demonstrates that after 40 years of "mental health" propaganda the public refuses to use "mental health" language or concepts to understand and explain human behavior. In addition, serious and responsible scholars question the applicability of the model of sickness and health to the minds and psyches of human beings. When dealing with a person who is thought to be emotionally disturbed, the psychologist does not assume that person is possessed of a disease entity analogous to the Koch bacillus. There is no alien, hostile, destructive virus external to the individual which causes the symptoms or the behavior. At least none has yet been found.

Another troubling area for the psychologist is the lack of any comprehensive, overarching theoretical position. With the demise of Freudian personality theory and treatment techniques, nothing has risen to take its place. Though still popular and possibly dominant in mass media and public consciousness, psychoanalysis has failed to demonstrate either meaning or effectiveness. For a time it appeared as if learning theory might occupy the place vacated by psychoanalytic theory, but it too has failed to provide either a theoretical position or techniques broad enough to cover the reality of what occurs in psychotherapy. Commenting on this situation Phillip Rieff writes: "So confused, psychiatrists and clinical psychologists, in their hospitals and consulting rooms, stand almost as helpless as their functional predecessors and sometime cultural opponents, the Clergy" [1]. A summary of the condition of psychology is offered by Lowell Kelly.

> In a word, the *practice* of clinical psychology is of necessity still largely an art because the *science* of psychology has not yet provided the basic knowledge and techniques which permit clinical psychology (or psychiatry) to be practiced as an applied science.[2]

---

[1] P. Rieff, *The Triumph of the Therapeutic* (New York: Harper & Row, 1966), p. 21.

[2] L. Kelly, "Clinical Psychology: The Postwar Decade," in *Current Trends in Psychological Theory* (Pittsburgh: University of Pittsburgh Press, 1961), p. 48.

Nevertheless, the mental health professionals continue to act and work to help and heal.

The most prestigious and most sought after psychological activity today is psychotherapy. A problem for any responsible psychotherapist is the fact that psychotherapy has not been able to demonstrate effectiveness of cure greater than that of the spontaneous remission rate. That is, available research studies, crude and inexact as they perforce must be, roughly indicate that about two thirds of the recipients of psychotherapy improve. However, studies also indicate that about two thirds of the persons with comparable degrees of disturbance improve if nothing is done by way of any treatment. Most psychotherapists resolve this difficulty for themselves by relying on their clinical experience, which for the most part indicates that treatment has helped people. At the same time it must be acknowledged that the many knotty and difficult problems in evaluating outcomes of psychotherapy are just beginning to be understood and unraveled. In the meantime, as psychotherapists, we must continue to respond to the needs of men and of the society by practicing the art as best we can, trusting that the labors of dedicated men and the tools of research will lead to greater understanding and ability to manipulate human behavior.

These two contrasting indicators of the current state of psychology — the external marks of vitality and the internal malaise — indicate that this discipline is ready for a change, prompted in part by feelings of frustration among its practitioners. This feeling is not necessarily caused by any crisis in the discipline, for it can be judged to be rather healthy in terms of its own traditional terms of reference. Rather the indicator of impending change comes from the growing conviction that somehow the whole tradition is out of step. Psychology is in a state of flux, of impending change. The direction which that change is likely to take is not yet clear, but there may be some clues scattered about that can be examined.

The shortage of broad, theoretical positions was mentioned above. Since about 1960 the new theoretical positions have been of a single type. They are termed "theories of cognitive consistency." A large number of theories have been put forward simultaneously and independently by researchers in the area. Common to all these is the notion that a person behaves in such a way as to lead to the greatest congruence within his cognitive system. In short, he acts by and large in accordance with what he believes to be the case.

With the advent of these theories, along with a considerable body of quite solid research data, cognition became a significant variable within psychology. Jerome S. Bruner's work at Harvard on the cognitive development of children lends support to the early importance and significance of cognition by human beings. It became quite respectable, psychologically, to be concerned with what people believed and thought. Research evidence for the importance of beliefs is accumulating rapidly. Rokeach's ingenious studies of belief offer the surprising finding that belief is more important than race in social choice. He concludes, "In other words, belief congruence will override racial or ethnic congruence except when the perceived cost is too great." [3]

Another possible harbinger of what may come in psychology is contained in a recent report that is unique in psychological research. Necessarily most psychological research is cross-sectional rather than longitudinal. This means that the typical research project looks at a cross section of people at a given point in time. We have very few longitudinal studies, that is, projects in which the same people are followed across a lengthy period of time. Consequently the longitudinal studies that do exist are highly prized and need to be regarded with more respect than the cross-sectional studies, provided good research standards are met. Recently material is becoming available on a group of adults who have been followed since infancy. An initial report concerns antecedents of good adult adjustment. The authors conclude:

> In this sample, the mother's own cognitive/coping skills appeared to be more relevant to adjustment (of her children in their adult life) than her emotional warmth. Despite the importance accorded maternal warmth in the literature this study suggests that intellectual competence, frankness and openness, and philosophical-moral value orientation discriminate more than warmth-coldness in distinguishing mothers of high optimal adjustment Ss (subjects) from mothers of low optimal adjustment Ss (subjects).[4]

---

[3] M. Rokeach, *Beliefs, Attitudes, and Values* (San Francisco: Jossey-Bass, 1968), p. 81.

[4] E. Siegelman et. al., "Antecedents of Optimal Psychological Adjustment," in *Journal of Counseling and Clinical Psychology*, 35, 3 (1970), 283–89.

Provided this finding is substantiated and accepted, American mothers (and fathers) will need to understand that their beliefs and values are more important for the welfare of their children than their affection and love.

Jessor and Feshback also emphasize the significance of beliefs and values, of the conscious, cognitive processes of which man alone is capable:

> . . . the "lockstep of learning theory" has been broken, and a fundamental concern for cognitive processes and functioning is manifest in nearly every area of psychology . . . all share a common interest in cognitive structure and functioning. . . . The importance of these developments lies, it seems to us, not simply in their immediate contributions and applications, but, perhaps, more important, in the potentiality of the work to generate a model of man more congenial to the moral and humanistic concerns of the clinician — a model of man as a *thinker and seeker after meaning.*[5]

The model of man as a "thinker and seeker after meaning" is also much more amenable to the theology of the Christian faith than a model of man as driven by biological needs or a model of man as a mechanical responding organism. With this background in the current state of psychology we can move to a consideration of the doctrine of providence as a psychological phenomenon.

PROVIDENCE AS A PSYCHOLOGICAL CONSTRUCT

In considering the doctrine of providence as a psychological construct and phenomenon we exclude any implications as to the truth value or the reality of the order postulated by the doctrine. To explore the psychological implications of the doctrine is not to assert anything dealing with the question as to whether God is or is not involved in sustaining the world of creation. This is the logical error into which Freud falls in dismissing the truth claims of the Christian faith as false because he has demonstrated that men have wishes and projections regarding God and His existence and favor. His treatise *The Future of an Illusion* is based on this fallacy.

To be sure, men may have a need for order in their existence. Men may have a wish for God to be actively involved in guiding and

---

[5] R. Jessor and S. Feshbach, eds., *Cognition, Personality and Clinical Psychology* (San Francisco: Jossey-Bass, 1968), p. 211.

controlling history. This says nothing at all about the truth or falseness of the assertion. If I discover that I have cancer of the colon, I am likely to have a great variety of very strong needs and wishes that my surgeon be a competent, skilled, and a highly qualified technician with the knife. I may even dream about his skill or lack thereof. I may talk at length with family and friends about his competence, really trying to convince myself. None of this emotional, cognitive, and volitional activity on my part is going to affect either the existence of my surgeon, his care for me, or his skill. If I want to settle that question, I must look at the facts. I will need to examine his credentials, find out where he trained, talk to others whom he has operated on, ascertain his success/failure ratio, and the like. I may even wish to obtain a personality measure on him, knowing that the closer he comes to being an obsessive-compulsive person, the better off I am going to be. In short, I look at the evidence and not at my feelings, emotions, or psychological processes.

Consequently in what follows the truth of providence is not in question. Rather, we shall attempt to probe the psychological processes of individuals who believe or disbelieve the doctrine. For those who believe in providence, such belief is a part of the total structure of beliefs, values, attitudes, and opinions by which meaning and significance is given to the raw facts of existence as experienced. Men possess belief systems, highly intricate and complex in their structure and relationships, and use their belief systems to process, code, store, and interpret the raw sensory input available to the individual in his interaction with the environment. Boring says: "The difficulty here is this: the man is not acting in a physical world but in a psychological environment where the reality is what he perceives or believes." [6]

The belief system that a man holds is, at least in part, causally related to his behavior. This point is made by Bergman:

> The difference is that I . . . have . . . a certain mental state, which is best called "verbal" whether or not I explicitly verbalize it to myself or others. If so verbalized or tagged, as it were, this kind of state variable takes the form of a proposition or series of propositions. This is what I mean by calling us "propositional animals."

---

[6] E. G. Boring, *History of Psychology* (New York: Appleton-Century-Crofts, 1957), p. 725.

But by calling us so I wish to imply more than that we are afforded the luxury of some sort of inner light by which we can watch ourselves act where the dumb creature merely acts. The presence or absence and the kind of propositional states makes a difference, or, as some like to say, a dynamic difference, in that, all other things being equal, the course of our behavior still depends upon them. In other words, our propositional states are themselves among the causal factors that determine our behavior. . . . Let me from now on call the system of a person's actual and potential propositional states his "rationale." [7]

Reflecting a long tradition of holding to belief systems as causal determinants of human behavior, Johann Albrecht Bengel wrote in 1742, "Dogmas exercise an influence on man's whole behavior."

The belief system a man holds is causative of his behavior in determining the meaning given to an event or episode which occurs in that man's life. Albert Ellis develops this insight into an entire system of psychotherapy in his rational-emotive system of psychotherapy. A key point in his system is the contention that it is never an event which causes me to feel what I feel, but rather what I am saying to myself about that event. If my wife fixes my breakfast egg too hard for my taste, it is not her behavior which angers me, but rather what I believe about my wife and my breakfast egg. If I become angry at her, I believe and then say to myself that my wife is doing something which I don't like; therefore she shouldn't be doing it. But since she is doing it, she is evil, awful, horrible, and blameworthy. Therefore I blame her and become angry. I must also believe that the only proper way for a breakfast egg to exist is in a slightly runny mode, and therefore this is not really a breakfast egg at all but rather an abomination which I may curse and reject. Epictetus said it over 2,000 years ago, "It is not things which disturb men, but men's view of things which disturbs men."

In addressing the Second Conference on Research in Psychotherapy under the sponsorship of the Division of Clinical Psychology of the American Psychological Association, Jerome D. Frank, one of the great figures of American psychiatry, explained the effectiveness of psychotherapy in these words:

---

[7] G. Bergmann, "Purpose, Function, Scientific Explanation," in *Readings in the Philosophy of the Social Sciences,* ed. May Brodbeck (New York: Macmillan Co., 1968), p. 128.

The therapist supplies an explanation for the feelings which the patient can accept as valid and this becomes the way he actually feels. . . . The new cognition is usually part of a self-consistent conceptual scheme which further helps the patient to organize his feelings. These cognitions also suggest certain lines of behavior which tend to lead to improved relationships with others. This further diminishes the feelings, and so the patient gets better. . . . In this sense the observation may be justified that the therapeutic effect of an interpretation depends not on its truth, but on whether both therapist and patient believe it to be true.[8]

Psychotherapy, in this view, consists of the substitution of one belief system for another by the influence and prestige of the therapist and the expectation of the patient that he will be helped. Thus the very existence of the profession and practice of psychotherapy support the significance and effect of a belief in the doctrine of providence on an individual's life and behavior.

If I believe the doctrine of providence, that is, if I have the propositions which form that doctrine embedded in my total complex of beliefs, values, attitudes, and opinions, I will perceive my world, my life, the people around me, and the circumstances of my life in a different manner than the person who does not believe in providence or who believes contrary to it. That difference in perception will result in different meanings being supplied to a given situation. The differing meanings, as indicated by Frank above, will result in different behaviors and differing emotional responses.

Consider the instance of a young woman, Mrs. A., whose husband is alcoholic. He continues to provide for her quite adequately. They have no children. Mrs. A. comes for psychotherapy complaining of her husband's inattentiveness, lack of consideration, undependable nature, and, above all else, the complaint that he shows no love to her and she no longer loves him. In the course of psychotherapy she reveals that she has been involved in an affair with a neighbor which she finds very rewarding and satisfying, for in this relationship she feels happy, loved, and valued. However, she comes to realize that the affair is self-destructive, unwise, and potentially damaging. Mrs. A. concludes it, with some regret, and

---

[8] J. D. Frank, "The Role of Cognition in Illness and Healing," in *Research in Psychotherapy*, ed. H. Strupp and L. Luborsky, II (Washington, D. C.: American Psychological Association, 1962), 9—10.

moves toward a more "self-actualizing," "self-fulfilling" stance toward her life. She recognizes her "passivity," practices greater assertiveness, grows out of her "dependency" behaviors, and finally obtains a divorce, even though she fears being alone and the need to enter the competitive struggle for a husband.

This fairly typical account of a psychotherapy situation and outcome derives from the initial step taken by Mrs. A. in seeking psychotherapy. In turn, that initial step depends on her viewing her life, her marriage, her aims and goals as centering on the maintenance of a state of emotional well-being. She needs to "feel good" all or most of the time.

Consider the same situation with a young woman, Mrs. B., whose belief system includes the doctrine of providence. The same situation and identical behavior patterns result in a different meaning imparted to them and thus in different emotional response. Mrs. B. believes that God is involved in the world and sustains it and her, and she sees her alcoholic husband within that framework. She may be able to verbalize: "Somehow this is a reflection of God's will for my life." She will search for a conceptual framework by which to understand more completely her role and her ideal course of action. It is not very likely that she will seek psychotherapy, for the totality of the marriage relationship is not defined as a problem which requires help-seeking behavior. Her behavior may be termed acceptance, resignation, denial, or irrational by others, but it remains stable and enduring. The environmental factors are the same but the problem is different. For Mrs. A it is to attain the highest level of happiness. For Mrs. B it is to find what God's intentions are for her and to be faithful to them. As long as Mrs. B. surveys her life and responds: "It is God's will for me!" she is not likely to seek professional help or to divorce her husband. She may or may not be happy. She may or may not be effective in addressing the problem of drinking by her husband. Other factors, including her personality and abilities, will affect such issues. She will likely be able to maintain hope, see meaning in her life, and continue to function as a wife.

The idealized cases described above are admittedly oversimplified. Such clean and sharp distinctions are not often found in real life with its richness, complexity, and diversity. When discussing belief systems and their relationship to behavior, it must be borne in mind that the relationships within belief systems are not in the nature of truth tables, do not conform to the principles of formal logic, and are not reducible to a set of axioms yielding perfect, 100-percent classification into propositions which are believed and disbelieved. Rather, the relationships within belief systems are in the nature of a psycho-logic system which is dynamic in movement and subject to change. As yet principles of psycho-logic are only dimly understood, but efforts are being made to gather further information about the psycho-logic quality of belief systems.[9]

An example may illustrate the distinction between a psycho-logic and formal logic approach to belief systems. "Dick loves Jane. Jane loves Bobby." Given these circumstances the formal principle: "If Dick loves Jane, then Dick also loves what Jane loves" applies to things like pizza, romantic movies, and classical music, but not to Bobby. Far from loving Bobby, Dick hates him. Common sense tells us that another principle is at work—the principle of romantic rivalry for the affections of Jane. Thus belief systems are not organized in strictly rational, logical form, but rather in a form of interlocking hierarchies in which a given hierarchy is brought to bear upon others in a process of judgment and evaluation of a given unit of perception. Dick will quickly learn to love pizza, which he formerly despised, as long as he judges Jane's love of him to be an attainable goal. Inasmuch as Bobby impedes progress to that goal, he is disliked, even if formerly he had been liked greatly by Dick.

Formal logic is almost all two-valued. The form of logic is: "If A, then B," or "+ or −," or "true or false," or "good or bad." Human beings display a much more finely graded response in assigning objects to dimensions along which they may vary. Also the human being ordinarily assesses any object along several dimensions simultaneously, though he may not be fully self-conscious of the assessment process. This complex ability is what the psycho-logician is attempting to honor and to plumb.

Recognizing the psycho-logic quality of belief-system functioning, we will not be surprised if and when an individual who believes in the doctrine of providence does not behave in strict accord with

---

[9] Robert Abelson, ed., *Theories of Cognitive Consistency* (Chicago: Rand McNally, 1968).

102

whatever may be the logical consequences of such a belief. We may only assert that belief if the doctrine increases the probability that such behavior will occur.

LAW AND GOSPEL
AND THE PSYCHOLOGY OF PROVIDENCE

Lutheran theology has a long and rather unique history of placing heavy emphasis on the proper distinction between the Law and the Gospel. The ability to properly discriminate between Law and Gospel has been seen as the key to Christian life as well as to theology, preaching, and church structures. For Lutherans, Law and Gospel is a construct that cuts across many others and assumes a central position in the faith.

In attempting to understand the psychological implications of belief in providence, we will need to pay attention to the overriding significance of the acceptance of the construct of Law and Gospel and the effects of a proper or improper discrimination between the two by an individual. Again, given the nature of belief systems, the place of Law and Gospel in a person's beliefs is subject to the psycho-logic quality of belief-system functioning. Nevertheless, Law-Gospel is seen as more central, stronger, and higher in the hierarchy of beliefs than the belief in providence.

Psychological processes are distinguished from all other phenomena in creation by their symbolic nature. The act of symbolizing is a triadic constellation whose terms are: the object A, the symbol B, and the third member, the subject, for whom the symbol *means* or *represents* the object. The crucial factor is the third member—the subject—who possesses the ability to lend meaning to the observed objects. The belief systems held by the individual function in the meaning-lending process to influence and shape perception of and response to the object. At this point the Lutheran theological tradition of distinguishing between Law and Gospel becomes meaningful in terms of the psychology of individuals.

A life lived under the Law is experienced as "demand" in its totality. Every interaction with the external reality is perceived and felt as an expectation to perform, to measure up, to meet the standard, whatever it may be. This living under demand is reinforced by the external world in a myriad of subtle and not-so-subtle pressures. The entire process termed socialization is expressive of the Law operating in the world through God's dealing with the world by the Law. The psychological consequences of this for the individual are evident in the ready ease with which he reacts to most situations in terms of what is expected of him and what other people will think of him. His sense of self-identity becomes dependent on what he does or does not do. His awareness of self-value, feelings of inadequacy or mastery, derives from his evaluation of his achievement.

Living under the Law means that in the constant process of self-observation he symbolizes or gives meaning to himself in terms of his behavior which, in turn, is evaluated along a success-failure, good-bad dimension. The pastor who notes a falling off of church attendance, a decrease in financial support, and the collapse of his young people's program probably will view himself as a failure. He turns to introspection to discover his failings and weaknesses, assumes responsibility for the "failures," and as he blames himself he blames his people. He may strive for humility in the conviction that this is the Christian way to cope with his sense of failure. As a result his conviction that he is "bad" is strengthened. But then the way to overcome being bad is to "do good things." Now, however, his entire identity is at question in every action. His anxiety level rises precipitously and he is nervous about everything. The end result is a downward spiral of failure, increased striving, repeated failure, and finally ulcers or some other psychosomatic illness.

As long as he is living under the Law he is in the position of the man who has begged, borrowed, stolen all the money he can lay his hands on, mortgaged home, wife, children, liquidated every possible asset, put it all in one sack, and taken a trip to Las Vegas. There the entire sackful, all the value of his life, is placed on 13 Black at the roulette wheel. Now he stands there watching the ball swirl around the wheel waiting for it to drop. The feeling he has is the feeling that the Law-bound have all the time about everything. Neurosis, for the psychologist, is primarily identified in terms of anxiety. By this understanding the life under Law is the neurotic life and the experience of demand the origin of neurosis.

Life under the Gospel, as Scripture indicates, is a life that is free from Law. Life is experienced as freedom, openness, and hope. The question of self-value and self-identity is in no way dependent on or caused by what a person does or does not do. The value which he possesses is determined by the act of God in freely loving him. His identity is a given, a *datum,* from which he begins. All of his interaction with external or internal reality is symbolized or given meaning realistically, apart from any consideration of his personal value or worth. His life is not at stake, but rather his life is opportunity. Under the Gospel he possesses a secure base of identity from which to impart meaning to objects in the symbolizing process.

He may not be totally free from anxiety, for his life is lived along the Law-Gospel continuum and he may fluctuate along that continuum: at this point closer to the Law, at that point nearer to the Gospel. The relationship between Law and Gospel is one of dynamic tension rather than categorical separation. Life under the Gospel thus becomes living within the tension between the two poles. For this reason Word and Sacrament is the vital energizing force in maintaining Gospel directionality. The Gospel is the power to overcome the fiery serpents of doubt, fear, and anxiety which afflict a person's sense of identity.

Given this dynamic wobbling along the tension line between Law and Gospel, the doctrine of providence will be associated with a clutch of possible attitudes toward self and the world. A schematic presentation of possible ways in which the doctrine of providence may lead to symbolic representation or impartation of meaning to reality is offered in Figure 1.[*] Note that any attempt to analyze the interplay of Law-Gospel and the doctrine of providence must seek to identify clear-cut categories, whereas in real people such clear-cut and discriminant positions are not likely to exist. Here types are offered as a way of exploring the implications of providence as a cognitive belief within a psychological process.

The two triangles represent Law and Gospel along the vertical dimensions. The horizontal dimensions represent closed and open attitudinal stances allied to Law and Gospel. The interface between the two triangles represents the doctrine of providence in interplay between Law and Gospel. The ends of the elongated rectangle of "Providence" represent the two poles of internal reality (self) and external reality (world). The phrases within the triangles indicate the stance of an idealized type of personality at each angle.

* See p. 106

105

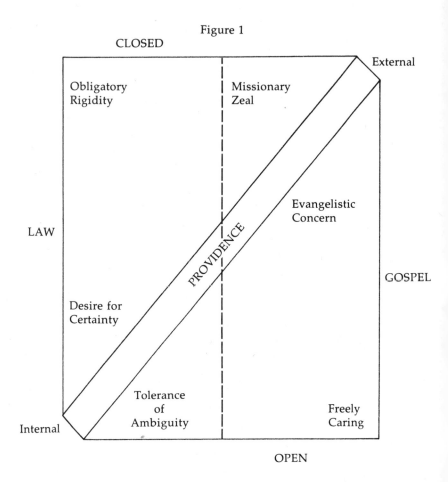

Figure 1

At the point of the Law triangle where Law, "Closed" stance, and "Providence" meet we find the attitude of "Obligatory Rigidity." Providence means that God's design and care for the world is of such a nature as to require a strict and closed attitude toward self and others. Here are manifested such attitudes as: "If God intended men to smoke He would have made them with chimneys." Again here would be located attitudes which say, for instance: "God has made Negroes to be inherently inferior to Whites. The curse of Ham has been placed upon them, and they must suffer the consequences of that until the return of Christ."

A great deal has been written and said regarding the presence of prejudicial or ethnocentric attitudes within the Christian church.

106

Principally the work of Glock and Stark in the area of anti-Semitism has gained a large measure of acceptance. They suggest that religious orthodoxy leads to theological anti-Semitism, which in turn leads to anti-Semitic attitudes and behavior. Though there are serious questions regarding the quality of their research and the fallacious drawing of causal relationships between religious orthodoxy and anti-Semitism, their research has demonstrated that there are those within the Christian church who are anti-Semitic. How shall this be explained? What can be done about it? The schematic representation offered here indicates a theoretical position which is subject to research and which, if supported by empirical studies, would clarify courses of action available to the church to cope with those aspects of an attitude judged to be theologically and socially undesirable.

Prejudicial or discriminatory attitudes toward others cluster together. A person who is anti-Semitic is highly likely to be prejudiced toward many other groups. There is a general "prejudice" factor rather than a single factor of anti-Semitism and a single factor of anticommunism, and so forth. The theory suggests that the dynamic source of the general prejudice factor is located in the interaction of Law and providence. Under Law the doctrine of providence gains the meaning of rigidity and of static categories established by divine will. The demanding force of the Law interacts with such a static view of providence to provide the rationale for prejudice and to lead to prejudicial behavior. Providence provides the aura of "rightness" and of "truth" that justifies holding prejudicial positions. If God made certain people to be hewers of wood and drawers of water and made others to be the chosen ones, who can fight it?

At the angle of the triangle where external aspects of "Providence" meet "Law" and "Closed" would be found the attitudes of "Missionary Zeal" which in extreme cases result in the "white man's burden" type of missionary work. Social and cultural norms get mixed into the missionary vision and as a consequence the subtle negative aspects of much of 19th-century missionary activity are explicable. Providence means that God has created and sustains the world with the expectation that Christians are to accept the responsibility for the conversion of all peoples.

Note that this angle of the triangle extends over the dimension of "Gospel" and "Openness." The Gospel will be preached and men will be converted. However, it is the influence of Law which will lead to imposition of cultural norms along with the Gospel. Thus "Mother Hubbards," the garments with which missionaries clothed nubile native women, become a necessary part of the task. "Jesus Loves Me" is translated into many languages, and standards of Western music and linguistic imagery are imposed upon disparate cultures. Capitalism is judged to be the economic system which must accompany Christianity.

Motivational level is likely to be high, and many people will be moved to sacrifice and devotion to such a task, for providence comes to signify that by such activity a share in God's providential activity is gained by man. He becomes a partner in the exciting work of shaping and molding the entire world. In fact, at times he is even able to feel that he is the senior partner. The vision of a world at peace, with everyone knowing Jesus as Savior, loving his neighbor, cleaving to standards of truth, justice, kindness, and right behavior, is captivating to say the least. In this sense the millennial vision of Marxism and "Missionary Zeal" types bear a close resemblance and roughly equal motivating power. The preaching of the Gospel becomes the means of ensuring a better world. "If everyone believed in Jesus, we wouldn't have any problems. War would be abolished. Famine and unequal distribution of wealth would disappear. The need for courts and police would wither."

The demand of the Law for "good behavior" is met, and people devoted to "Missionary Zeal" are able to feel relatively good about themselves. Ego strength is likely to be high (it needs to be in order to impose one's own will upon entire cultures) and psychic rewards are great. However, when the missionary returns home on furlough, he is able to accept lionization and adulation without becoming in the least bit aware of what is happening. It is simply right that people should admire him for his sacrifice and should provide meals, lodging, care, money, for after all he has given up so much.

"Missionary Zeal" is not confined to foreign mission work, but also manifests itself in a broad variety of causes. It may be a temperance campaign, or a drive to remove *Playboy* from drugstore magazine racks, or leading pickets against a performance of the musical play *Hair*. It may take the form of a vigorous and effective campaign for Christians to tithe as a matter of course. The stewardship campaigns in the churches of the forties and fifties which stressed percentage giving often gave the implication that God's providential care was assured to the tither. Tithing became the way to a happy life, richly blessed with health, money, strong and secure family life. Evidences of God's providence take the form of business successes, unexpected good fortune, preservation of life and limb.

The angle at which the internal (self) dimension of providence interacts with the Law triangle produces the personality characteristic of desire for certainty. Again the theory offered here provides a researchable point, for it has been established that persons differ in the need to impose a certain and well-ordered structure upon the ambiguities of life. Rorschach tests, as well as other projective psychological tests, depend on the fundamental assumption that when presented with an ambiguous stimulus, we impose varying degrees and kinds of structure on the ambiguity. All men must do some of this, but some more so than others. The hypothesis implicit in the theory advanced here is that those for whom life is experienced as a demand, whose stance toward life is a closed one, and for whom providence becomes primarily a principle for order and structure, will possess a higher degree of desire for certainty. Such persons need to know precisely and truly. No uncertainty is allowed. Every dilemma is resolved swiftly and surely, though not necessarily accurately. The simple and immediate solution to any issue or problem is as far as this personality type can tolerate exploration.

In interaction with Law the doctrine of providence shifts in the emphasis abstracted from it. It may signify most strongly rigid, static categorization imposed by the will of God on all of creation. For others it becomes a support for dominance and impetus to a millennial vision. Finally, for some it becomes a model for order and structure necessary to cope with the ambiguous flux of human life.

Shifting now to the Gospel triangle and the interaction of the doctrine of providence with the Gospel and the open stance toward life derived from a stable, secure base of self-value and identity, different types emerge. At the angle of "Gospel-Open," "Providence" supports a "Freely Caring" typology. The fact of God's sustaining presence and power in redemptive, healing action allows for all of creation — including persons to be valued — to be seen in a realistic fashion with warts, blemishes, and weaknesses, and yet as loved and cared for by God. Providence is an open, positive caring by God for all that is His. Persons, whatever their given characteristics, are His children. Here is the antidote to ethnocentrism and prejudice, but note that it is only in conjunction with the Gospel. The failure of at least a generation of propaganda for world brotherhood and the attempts to persuade us that we are all the same, by this theory, is related to the lack of the dynamic power of the Gospel in such programs. On the other hand, a strong argument for tolerance advanced by a historical figure is that of Oliver Cromwell, who during his tenure as Lord Protector enforced a charitable, open, and freely caring policy upon a recalcitrant English Parliament. His rationale and conviction derived from the interaction of "Gospel" and "Providence."

At the angle of "Gospel-Open-External," as opposed to "Missionary Zeal," "Evangelistic Concern" is postulated. Providence interacts with Gospel to support an attitude of concern for others, but the concern is not as programmatic, cultural, and imperious as it is individual and supportive, healing human hurt wherever God's Providence places me. This may account for the observation historically that the great periods of intense missionary activity do not coincide with the periods when the Gospel is most at issue and most clearly preached — the apostolic and Reformation eras.

To be sure, mission work, in the sense of preaching the Gospel to persons not having heard it, was carried on during the apostolic and Reformation periods. However, such activity was in a different key than that of the 4th to 6th centuries and that of the "Great Century" (19th and early 20th) surge of missionary work. The difference appears to lie in that the emphasis is more on reaching out, one by one, to the poor, downtrodden, hurting persons rather than the broad sweeping vision of "evangelize the world in our generation" or converting entire nations or tribes through the ruler.

The difference is one of degree and strength of emphasis rather than an either/or dialectic. Yet it is just such shifts of emphasis we would expect based on the theory of flux along a Law-Gospel tension. Under "Gospel," "Providence" signifies a concern with the individual in his life, unique and idiosyncratic as it is. God's love is for each man. His care is lavished on all, believer and unbeliever alike. This permits acceptance of alien cultures and recognition that

110

this strange culture results from God's providence and His continued involvement in the world. Universalism is not a necessary consequence of the interaction of "Gospel-Providence," for Gospel can be based only on the acts of God in Christ, revealed in time and history. The vision engendered is not one of a millennial kingdom of conformity to Law but rather of a redemptive fellowship in which caring and concern with others allows for them to be what they are — redeemed and forgiven sinners rather than exemplary citizens of a theocracy.

At the angle of the "Gospel-Open" triangle where the internal pole of "Providence" interacts, the expectation is that a personality characteristic of "Tolerance of Ambiguity" would emerge. Providence signifies that God's care is granted the person as he is. He can look at himself as a complex, highly volatile organism and accept the plurality of his motivations, cognitions, and emotions. Secure in the Gospel-granted sense of self-value, he can accept that which is not very nice about himself. He can tolerate feeling bad, depressed, or uncertain. He does not need to deny either his dark side or that of the world. He need not be defensive about his failure to meet the demand, for he knows it does not affect his value and worth.

Consequently the essential ambiguity of life, witnessed by the recognition of a duality in all religion and metaphysics, as well as the extreme difficulty in ascertaining just what "right" or "wrong" behavior is, does not panic the Christian. He has the courage to act, not knowing for certain either the quality of the act or its consequences, because the Gospel assures forgiveness and providence assures him that God can use his actions in pursuit of His goals. The Spirit uses the forgiven sinner to serve the redemptive fellowship.

"Gospel-Open" interacts with "Providence" at different points or levels to tend toward distinct emphases. "Freely Caring" is associated with providential emphasis of God's total commitment to His world. "Evangelistic Concern" places a greater stress on the individual nature of God's providential care. The reality of God's divine will for the Christian as regnant allows for "Tolerance of Ambiguity" in his stance toward the whole of life.

Each of the six clusters of attitude and behavior hypothesized here are subject to empirical test. The dimensions plotted in Figure 1 are capable of being described in terms of their function and predictions being made as to specific behaviors associated with the six angles of intersection. Such research may well prove to be the most fruitful way of relating psychology and its skills and techniques to theology and its body of revealed knowledge. Where the above theoretical guesses are to be supported, a great deal would need be said regarding preaching, pastoral counseling, and the educational activities of the church. Such implications as may be drawn for the church's life from the theory suggested had best wait for the research to be done before speculating.

Sociology's Reluctant Participation in the Dialog Concerning Providence

David S. Schuller

A strict phrasing of the question regarding providence, put to sociologists of religion during the early seventies, would have received a simple but conclusive answer. This has not been a problem to which they have devoted research or much thought. But if we set the question in a broader frame, we find several areas that provide significant background for our investigation. Four areas of concern emerge: the role of religion in society, the problem of theodicy, transcendence in an age of secularity, and alternatives to providence.

1. *The Role of Religion in Society.* How does a discipline that seeks to deal with empirical social data — and yet strives to arrive at analysis and theory lying beneath the raw facts — deal with the phenomena of religious concepts, beliefs, and practices? While this looks distressingly broad as a means of securing insight into changing human responses to concepts of providence, it forms a foundation for a sociological interpretation of the role of religion. It also indicates the limits of the sociological answer. The sociologist *qua* social scientist must insist on framing the question in such a way that he can utilize a methodology that will be defensible within the canons of his own discipline. As a Christian, mystic, or agnostic he may additionally possess strong reactions to his own findings. Moreover, he quickly comes to the limits of his craft where he must confess that an explanation of the rise or current role of religion in a society does not thereby preclude the possibility of an objective reality that lies beyond the human dimension. It does lie beyond the purview of sociology to make any judgments about this probability. To demonstrate the rootage of religion in the human group is not to preclude a superhistorical or transcendent dimension to religion.

2. *The Problem of Theodicy.* The commonly held explanations of the human plight as evidenced in suffering, injustice, evil, and death

have come under increasing attack. In order to face life as a reflecting human being, a man must adopt some view of the universe that will provide him with meaning for the individual evidences of evil and death that overtake those he loves and eventually destroy him as well. The average human being does not construct a world view *de novo*, but tends to absorb the folk wisdom of his culture. While idiosyncratic at points, his interpretation of the meaning of life reflects the nomic interpretations of his society. It is axiomatic that an individual subjects himself to the ordering of his society as he internalizes explanations of life that place his subjective biography into the broader frame of humanity. A series of factors has caused the credibility of such theodicies to be questioned seriously. The project that produced this book is evidence of this fact.

3. *Transcendence in an Age of Secularity.* Those sectors of Western civilization which tend to forecast changes that slowly spread to the rest of the culture have been moving steadily toward greater secularity. This movement can be measured by the growing freedom from ecclesiastical domination, by the decreasing centrality of theological questions, and by the tendency of the average man to minimize the role of God, religion, the transcendent, or the holy in his value system and behavior. The Renaissance, the Enlightenment, the Industrial Revolution, the Cybernetic Revolution—each marks a milestone on this path. This secularity has made serious inroads in the thinking of Americans. Most recently, however, some sociological researchers and theorists have marshaled strong evidence questioning any facile acceptance of this secularization hypothesis. We are again dealing with a process in which the religious factor is involved in a dialectical relationship with the rest of a culture, both influencing other structures and in turn being influenced by them.

4. *Alternatives to Providence.* If modern society is critically reexamining its traditional sacral approaches, it will prove useful to explore how churches are addressing the worldwide problems of hunger, poverty, overpopulation, illness, and injustice. If simple appeals to God's providence are no longer adequate, what concepts are taking their place? Additionally, what values and actions arise from the new guiding concepts? Throughout the developing nations the emerging urban populations are inclined to reject traditional religious institutions. In place of an appeal to divine beneficence,

attention is directed to technological rationality. Man looks to science to control natural forces and the environment.

We shall examine each of these four areas in more detail as a means of probing potential sociological perspectives about a contemporary approach to the concept of providence.

I. A Sociological Interpretation of Religion

Two sociological theorists who have distinguished themselves by their interest in the questions of contemporary religion are Peter Berger and Thomas Luckmann. They have been critical of the sociologists of religion who have been content to deal with public opinion poll information about religious beliefs or practice. Concerned with more basic questions, they have sought to uncover fundamental understandings about the role of religion in our society. We shall follow the basic flow of their interpretation.[1]

Man is distinguished from the nonhuman animal world by his creation of a society that is not restricted to an instinctual structure. Man lives in a world that is open and not bound by a specific environment limited by his own species. Man is different from other mammals, then, in that he is not only placed in a world already structured as a given existing beyond his control, but also participates in making the world in which he lives.

Culture is an aspect of the world which man builds. For a particular individual, human culture is a given, a necessary ingredient in the world which will finish the process of making him human. The sociological axiom that man is a social animal is taken seriously. A man in continued isolation from human contacts begins to lose his humanity. This means that the "world building" activity of man is always a collective endeavor.

We are dealing, however, with a reciprocal action. Humans produce a "world" of material and nonmaterial culture. The very way in which they conceive of their lives—birth, death, work, the material universe, good and evil—is a product of this culture. This world

---

[1] See primarily: Peter L. Berger, *The Sacred Canopy: Elements of a Sociological Theory of Religion* (Garden City: Doubleday & Co., Anchor Books, 1969). The book was originally published in 1967; Thomas Luckmann, *The Invisible Religion: The Problem of Religion in Modern Society* (New York: MacMillan Co., 1967). First edition in German was published in 1963.

confronts the individual as an objective reality outside himself. An individual's language and the institutions of his society are all there as powerful determinants before his birth. Society, then, although a product of human activity, assumes an objective quality beyond the individual.

A society always exerts a coercive power. It is society that controls individuals, employs sanctions, and punishes individuals who do not conform. But the most significant coercive function does not lie in the political or legal institutions of a society. It lies "in its power to constitute and to impose itself as reality." [2]

As this objective reality is outside the person, society provides a "world" that man can live in. An individual's own biography is comprehended within the structures of the social world. A person's life becomes real to him and to others as he locates himself on the grid of a social world to which others subscribe. His identity, his knowledge of himself in a sexual role, his roles within a family, his calling within an economic structure, his position in a particular community comprise more than a series of roles that he may assume. His identity arises from these roles, for he not only plays the role of being a man or a husband or a father, but he is also indeed a man and a husband and a father. Society expects him to "be" a man or a father in a sense that encompasses more than functions. A person is able to reflect on these social roles, confronting himself consciously with the realities of the social world as they impinge upon his life. This social world, we are saying, is socially constructed. It is received by the individual, internalized, and recognized as an objective reality. But this is not a process in which the individual is passive, merely appropriating or being fashioned by his social environment. The individual is a participant, a "co-producer" of this world. His recognition of this world, his acknowledgment and use of it, his feedback into it — all aid in maintaining it.

Man demands meaning. This anthropological need to impose order upon the universe, Berger suggests, has virtually instinctual force. The process of constructing a social world is the process of ordering experience. This is fundamentally conveyed in language and in the traditional wisdom of the group. The task of socializing

---

[2] Berger, p. 12.

the young is to form them through training them to know and to appropriate this order. The social world makes possible an ordered and meaningful life for the individual. "Society is the guardian of order and meaning not only objectively, in its institutional structures, but subjectively as well, in its structuring of individual consciousness." [3]

This process of providing order and meaning conveys more than an enrichment of an individual's life. It stands as the bulwark against the horror and terror of an individual's never becoming fully human. It is the shield against alienation, anomie, the madness of experiences devoid of meaning. Participation in a socially ordered world demands some surrender of total individual freedom and determination. To live apart from the socially ordered world results in assigning to a human being the unbearable condition of existing as an animal in a senseless world.

The greatest threat to this world of meaning comes from death. If the world of ordered meaning is the tiny clearing of light in a jungle of darkness, then the greatest threat to this small island comes from witnessing the death of others and anticipating one's own death. Death is the greatest threat to all basic assumptions of order on which society depends. No other experience so radically challenges all social definitions of reality. Any marginal situation (one that lies outside "everyday realities," such as the experience of dreams, nightmares, the transition state between sleep and wakefulness, "ecstasy" resulting from chemical or other causes) challenges the neatly ordered universe of meaning by providing an experience that lies beyond normal interpretations and supplies a point of reference outside daily routines for seeing them from a new perspective. The credibility of all order in the face of chaos is supremely tested by the encounter of death. [4]

We sense how fragile every fabric of social ordering is, how vulnerable is the dike separating social meaning from the darkness of ignorance, self-interest, and death itself. Socialization and social

---

[3] Ibid., p. 21.

[4] The concept of marginal situations comes into recent sociological writing originally from Karl Jaspers. It was Martin Heidegger who most clearly described death as the supreme encounter with the marginal situation.

control, we have indicated, are the two chief processes by which a society preserves its social world. A final process that must be noted is that of legitimation. Legitimation encompasses the "knowledge," that is, the interpretations given to explain and justify the social order. Legitimations answer the question of "why" to both individual experiences and institutional arrangements. These legitimations are normative in that they represent the group's understanding in contrast to any purely individual thought about the "why" of life and society.

Legitimations form part of the social world. Since few people are interested in ideas as such, legitimations tend to be largely pre-theoretical in character. Most legitimations appear "self-evident" to people in a given society. Their facticity is grounded initially in simply being there. Higher levels of legitimation naturally occur, but they need not be detailed here. But when a challenge to the facticity of any legitimation occurs, this taken-for-granted quality disappears. New ways of providing answers must then be sought.

The function of religion in this interpretation of the social world-creating and -maintaining process is now obvious. As an empirical phenomenon these sociologists describe religion as "the human enterprise by which a sacred cosmos is established." [5] They insist further that such a definition is given as a tool which by the very nature of a definition cannot be judged as "true" or "false." They argue that historically religion has been both the most widespread and the most effective means of legitimation, for it seeks to relate experience with ultimate reality. Social institutions receive the strongest type of validation when they are located within a sacred and cosmic frame of reference. It may be one thing to conceive of government as deriving from the consent of the governed; it may be quite another to view government as God-ordained and God-sanctioned. The humanly constructed social world is given a cosmic status. "Religious legitimation purports to relate the humanly defined reality to ultimate, universal and sacred reality." [6]

Religion is thus rooted in everyday life. Religious explanations

---

[5] Berger, p. 25. See his Appendix I for "Sociological Definitions of Religion," pp. 175–77. See Luckmann for necessary distinctions in the use of this concept.

[6] Berger, p. 36.

are not the creation of a few religious geniuses or theoreticians to be applied *ex post facto* to certain situations. The need arises first among those engaged in living. The same process noted before functions here. After a particular religious legitimation is crystallized, it achieves a degree of autonomy itself. It then begins to exert influence as it becomes an objective social fact that acts on daily life. The role of ritual similarly serves to continue to remind people of major pieces of such legitimation which they may be in danger of forgetting or corrupting.

Two disclaimers are voiced by Berger: "It must be stressed very strongly that what is being said here does *not* imply a sociologically deterministic theory of religion. It is *not* implied that any particular religious system is nothing but the effect or 'reflection' of social processes." [7] He is suggesting a dialectical process because he sees the same human activity behind the forming of society and of the creation of religion.

A complete understanding of a sociological interpretation of religion requires the reader to sense this self-imposed limitation of the discipline. Furthermore: "The implication of the rootage of religion in human activity is *not* that religion is always a dependent variable in the history of society, but rather it derives its objective and subjective reality from human beings, who produce and reproduce it in their ongoing lives." [8]

What does this material contribute to our understanding of providence today? We have depicted a society in which the realm of the sacred and of the transcendent can be granted, but cannot be taken for granted. As we have noted, most contemporary sociologists take great pains to indicate that the social sciences cannot in any ultimate sense prove or disprove the existence of God. But as Charles Glock has argued, when religious conceptions move beyond this simple assertion to speak of beliefs about God's intentions for man, his responsibilities to God, and God's capacity to enter into human events, we find a realm in which the social sciences cannot operate. [9]

---

[7] Ibid., p. 47.

[8] Ibid., p. 48.

[9] Charles Y. Glock and Rodney Stark, *Religion and Society in Tension* (Chicago: Rand McNally & Co., 1965), pp. 291 ff. See also Peter Berger, *The Noise of Solemn Assemblies* (Garden City: Doubleday & Co., 1961), p. 106.

In spite of the rapprochement between the natural sciences and religion within recent decades, the social sciences suspect that the real threat to religion in the future will come from the natural sciences. Sociologists have noted that while some of the philosophical and intellectual differences have been resolved, the more fundamental separation in basic value orientation has not been adequately explored. It is asked: "Why do people deeply committed to a scientific perspective typically find it difficult to also entertain a religious perspective and vice versa?" [10]

The basic world views remain contradictory. Every theological system postulates a divine or supernatural force which lies behind nature, both having created it and continuing to act upon it. This divine force furthermore is also capable of contravening natural laws through its own will, through direct intervention in what is described as a "miracle." In contrast, the basic assumption behind any science is the belief that every event in nature is determined by prior natural events and that the character of this determinism can be discovered through the use of scientific investigation.

Obviously an element of trust lies behind both faith and science. Because of its naturalistic model, science is able to validate at least part of its assumptions with "irrefutable scientific evidence." Because of the different base of the faith commitment, such evidence is not available.

If a new controversy is to emerge, this time between religion and the social sciences, the points of dispute will concern the nature of man. In their development the social sciences borrowed both theory and methodologies from the natural sciences. As a result there still exists an assumption that man's behavior is determined in the same way as that of natural phenomena, that is, man's actions can be understood and to an extent predicted on the basis of antecedent factors which will determine that action.

At this given point in time the social sciences would admit that they can identify causes for only a small part of human behavior and by no means for all causes within a given model. While the individual social scientist may admit the limitations of any deterministic model [11] for providing all answers regarding man and human society

---

[10] Glock, p. 290.

[11] Deterministic models regard human behavior as the "invariant" outcome of prior conditions. Such outcomes usually will be stated in degrees of probability.

within the realm of his discipline, he has no alternative than to improve the models in the hope of explaining more causes with improved theory and methodology.

Any conflict that may arise between religion and the social sciences would concern the relationship of man's free will [12] and divine intervention in human affairs. Religion must answer the question of God's authority and of man's accountability. If God's power is posited as absolute without the image of free will for man, man's fate is entirely in the hands of God; responsibility is removed from men and shifted to God. If, on the other hand, man's free will is posited by religion, his destiny is in his own hands. Responsibility is shifted from God to man. Social scientists question any great latitude of freedom in human choice, as well as God's intervention.

> . . . human behavior which would be explained from a religious perspective as God's will or as a result of man making a conscious and responsible choice to accept or reject God's will, is questioned by the results of social science research. Not only is the intervention of God rejected as a causal factor, but the idea that man's freedom is as extensive as religion allows is rejected as well.[13]

While it is difficult to assess the role of the social sciences in the overall process of secularization, one finds that both friends and foes of these disciplines grant an influence among the literate sector of the population. Specific studies have indicated that the members of some religious groups are relatively untouched by the findings of the social sciences about human behavior. In other cases one senses a reinterpretation of traditional beliefs in order to take into consideration knowledge and insights arising from the social sciences. Many of the contemporary theologians interpreting a secular theology are in obvious dialog with the social sciences.

The final outcome is difficult to predict. Since a current movement in our society is seriously questioning the final wisdom of a scientific methodology which reduces the scope of humanity, one is not inclined to predict the ultimate victory for the hypothesis of an untrammeled determinism. At the same time theologians of the stature of Reinhold Niebuhr warn that "without the constant in-

---

[12] In contrast the approach of free will rejects the idea of prior causation and grants the individual the maximum possibility of individual choice in his actions.

[13] Glock, p. 298.

fluence of rational and empirical disciplines, however, religious life would degenerate into an obscurantist effort to restore prescientific symbols to the post scientific absurdities." [14]

Speaking directly to our fundamental question and our immediate question, Niebuhr added:

> Without an emphasis on the universality of natural causation, religion is tempted, in place of the simple securities of the parental frame of reference, to create childish securities under a "special" providence. This absurd sense of security is established by imagining that the divine source of being and order will interfere with natural processes for the sake of the security of the righteous devotee.[15]

But the causal chain can only be explored so far. At that point sociology sees the necessity for interpretations that utilize the area of the sacred and the transcendent. Predictions can safely suggest little more than both the continued existence and change of the role of religion in modern society.

II. THE PROBLEM OF THEODICY

One significant aspect of the concept of providence has to do with theodicy: explanations of phenomena in terms of religious legitimations. We said before that the specific legitimation serves the individual by placing his life with its various joys, frustrations, and tragedies into a broader fabric of meaning by relating it to a sacred order that transcends nature. In this section we shall explore this process more closely and focus in particular on the fact that traditional theodicies are declining in plausibility. The old legitimations of power and privilege are being swept away in a day that turns to revolution as a means of initiating a new order. Albert Camus described this process as that of replacing the reign of grace with the reign of justice.

The task of theodicy is to offer an explanation for the suffering, injustice, and death that every man must face. One of the most dramatic illustrations of the collapse of theodicy was the appear-

---

[14] Reinhold Niebuhr, "Forward," *The Religious Situation: 1968*, ed. Donald R. Cutler (Boston: Beacon Press, 1968), p. xii.

[15] Ibid.

ance of Rabbi Richard Rubenstein's volume in 1966 entitled *After Auschwitz*.[16] Rubenstein was so horrified by the death of 6 million Jews in Hitler's Germany that the pillars of the Jewish faith collapsed for him. Specifically, he could no longer affirm a God who controls history, nor could he believe that the Jews were the special concern of God as a covenant people. He found himself forced to agree with Camus that in order to retain one's integrity it was better to cast off a framework that struggled vainly to give meaning to inevitable but unearned suffering, and to confess that the world is indifferent and that human suffering and death are meaningless. To affirm God as Lord of history was to make Him the ultimate author of Auschwitz. He could acknowledge God as "the holy nothingness," [17] but utterly rejected Him as a source of meaning or consolation before the vicissitudes of human existence. In this modern Jew we find a repudiation of God and the charge that He is the source of disillusion. Nihilistically Rubenstein welcomes death as the only Messiah: "There is only one Messiah who redeems us from the irony, the travail and the limitations of human existence. Surely he will come. He is the Angel of Death." [18]

Although Rubenstein's thought is cast in a uniquely Jewish mold, he was immediately seen as the Jewish equivalent of the Protestant radical theologians who proclaimed the death of God. One of the concerns of virtually all those who interpreted some sort of "death" of God was the awareness that modern man had become a creature of doubt who could no longer assent to theological or metaphysical explanations for natural events that did not square with secular explanations.

For primitive man all of life was sacred. As Mircea Eliade has demonstrated, religious experience at its source is not a matter of theoretical speculation but of an experience that precedes reflection. Man's daily life — including bodily functions, work, and community — at point after point is a reflection of a divine cosmos. He lives out on a natural level a pattern that reflects an ideal image revealed to

---

[16] Richard L. Rubenstein Jr., *After Auschwitz* (Indianapolis: Bobbs-Merrill Co., 1966).

[17] Ibid., p. 204.

[18] Ibid., p. 205.

him by myths. While he is aware of the physical world as distinct from the religious, cosmic symbolism adds another dimension to life. "Openness to the world enables religious man to know himself in knowing the world—and this knowledge is precious to him because it is religious, because it pertains to being." [19]

Theodicy, then, provides meaning for man. It provides the plausibility structure that enables him to understand his position in society, his work, his relationship to a family, the joys and pains that mark human life, and eventually interpret his old age and approaching death. As important to life as the basic physical requirements of food, clothing, and shelter are the mental/spiritual requirements for meaning. A man must sort out the significance of what is happening to him. Thus a person who is suffering intensely from disease or from persecution by others desires relief from the pain. But equally intense is his desire for an answer to the question, "Why?" Indeed in cases where the pain cannot be removed, the question becomes primary.

Theodicies provide a "place" in the broader scheme of life for individuals and for groups. An entire race may ask why it is discriminated against; a nation may ask why it was defeated and occupied by enemy forces. Specific theodicies seek to provide the answer. This indicates an important *social* function of theodicies. They provide a rationale for the inequities of position, power, and possession found in every society. A theodicy must not be seen as an ideological device fashioned by those in power to protect their privileges. For the theodicy provides meaning and interpretation for the peasant as well as for the king.

As is apparent, theodicies are found in every type of society and on every cultural level. There are great variations in their level of rationality and sophistication. Among primitive peoples the life of the individual is closely identified with that of the family, clan, and tribe. Consequently there is a blurring of the individual biography into that of the collectivity. The success of the tribe brings joy to him; the threat of his own death is lessened in the awareness of the continuity and ongoing life of the larger group. The pattern

---

[19] Mircea Eliade, *The Sacred and the Profane: The Nature of Religion,* trans. Willard R. Trask (New York: Harcourt, Brace & World), p. 167.

of his individual life is incorporated into cosmic cycles that relate him to the larger rhythms of nature and to a larger family that transcends immediate space and time, for primitive theodicies typically relate him to his ancestors and to future generations.

On a much higher level of sophistication we find the concept of *karma* in India. Within this system one finds an explanation for every contingency of life, for an inexorable law of cause and effect is seen at work in the universe. Combined with *samsara*, the wheel of rebirths, one finds himself placed in time both backward and forward. Furthermore, whatever comes to the individual is his just due; it is reward or punishment for his own past actions. The harsh lines of Hindu theodicy were softened by the people through magic, intercession with the deities, and other forms of devotionals that would aid a man in this life or his next incarnation.

In mysticism, as another example, the individual escaped the force of human travail through union with the deity or with sacred beings. One's own suffering, poverty, or death is trivialized when measured against the overarching reality of incorporation into the divine. Life in the world becomes illusionary; only absorption into the divine is real.

In dualism the universe becomes an arena for the cosmic struggle between the forces of good and evil. Good and evil take various forms; the conflict may be between spirit and matter. The material world may then be seen as evil. Man may be conceived of as coming from another realm, not truly part of the earth's disorder. Life becomes a matter of severing oneself from the prison of this world. The theodicy provides an explanation for evil and suffering and projects a path for man to follow. Man's redemption lies in his return to his true home, which is far removed from the darkness of the world. In such dualistic schemes, of which there are many, the world is typically devalued; ascetic practices purport to aid the person in breaking the chains of his earthly prison cell.

While every religious interpretation of life involves theodicy, the problem becomes central in the monotheism proclaimed by Biblical faith in both the Old and New Testaments. When there is no other deity, when God is central and the source of all ethical values, the problem of theodicy becomes unbearably acute. "Indeed, more than in any other religious constellation, it may be said that this type of monotheism stands or falls with its capacity to solve the problem of theodicy, 'How can God permit . . . ?'"[20] Where God is totally powerful and righteous, creator of both man and the universe, the problem is posed in the form experienced by most Christians.

The Book of Job is significant both because it faces this problem in a classical form and because its answer is peculiarly unsatisfying to the modern Western mind. The answer that Job gives to the overwhelming suffering experienced by man is one of submission and continued trust. "Though He slay me, yet will I trust Him" is the confession of Job. In sackcloth and ashes he repents before the majesty of God, who permitted destruction, loss, suffering, and death to ravage everything and everyone about him. Before the wisdom of God Job recognizes his ignorance; before God's majesty he acknowledges his humility; before God's power Job confesses his weakness. Submissive, he continues to trust.

The thing the modern reader finds unconsciously disturbing is that the problem has been subtly shifted. The concern at the beginning was theodicy: How can a righteous, loving God permit such things to happen to a man who loves and serves him? The answers posed by Job's friends are categorically rejected. The argument suddenly turns and we are confronted by "anthropodicy" where the question of human sin replaces the original question of divine justice and goodness. The original question is declared illegitimate and a symptom of the very human problem that now has been lifted to prominence. The modern reader who persists with the original question leaves Job with the sensation that he has been outtalked but probably not convinced on the level of his thoughts and feelings.

The problem of theodicy lies at the heart of Christology. For the unbearable tension posed by a righteous God and suffering humanity is resolved in the incarnation, when God becomes man, and as the God-man suffers and dies vicariously. The suffering of the cross is crucial for theodicy. Without the cross incarnation alone does not get at the root problem. It must be *God* who suffers. Undoubtedly this awareness was crucial in the Christological formulations developed at Nicaea, namely, that it be clear that in the suffering of Christ God Himself was suffering. The problem finds

---

[20] Berger, p. 73.

resolution only if full humanity and full deity are involved in the action of the cross.

Some may argue that the difficulty we faced in resolving the problem in Job is still with us, for Christ is clearly portrayed as suffering for the sins of mankind. To this extent the question has shifted from any accusation against God to one against man.[21] Instead of asking about God's justice, we again are confronted with a substitute question, namely, that of the sinfulness of man. For Christ's suffering and death are clearly to justify man, not God.

The problem of theodicy for Western Christian society revolves around the plausibility of these explanations. From one standpoint the difficulty is not unique. In other centuries when plague devastated a population, when war ravaged a nation, or an earthquake destroyed a city, people asked the question of God's presence and justice. Repeatedly in the face of mass destruction the question of theodicy was raised and the validity of the Christian solution discussed. Some historians in documenting the rise of secularism suggest a rather steady devaluation of Christian theodicy. In more recent and more secular decades the question has been likely to shift from one of theology to one of anthropology — not asking: "How could God permit this?" but: "How can human beings do this?" As we saw in the case of Rubenstein, the massive horrors of our own day have caused questions of the Biblical God to be raised in their starkest forms.

One of the dominant characteristics of our modern secular age is a strong sense of contingency.[22] As secular man searches for causes, he finds it difficult if not impossible to see the controlling hand of reason, history, or God. What is given is arbitrary; it is pointless to seek an ultimate order or reason behind what is. Gilkey describes the present secular attitude:

> Our environment, taken even in its widest sense, exhibits neither
> a holy eternal order, as it seemed to the Greeks, nor one eternally
> willed by a holy sovereign Lord, as in the Biblical tradition; and

---

[21] For a significant discussion of the essentially masochistic attitude demanded of man by Biblical religion see Berger, pp. 73–77.

[22] Langdon Gilkey, *Naming the Whirlwind: The Renewal of God-Language* (Indianapolis: Bobbs-Merrill Co., 1969). For his excellent analysis of contingency see pp. 40–48.

our life, therefore, is not dependent on a sacred order or a transcendent divinity for either its existence or its meaning.[23]

This sense of the accidental is strong today. The very idea of an explanation or reason seems to be ruled out. This has been asserted by existentialists, such as Martin Heidegger, who see existence as simply "being there."[24] Like dice, existence is thrown, but one cannot look for a thrower or for any reason for the throw. This sense of radical contingency is being met in two different fashions. In broad terms the American response has remained essentially optimistic. The liberally educated man is likely to go ahead and live the good life with the proximate meanings that intelligence can create. The European mood has been darker and more pessimistic with a far greater concern that a blind fate ultimately rules and mocks the fragile meanings that man may create.

For both the final meaning is the same: There is no ultimate order within the universe nor is there a transcendent source. Any meaning or value cannot come from outside a man's life. A meaningless void occupies the center of life. While not evil, it is neutral and devoid of purpose. Theodicy becomes impossible. There is no transcosmic source of meaning or security. Man is alone in a random, accidental universe. Against this background we can understand the Judeo-Christian cry of anguish of the late sixties that God was dead.

III. Transcendence in an Age of Secularity

Much of what we have said thus far has pointed toward a modern secularity in which there is missing a sense of a transcendent God who orders life for the good of His creatures. Any purpose or meaning that modern man can claim for his life now must be found within a relative, contingent world. A man may respond by finding life meaningless, burdensome, and absurd; he may never search for transcendent goals and may content himself with the calm desperation of familiar routines and demands, spiced occasionally by the minor enjoyments of pleasure and the excitement of the

---

[23] Ibid., p. 38.

[24] Martin Heidegger, *Being and Time,* trans. J. Macquarrie and E. Robinson (New York: Harper & Row, 1962), p. 321.

unusual. To the extent that he has been exposed to the philosophic and theological writings of our day—whether through theater, novels, or the popularization coming through magazines or television—he is made aware of the eclipse or death of God and is reminded that modern man is expected to have outgrown his need for mythologies. In a frenzy bewildering to those outside the church, many professional theologians and churchmen have added their weight to the denial of a Biblical God that inhabits a three-storied universe, who exists in transcendent splendor, and who enters our world only at odd moments to judge or rescue. For the most part they have stopped short of the radical answer of atheism and predictions of the rapid death of the church. Instead they have sought to reinterpret the Christian conception of God and the mission of the church to conform to currently popular humanistic expectations and cultural goals.

Serious questions are being addressed to the radical theologians, suggesting that they have not been radical enough. While ostensibly making concessions to the modern spirit, they have failed to be consistent, for example, in the area of Christology. They want to reserve a special place for the contemporary influence of Jesus Christ that is not explained by the rest of their approach. For moderns in the postmoral, postindustrial age to return to a man of the first century for direction and guidance in ethical decisions for the latter third of the 20th century remains an act of faith. Any power or positive influence that this first-century man can actually exert over my life—beyond that of Luther or Lincoln—involves a tacit reliance on an earlier Christology that is otherwise denied.

The problem we face is much more troublesome than the one Bultmann sought to solve. Bultmann wanted to relieve contemporary man of the "crude and unbelievable mythological machinery"[25] that the Scriptures seemed to impose on faith. He was able to redirect our concerns from a God "up there" or "out there" and to depopulate the world of angels, demons, and other assorted spirits. But the deeper problems remained untouched: Is there a "divine"

[25] See Gordon D. Kaufman, "On the Meaning of 'God': Transcendence Without Mythology," Transcendence, ed. Herbert Richardson and Donald Cutler (Boston: Beacon Press, 1969), p. 115.

or "other worldly sphere" at all? Is there a reality beyond the world of our senses? Is there a "God" who acts in the lives of men?

Earlier ages used elaborate mythologies and theologies to interpret the world around them not only to explain "supernatural" happenings but also the everyday world of home, field, forest, and sea. As scientific explanations developed and technological control increased, man became less dependent on the mythologies for daily life and work. The realm of the gods shrank to the preserve of "religion" and the diminishing realm of the yet unexplained.

The sociology of religion has posed the question quite bluntly: "Is there a central function of the idea of Transcendence that might be retained even while the traditional arguments for it must be abandoned?" [26] The question suggests that while it may no longer be meaningful to speak in older physico-local terms of anything "outside the world," the function—the appreciation of something independent of men and their cultures—is highly significant.

One discovers this need for the transcendent on both the personal and social levels of reality. An individual experiences certain longings and desires that remain unsatisfied, characterized by Abraham Maslow as "deficiency needs." [27] Some would argue that the human creature has desires so profound that they cannot be met within the confines of human existence. His deep cry is for contact with the transcendent. Men like Paul, Luther, or Pascal are miserable in their existence until an experience of transcendent reality gives a sense of wholeness and rightness to their entire lives. Usually we identify such conversion experiences with religion, but Maslow reminds us that such peak experiences are not confined to the "conventionally religious sphere."

Individual religious experience can be validated only as it is shared and compared with the experiences of others. Further, the insight or experience of the individual can never influence others until it is shared. If not shared, it dies with him. Within the social group as well as individually, people experience a need for reference

---

[26] See Robert N. Bellah, "Transcendence in Contemporary Piety," Richardson and Cutler, p. 85.

[27] Abraham H. Maslow, *Toward a Psychology of Being* (New York: Van Nostrand Press, 1962), see chap. 3.

beyond the group. Society finds itself forced to anchor appeals for commitment or definitions of goals and values on a level of reality above itself. One finds the same principle at work in the life history of the individual or in the collective experience of the group. Bellah summarizes this need for transcendent rootings in the social sphere:

> The kind of symbolism which societies develop to indicate their commitment to higher values and to define their legitimacy varies in historical perspective. But there is no society which can avoid such symbolism; it is necessary even in the most complex modern societies.[28]

In an essay on the sources of social transcendence Harvey Cox provided a significant footnote to our immediate concern. In speaking of how the religious vision — such as the kingdom of God or the new Jerusalem — has affected cultures, Cox outlines three ways in which the catalytic power of a social vision can be undercut. The first method is to postpone the new world entirely to an epoch beyond time and history. Historically this portrays the church as a small conventicle enduring the travail of an evil world, confident of a new order beyond earthly limitations. The second way of diffusing the catalytic power of religious vision is to identify it with a particular institution or series of reforms so that when these are attained or lost, the tension is reduced. Historical illustrations could be drawn from any of the utopian groups that identified Christianity with a particular theological-political ideology. The third way to destroy the potential effect of the religious vision is to equate the religious institution itself with the kingdom of God and then either spiritualize or individualize the radical hope until it becomes trivial. In the history of the church the Constantinian-Roman model with its modern applications, even among Protestants in North America, illustrates this approach.[29]

An increase of secularity is a contemporary reality. Sociologists of religion have noted that "churchly" religiosity has declined in Europe in a different fashion from the United States. In Europe there has been a progressive decline in institutional participation; fewer

---

[28] Bellah, p. 91.

[29] Harvey Cox, "Feasibility and Fantasy: Sources of Social Transcendence," Richardson and Cutler, pp. 55–56.

people attend worship services and partake of the sacraments. The American pattern has been characterized by continued participation in the cultic life of the church, but a "secularization from within" makes it evident that religious beliefs are becoming devoid of meaning. In each case we find a growing group of people who seem to be getting along without a sense of the supernatural as a significant and meaningful reality.

Gilkey has distinguished three social and institutional changes that have accompanied the transformation of attitudes and values involved in secularity. First, with the growth of technology and urbanization man is less dependent on the order of nature. Attitudinally men feel they have moved from God's world, where they were participants in an eternal order, to one where they have become the creators and determiners of a changing order. Second, this has reordered man's view of human institutions and customs. Former authorities, once unquestioned expressions of a divine order, are now forces with which one can negotiate. Finally, the world has become desacralized; the world is material, a natural and social environment that can be fashioned in virtually any shape we desire.[30]

Against this background of increased secularity are found a variety of ecclesiastical responses — from Protestant conservatism, which militantly attacked the charges as apostasy, to radical churches, which embraced the charges with a call to celebration. Sociologists used two sets of categories to understand the phenomenon: (1) Those who did not share the majority world view of secularity became a "cognitive minority," a group that consciously formed itself around a body of knowledge which it professed in contrast to the rest of society. Such a group consciously supports itself in what is usually a defensive posture because of its confession of certain realities denied by the majority culture. (2) At the opposite end of the pole one finds surrender. Modernity is embraced with a passion. Traditional religious concepts are retranslated to be consistent with the new world view. In this case supernatural elements were translated into a naturalistic frame; all otherworldly accents were proved to have had this-worldly referrents all the while.

---

[30] See Gilkey, pp. 36–38, and Sydney E. Ahlstrom, "The Radical Turn in Theology and Ethics: Why It Occurred in the 1960's," *The Annals*, 387, (January 1970), 7–9.

During the very period in which it seemed so obvious that Western society was moving toward an evermore complete secularity, it became clear that a strong sense of the sacred — "signals of transcendence" — was very much alive. A series of analysts began to interpret the conflicting evidence by suggesting that while organized religion was losing ground in certain areas where its presence had been evident, many contemporary individuals refused to live in a totally desacralized cosmos. Some who represented the elitist vanguard of that society were turning phrenetically to any belief system that offered salvation from the sterility of positivism.

In a widely quoted article Huston Smith[31] documented this countermovement among university students. He indicated that some of the most brilliant young people in the best universities of the land were those who were studying Asian philosophy, exploring yoga, Tibet and Zen, the kundalini, parapsychology, even witchcraft and magic. Here one saw a clear rejection of a mechanomorphic interpretation of life offered by modern science and a demand for a world view in which transcendence, mystery, and the supernatural can still break into an overly tidy world of scientific explanation and systems analysis.

Smith suggested the criteria of incomprehensibility and indomitability for discovering areas of contemporary life where the sacred seems to manifest itself in our secular world. Three areas where a sense of the sacred is felt are: (1) the unconscious; man's psychoanalytic understanding of the deep unconscious springs of his being continue to exist on a primitive level; (2) the awareness of one's own existential death; and (3) the intersection of lives at depth levels.

Peter Berger wrote *A Rumor of Angels* to deal with this same phenomenon. His signals of transcendence are "phenomena that are to be found within the domain of our 'natural' reality but that appear to point beyond that reality."[32] He discusses such signals as man's propensity for order, the role of play, his tendency to hope for the future, his sense of moral outrage before a particularly hei-

---

[31] "Secularization and the Sacred," *The Religious Situation, 1968,* ed. Donald R. Cutler, pp. 585 f.

[32] *A Rumor of Angels: Modern Society and the Rediscovery of the Supernatural* (Garden City: Doubleday & Co., Anchor Books, 1970), p. 53. First edition in 1969.

nous offense, and the phenomenon of humor which arises from a sense of incongruity or discrepancy. He concludes that "modern man" has not lost his propensity for awe, for the uncanny, for those "subterranean rumblings of supernaturalism." [33]

IV. ALTERNATIVES TO PROVIDENCE

One final perspective will prove useful. In the light of the changes we have discussed regarding the concept of providence, what are the new guiding concepts that have arisen to take its place? How does the church define its role in the midst of rapidly changing cultures? How does the Christian see himself as an agent of God in the midst of the revolutionary changes taking place in technology, economics, and politics? In order to gain a geographically broad and theologically "mainline" response, we shall examine primarily the approximately 80 essays prepared for the Geneva meeting addressed to the theme: "Christians in the Technical and Social Revolutions of Our Time." [34] What appeals to God's providence do we find today among Christians representing every segment of the globe as they address problems related historically to the idea of God's providence?

In surveying the theological bases of Christian social policy over some 40 years, several underlying themes arise:[35] (1) Until World War II one finds an ongoing debate between an essentially optimistic, evolutionary view of the Kingdom's growth on the earth (expressed primarily by American and English theologians) and a European view that discounted any essential relationship between God's kingdom and the economic and political developments taking place in history. The persuasiveness of Karl Barth and the horrors of the war undermined the optimistic, evolutionary view. More recently "ecumenical thought has sought to discern the divine providence working through the secular movements and revolutions

---

[33] Ibid., p. 30.

[34] The four volumes are: *Christian Social Ethics in a Changing World, Responsible Government in a Revolutionary Age, Economic Growth in World Perspective,* and *Man in Community.* For more detailed information see the following references to particular essays and volumes.

[35] Thomas S. Derr, "The Development of Modern Ecumenical Political Thought," *Responsible Government in a Revolutionary Age,* ed. Z. K. Matthews (New York: Association Press, 1966), pp. 301–3.

of our time, without making trust in God an excuse to evade the responsibility for Christian participation in the struggles of this age."[36] While the question of providence was often ancillary, this theme did deal centrally with the question of God's role and action in history. (2) The second theme related the presence of the Kingdom to the church's concern with the whole man in his social setting. The 40 years of development here might be read as preserving a tension between the transcendent and temporal aspects of the social order. Transcendence was preserved in all of the prophetic utterances that judged society for losing its ultimate perspective, its necessary spiritual center, or a sacred sense of life. The temporal has received a heavier accent in the last dozen years in finding God at work in the secular world, in calling the church to its servant role, and in seeking to find a new solidarity with all men. (3) The concept of the church has also undergone a significant shift. In the 1920s the church was interpreted largely in purely sociological categories; it was seen as a voluntary organization that was able to exert some power and persuasion. A much more theological interpretation of the church now holds sway. Its transcendent, eschatological dimensions are highlighted as attempts are made to rescue the church from its cultural, racial, and national patterns. (4) The fourth theological concern has sought to define a method by which responsible decisions might be made. Two conflicting answers have been in dialog over two generations. In the early years ecumenical leaders attempted to develop what can be called "middle axioms" to guide decisions. In the tradition of natural law this was an effort to provide "principles" sufficiently broad yet specific enough that ethical guidance could be provided. In turn the "contextualists" sought to avoid the sterility of fixed principles in order to be responsive both to the Word of God and the new situation. These two points of view remain in contention today. Each added response may be seen as correcting a potential difficulty in an earlier position.

In a word, during the past generation and a half we have seen the rise of a theological humanism. It is theological; it has not abandoned the Christian faith. At least a few modern spokesmen, in spite of what may appear to be novel or tortured exegesis or theological

---

[36] Ibid., pp. 301–2.

135

judgments, nevertheless are concerned that they make their point within a theological frame of reference. But it is also humanistic, with a heavy contemporary accent on the necessity for the humanization of life and a call to Christians to sense their solidarity with all men.

In one of the concluding essays in the volume on economic development Charles Elliott, an English Anglican priest who teaches economics, consciously speaks of a "secular redemption."[37] In arguing that the task of the Christian economist is to assure that economic growth will always be a means and not an end, he calls for an eradication of the environmental factors that limit and corrupt the human spirit. As economic activity fights disease and ignorance, as it reduces mortality and offers education and challenging, stimulating jobs, it is serving a "redemptive" end.

This same conclusion arises when one looks specifically at the social involvement in ecumenical history. In an earlier period churches relied heavily on joint actions addressed to the social order, particularly in the form of formal statements. Attempts to influence governments through proclamations or direct social action alternated with the counterpoint concern that churches provide the worship and programs of theological education that would permit lay Christians as the body of Christ to fill crucial positions in the world in order to influence institutions. Since World War II we have seen a reemergence of contextualism in ethics with a rejection of the old Christian blueprints for a more humane and just society. While there has been a rejection of uniquely Christian political movements, there has been an increased concern to have the church join other groups in fighting for the poor and dispossessed. In a rejection of institutional rigidity, individuals have tried to form ad hoc groups that would bind themselves together only long enough to accomplish a specific goal.

The basic concern remains a practical one dealing with the lives of people. Thus theology, economics, and sociology remain strictly tools to be used to build a superior quality of life for people. In summarizing how Christians should cooperate with non-Christians,

---

[37] "Ethical Issues in the Dynamics of Economic Development," *Economic Growth in World Perspective*, ed. Denys Munby (New York: Association Press, 1966), p. 340.

a Japanese professor of political science insists that in newly independent countries struggling for social justice and minimum welfare for masses of people, "Christians should set aside their controversies with non-Christians over the ultimate question of God or atheism and should engage at once in the urgent task of nation-building." [38] He does not deny the need for apologetics, but he reminds Christians that a preoccupation with dogma and ritual to the neglect of the needs of the people is a denial of the love of God.

This concern is illustrated in the economic analysis presented under church auspices. The analysis builds almost exclusively on the data provided by the appropriate discipline. When the working life of a developing society is under discussion, the migration of people from agriculture to industry, the loss of economic independence, rates of unemployment, the movement from manual work to automation, the same type of analysis could be found in a United Nations publication. In most of the essays a final section will focus on the moral, ethical, and "human-spiritual" implications of the data. Advice is given to the churches concerning how to reach the workers in certain cultures and which needs appear most pressing. Typical would be this final paragraph by a Dutch churchman and economist:

> The churches must consider how they can put Christianity's ancient message of freedom, simplicity and joy into such understandable and relevant terms that it will once again appeal to and liberate the agitated, nervous, and often unhappy people of this industrial civilization. [39]

The focus is on the hard data provided by economists; a broadly humanistic, compassionate concern is evident; the church and other agencies are appealed to. But the sections of theological analysis tend to be segregated. Little theological insight of any profound dimension informs the discussion dealing with the policy level or technical questions confronting an economically developing nation. As a result the question of how God relates to these concerns — by way of providence or otherwise — is not raised.

---

[38] Yoshiaki Iisaka, "Christians and Political Life in a Dynamic Asia," Matthews, p. 334.

[39] Pieter Kuin, "Economic Growth and Welfare in the Industrialized West," Munby, p. 53.

This is even more evident in the consideration of the current challenge to political institutions. The tone of current analysis and prescription is not one of utopian dreaming. Modern man is seen as living in a revolutionary period in which he is destroying existing structures in order to build new ones more responsive to human needs. Speaking specifically to this issue, André Philip calls for conscious action and attempts to influence events supported by technical analysis of the given problem. "Such action must be technical in character and in no way revolutionary or violent." [40] Because the technical structures are so elaborate and interrelated in industrialized countries, revolutionary or violent means have become impractical quite apart from ethical considerations. This obviously is not true in the new nations of the world. Here the struggle and conflict involved in creating a new nation may involve the violence that Europe experienced during its nation-building period of the 14th to the 16th centuries. But whatever the form of the crisis or the revolution, man clearly is on center stage. The old authorities of king, pope, or parliament no longer appear as absolutes. For most appeals to God's providence do not provide the data or the psychological motivation necessary for making the decisions required in building new political structures. Men hold in their hands the power to destroy and create, to establish new values and form new institutions that will better serve human need.

Nowhere is this process seen more clearly than in the question of establishing peace in the face of possible atomic warfare. Within the ecumenical movement widespread agreement developed in the rejection of traditional arguments for the use of force in the light of the new atomic possibilities. "God's law says 'No' to atomic war." "The church must speak out clearly against atomic war." "Atomic war can no longer be a means of enforcing justice, as a *bellum justum* was in the past." [41] It is significant that in an area where the church has developed a stance — as in the case of the concept of just war —

---

[40] "The Revolutionary Change in the Structure of European Political Life," Matthews, p. 120. For a contrasting point of view see Richard Shaull, "Revolutionary Change in Theological Perspective," *Christian Social Ethics in a Changing World*, ed. John C. Bennett (New York: Association Press, 1966), pp. 23–43.

[41] Helmut Gollwitzer, "The Christian in the Search for World Order and Peace," Matthews, pp. 51–52.

any new pronouncement must begin with God's commandment. In speaking judgment upon a new situation, theologians have struggled to avoid sounding arrogant or fanatic. They were also concerned that their "no" would not be heard as abstract principles incapable of immediate translation into specific action.

Since this series of Geneva essays was written during the period in which Harvey Cox was enjoying great popularity in the United States, we might focus on his line of argument in developing "The Responsibility of the Christian in a World of Technology." [42] Basic to Cox's thinking is the conviction that our contemporary scientific technology would be unthinkable without the freeing influence of the Biblical faith as it culminated in the Gospel of Jesus Christ. "The Christian Gospel, rather, is the Word of God calling men in every age and within any social or cultural ethos to take responsibility for himself and his neighbor in history before the living God." In his well-known argument, modern technology could only arise after the world of nature was disenchanted. Only after a concept of the Biblical God had demythologized the world could it become available as neutral material to be worked. Similarly work had to be elevated from the domain of slaves where physical work was a lower form of activity to where it was respected and material accomplishment was honored. The third prerequisite for our modern world was the belief that change was both possible and good. The former "closed" universe was opened when God was conceived of as the fashioner of new things and Himself creating change.

Cox seeks to integrate his theological and technological understandings. He invites Christians to call the "technicians" and "humanists" today to a glorious celebration of *what God has done* for man and *what man can do in response.* For him technology is more than a new bag of tools. It has transformed life itself and has presented us with a new set of challenges. We are no longer terrified before the forces of nature. Man has become the new source of terror. But Cox's final affirmation focuses on the God who has brought us to this moment:

> But we know that the God and father of Jesus Christ is not just the God of nature. He is also the Lord of history, the supreme

---

[42] Munby, pp. 173–92.

sovereign of political and economic life. He is now demytholo-gizing the structures of corporate human existence and bringing them under human control, just as he once conquered the natural forces. He continues to dethrone the principalities and powers, making them available to man as his captives, as instrumentalities for the building of human community. The God of Abraham, Isaac, and Jacob, is also the Lord of technological man. [43]

At the present moment, then, Christians recognize that they are at a crossroad where significant decisions must be made. They have heard through demonstrations and revolutions that many past practices represented an uncritical baptizing of the status quo. Dangers adhere to economic affluence and political power. Churches are trying to face up to the demands of the faith in hearing Christ's warnings about riches and power. But most significant is the aware-ness that for the first time in the history of mankind it has become technically possible to remove the ravages of poverty, squalor, and disease. Churches are faced with the challenge of doing more than "ambulance work" — of asking how structural changes within society can destroy in this generation the crippling effects of abject poverty and hunger with their attendant suffering. For the first time in history the question was not one of dividing relative scarcity among many people but redistributing relative abundance. It meant shifting our concerns from questions of individual ethics and stewardship to asking about corporate, institutional responsibilities.

Ronald Preston of the United Kingdom provides the simplest but probably the most accurate lead to speaking to our question of where people see God in the great economic and political revolutions of our day. In commenting about our recent increase of affluence he says simply: "Christians have for the most part accepted it without comment. Those who have thought about it have welcomed it as a gift from God." [44] Modern concern has been forced to deal with urgent and highly complex technical questions. As a result founda-tional or source concerns of God's relation to the process have rarely surfaced. When theological concerns are raised, they tend to be ethical questions addressed to practical concerns dealing with the redistribution of wealth and power in a day when men feel clearly in control of the decision-making process.

---

[43] Ibid., p. 192.

[44] "Christians and Economic Growth," Munby, p. 110.

140

The Concept of Providence
in Modern Historical Thought

Carl S. Meyer †

St. Augustine of Hippo in emphasizing providential control set the pattern for much of the historical thought in the Middle Ages. Even in the period of the Renaissance and Reformation, despite Guicciardini and Machiavelli, Augustinian ideas about the meaning of history prevailed. The theologies of Thomas Aquinas (d. 1274) or Martin Luther (d. 1546) did not differ radically from Augustine on this point, so that its basic thrust remained. John Calvin (d. 1564) and Jacques Bossuet (d. 1704) were closer to Augustine's concepts of providence than were Luther or Aquinas. The Age of the Enlightenment neglected or denied this concept and the idea of progress supplanted it. That idea persisted into the 20th century, when the traumatic experiences of world wars, destructive nuclear weapons, and futile conflicts questioned and for many nullified the idea of progress and steeped many into a pessimistic *Weltanschauung*.

A reconsideration of the idea of providence by an investigation of its use in historical writings since the middle of the 16th century seem useful and the writer has here attempted such an investigation.[1] In the Age of Enlightenment man, like Faust, sold his soul and denied his Maker. History is not, as J. B. Bury once pungently remarked, "the dossier of an incompetent Providence." It is a mystery, or, in Jacques Maritain's phrase, it is "God and the mystery of the world." The relationship between "the defectible freedom of man" and "the eternal freedom of God" is to Maritain "the absolutely primary problem for the philosopher of history."[2] It is a problem that must begin with a study of the meaning of history and the basic

---

[1] See above, pp. 19—43, for the essay by Martin Scharlemann, "Divine Providence: Biblical Perspectives," and pp. 45—66, for the essay by Richard Baepler, "Providence in Christian Thought."

[2] *On the Philosophy of History*, ed. Joseph W. Evans (New York: Charles Scribner's Sons, 1957), p. 123. G. Barraclough points out that many historians are way off

relationship between good and evil in the world and the designs of God, who preserves, rules, and governs the world and concurs in its happenings, at times gracious and merciful, at times permissive and tolerant of evil, at times wrathful, sometimes concealed, sometimes revealed. It is this problem that is subsumed under the concept "providence" and which is here surveyed in philosophies of history and historical accounts since the Age of the Reformation.

I

The Age of the Reformation was a polemical age, and history had to serve the cause of religious polemics. Then, too, history had its lessons to teach, not least about the providential guidance of God for the welfare of the church.

Among the first generation reformers Philip Melanchthon (d. 1560) was the only one who can properly be designated as a historian. Not that he was an outstanding historian, but the theocentric orientation of his view of history and his Law-Gospel emphasis place him in a unique position. Melanchthon believed that natural, unregenerate man approaches divine laws with grave doubts concerning providence.[3] Melanchthon stressed the government of God particularly in the affairs of the church. "God governs and serves the church of His Son, our Lord Jesus Christ, who was made a sacrifice for us." The phrase *Deus gubernet et servet Ecclesiam* occurs now and again in Melanchthon's letters.[4]

While Melanchthon did not use historical writing primarily for

---

even searching for meaning in history under the guise of simple searching for facts. He writes: "I believe that 'it is by returning again and again to the great central problems that history has renewed itself,' and that the tendency, now inbred in historians, to treat all historical facts (as a cynic once observed) as though they were born free and equal, stands in the way of this renewal. If we say that some phases of the past are more important than others *for us*, we do not, after all, mean to imply that all are not (or may not be) equally important (or unimportant) in the sight of God: we simply mean that there are certain affinities or similarities in circumstances, or in the questions with which men are coping, that make (or are, we think, likely to make) their study practically rewarding." "The Historian in a Changing World," *History in a Changing World* (Norman: University of Oklahoma Press, n.d. [1958]), p. 13; see also pp. 15−17.

[3] *Melanchthons Werke in Auswahl,* ed. Robert Stupperich (Gütersloh: C. Bertelsmann Verlag, 1952), II, 1, 242/14-15.

[4] Philip Melanchthon to John Hess, 16 Feb. 1541, *Corpus Reformatorum,* ed. Karl Bretschneider (Halle, 1832), IV, 101−2, No. 2145.

polemical purposes, Matthias Flacius Illyricus (d. 1575) did. Flacius was responsible, with the help of co-workers, for the *Magdeburg Centuries,* a massive 13-volume collection of sources from the first 13 centuries of the history of the Christian church. The history of the church echoes the goodness and power of God, according to Flacius. This aspect, not the polemical aspect of Flacius' *Centuries,* is of consequence here.

Besides God's power there is also a demonic element in the history of the church. The subject of the first sentence of Flacius' dedicatory Epistle at the beginning of the first *Century* is the devil. In the church the devil arouses men to fanaticism, blinds them, and leads them into horrible perversions of the Christian religion. The devil causes the barbarian devastation of schools and books. The devil deforms the church by scandals and heresies.

However, the devil does not have free or even primary rule in the world, for God restrains him, according to Flacius. God prevents the faithful from being drowned in the devil's sea of lies, deceptions, and darkness. Providence, for Flacius, does not mean only God's victories over the devil, but also God's control of the demonic in history.

From heretics within the church and from wicked men outside, God preserves the faithful. When empires fall, God maintains a remnant, the church. The cruelties of the tyrants and the crimes of the impious are broken, turned aside, and punished. However, the mark of the true church is that she lives under the cross. Flacius has conceived of church history as the struggle between God and the devil, God being the divine mover in history and history being the record of God's will. In each of the 13 volumes Flacius has a section *De miraculis.* The incidents recounted are evidence that Flacius believes in God's active intervention in history. However, Flacius is primarily concerned about the church's doctrine in each century and her teachers. According to Flacius even that great "German prophet" of the latter days, Martin Luther, is important because of his voice and ministry whereby the light of the Gospel was recalled as if from the darkness of Egypt and shone again as in apostolic times.[5] This happened because God uses men as His agents.

---

[5] Matthias Flacius Illyricus et al., *Centuriae Magdeburgenses . . . . ,* ed. Sigismund J. Baumgarten and Johannes S. Semler (Nuremberg: Johannes Leonard Lang, 1757 to 1760), I, i; II, i; III, i.

Flacius owed much to Augustine and the Augustinian tradition of writing history. He borrowed, it seems, Luther's concept of the *Wundermann,* applying it to Luther himself. Flacius placed a theological accent on the interpretation of history, thereby reversing for a time the humanistic accent of Machiavelli and Guicciardini and other humanists.

In answer to the *Magdeburg Centuries* Caesar Baronius (d. 1607) compiled the *Annales Ecclesiastici.* He was certain that his labors were under the protection of God and that the Roman Catholic Church through the centuries enjoyed the protection of the Almighty.[6] His view of providence did not differ greatly from that of Flacius, except that which was Flacius' heresy was Baronius' orthodoxy.

Both Flacius and Baronius were polemicists. John Foxe (d. 1587), too, wrote, at least in part, with polemical purposes. In the preface, dedicated to Queen Elizabeth, of his *Acts and Monuments,* Foxe said that by a knowledge of ecclesiastical history the people "may have examples of God's mighty working in his church, to the confirmation of their faith, and the edification of christian life." He postulated that there was "light and profit" for the church from a knowledge of "the acts of Christ's martyrs,"

> besides other manifold examples and experiments of God's great mercies and judgments in preserving his church, in overthrowing tyrants, in confounding pride, in altering states and kingdoms, in conserving religion against errors and dissensions, in relieving the godly, in bridling the wicked, loosing and tying up again of Satan the disturber of common-weals, in punishing transgressions, as well against the first table as the second.

In another preface Foxe maintained that "the true church of Christ" remained, even though it was persecuted, "by the providence of God" and "stood in open defense of truth against the disordered church of Rome." He invoked "the God of peace, who hath power both of land and sea" for the unity of the church. From the

---

[6] Matthew A. Fitzsimons, "Church History during the Protestant Reformation and the Catholic Reform," *The Development of Historiography,* ed. Matthew A. Fitzsimons, Alfred G. Pundt, and Charles E. Nowell (Harrisburg, Pa.: The Stackpole Co., 1954), pp. 126—27.

story of the martyrs "we may learn a lively testimony of God's mighty working in the life of man, contrary to the opinion of Atheists, and all the whole nest of Epicures." Foxe wrote his account of the martyrs of the church that "the wonderful works of God might appear to his glory." Even in the midst of "enormities" God guarded his elect.[7]

Foxe's language and concepts are sufficiently similar to those of Flacius that they would indicate a degree of dependence or interdependence. Their point of view was shared by theologians and historians of the second half of the 16th century.

II

Within a generation after the death of Foxe, Sir Francis Bacon (d. 1626) wrote *The Advancement of Learning* (1605). In this book Bacon advocated the study of history to remember the past and by so doing, in the judgment of Robert Collingwood, he "negates the idea that the historian's main function is to detect a divine plan running through the facts."[8] J. B. Bury judges, however, that Bacon formally acknowledged "the doctrine of an active, intervening Providence, the Providence of Augustine," but that he "did not press it or emphasize it."[9]

Foxe and Bacon belonged to an age that knew that "there's a divinity that shapes our ends, rough hew them as we will." Puritans and Anglicans appealed to providence as witness to the rightness of their cause.

We get a glimpse of the Puritans' belief in providence from Thomas Carlyle's description of Oliver Cromwell's speech to Parliament. Carlyle writes:

> He [Cromwell] talks about "births of Providence": All these changes, so many victories and events, were not forethoughts, and the theatrical contrivances of men, of *me* or of men; it is blind

---

[7] George Townsend, ed., *The Acts and Monuments of John Foxe* (London: Seeley, Burnside, and Seeley, 1843), I, viii, for the quotation; ibid., I, xxi–xxv.

[8] R. G. Collingwood, *The Idea of History* (New York: Oxford University Press, Galaxy Books, 1956), p. 58.

[9] J. B. Bury, *The Idea of Progress: An Inquiry into Its Origin and Growth,* reprint of 1932 ed. (New York: Dover Publications, 1955), pp. 88–92.

blasphemies that will persist in calling them so! . . . These things were foreseen by no man, he says; no man could tell what a day would bring forth: they were 'births of Providence,' God's finger guided us on, and we came at last to clear heights of victory, God's cause triumphant in these Nations; . . . I have no Notary's parchment, but only God's voice from the battle-whirlwind, for being President among you! [10]

Cromwell's contemporary, John Milton, composed his *Paradise Lost* to "assert eternal Providence" and to "justify the ways of God to men." A mention of one of the histories written in New England will show that among the Puritans of New England this same strong belief in providence is to be found, viz., *Wonder-Working Providence of Sions Saviour in New England, 1628 — 1651.*

One of the most prominent theologians and historians among the New England Puritans, Cotton Mather (d. 1728), began his *Magnalia Christi Americana* with an avowal of divine Providence without, however, defining his term:

I WRITE the *Wonders* of the CHRISTIAN RELIGION, flying from the Depravations of *Europe*, to the *American Strand*: And, assisted by the Holy Author of that *Religion*, I do, with all Conscience of *Truth*, required therein by Him, who is the *Truth* itself, Report the *Wonderful Displays* of His Infinite Power, Wisdom, Goodness, and Faithfulness, wherewith His Divine Providence hath *Irradiated* an *Indian Wilderness*.[11]

Mather liberally applied the concept of a "peculiar people" to the 17th-century church in the wilderness. There, when the faithful hungered, "the good Providence of God relieved them, and supplied them." There God gave them "a Moses" to lead them in the person of William Bradford and "our New-English Nehemiah" in the person of John Winthrop. Their laws, wars, and judges were proof positive that God was with them. Mather wrote:

When the Great God of Heaven had carried his *Peculiar People* into a *Wilderness*, the *Theocracy*, where he became (as he was for *that Reason* stiled) *The Lord of Hosts*, unto them and the *Four* Squadrons

---

[10] Thomas Carlyle, *On Heroes, Hero-Worship and the Heroic in History*, ed. Annie Russell Marble (New York: Macmillan Co., 1924), p. 313.

[11] Kenneth B. Murdock, ed., *Selections from Cotton Mather* (New York: Hafner Publishing Co., ca. 1926), p. 1. Capitalizations and italics in the original.

of their *Army*, was most eminently display'd in *his* Enacting their *Laws, his* Directing of their *Wars*, and Electing and Inspiring of their Judges.[12]

Theophilus Eaton and John Davenport were the "Moses and Aaron" of the Connecticut colony. Among those especially favored by God was Sir William Phips. Phips was instrumental in restoring the charter to Massachusetts—a great deed done by the sovereign God. Despite disasters "by an evident hand of Heaven," almighty God nevertheless gave the colonists abundant cause for thanksgiving.[13]

The emphasis of the Puritan historians on providence is not a unique contribution to the development of historiography. Yet in their portrayal of events and their preoccupation with the will of God these historians did not neglect the social and economic context in which the events took place. They regarded it as their obligation "to search faithfully for an understanding of God's revealed will in the ambiguous evidence of the historical world."

This was not the major concern of Jacques Bossuet, bishop of Condom and later of Meaux. In his *Discourse on Universal History* (1681), in his famous sermon on providence, and in other writings Bossuet defended the doctrine of providence against the skeptics of his age, like René Descartes (d. 1650) and Nicolas de Malebranche (d. 1715). Descartes virtually set aside the idea of providence by advocating a mechanical theory of the world and the doctrine of invariable law. Malebranche argued that the universe was as perfect as it could be, having been made by the Creator by general and simple methods. This he called providence. God acts only by means of general laws.[14] Bossuet wrote against Descartes and Malebranche and those whom he labelled "freethinkers":

> The freethinkers declare war on divine providence and they find no better argument against it than the distribution of good and evil which seems unjust and irrational since it does not discriminate between the good and the wicked. It is there that the godless ones entrench themselves as in an impregnable fortress from which they throw bold missiles at the divine wisdom which rules

---

[12] Ibid., p. 49.

[13] Ibid., see especially pp. 126, 161, 169–70, 184, 202, 227.

[14] Bury, *Idea of Progress*, pp. 73–76.

the world, falsely convinced as they are that the apparent disorder of human affairs is an evidence against this very wisdom.[15]

Bossuet was forced to face the problem of disorder, a seeming lack of purpose in human affairs. Augustine, too, had faced this problem. Augustine had used the analogy of orchestral music, which is distorted, if one stands too close to one section of the orchestra. A modern analogy would say that the affairs of man are like the helter-skelter movements of passengers in an air terminal or even of incoming and outgoing planes. But there are reasoned plans and air tower control personnel that belie the seeming confusion. Bossuet argued:

> If you know how to fix the point from which things have to be viewed, all iniquities will be corrected, and you will see only wisdom where before you saw disorder.[16]

In this observation Bossuet did not go beyond Augustine. He took a step beyond Augustine, however, when he argued that the doctrine of providence contributed to morality and civic righteousness. Bossuet maintained that to "the arrogance of libertines" the consciousness that they are under "this ever watchful eye of Providence" appears insufferable. They want to shake off "the yoke of this Providence" so that they can be independent "to live at their own fancy, without fear, discipline, or restraint."[17] History not only provides examples of God's wrath, it tells also that God is a superior police officer. "Big Brother is watching you," is a slogan Bossuet could have understood. Coupled with the certainty of God's ways of dealing with men, "he discovers the precise details of God's purpose in every historical nook and cranny."[18]

III

Bossuet was one of the last, if not the last, of the outstanding theologically oriented historians. In the 18th century Giambattista

---

[15] Quoted from the *Sermon sur la providence* by Karl Löwith, *Meaning in History*, fourth impression (Chicago: University of Chicago Press, 1957), p. 137.

[16] Quoted from the *Sermon sur la providence* by Löwith, p. 137.

[17] Quoted by Bury, p. 74.

[18] Frank E. Manuel, *Shapes of Philosophical History* (Stanford, Calif.: Stanford University Press, 1965), p. 34.

Vico (d. 1774) wrote much about providence, but he was much less certain than Bossuet of the manner in which it operates. The claim can justly be made that with Vico "the modern philosophy of history begins." Vico put truth and the created into juxtaposition to each other. This is the principle *verum factum* — the true and the created are identical and are related to God's omniscience. He repudiated the ideas of fate and chance, as held by the ancient Stoics and Epicureans because both deny providence; he applauded the Platonists because they agree that there is a divine providence. Divine providence is the "divine legislative mind." All nations, according to Vico, "believe in a provident divinity" who administers divine justice to preserve human society. For that reason he concluded:

> Our new Science must therefore be a demonstration, so to speak, of the historical fact of Providence, for it must be a history of the forms of order which, without human discernment or intent, and often against the designs of men, Providence gives to this great city of the human race. For though this world has been created in time and particular, the orders established therein by Providence are universal and eternal.

Divine providence, therefore, is responsible for the process by which primitive society embraces national life, the Vichian "reason of state." Providence also orders the form of religion on which the societal structures are based.

This must not be interpreted as an evolutionary or lineal theory of history. Nor can it be described as cyclical. Vico's theory of recurrence *(ricorso)* postulated a pattern of history that is a spiral-like movement. In the *corso* and *ricorso* of the three ages of man, "the Best and Greatest God has made the counsels of His Providence, by which He has guided the human beings of all nations, serve the ineffable decrees of His grace." [19]

In his *New Science* Vico, in his own words, "develops an ideal eternal history based on the idea of the providence by which, as he shows throughout the work, the natural laws of the people are

---

[19] Ronald H. Nash, ed., *Ideas of History* (New York: E. P. Dutton & Co., 1969), I, 27–29; excerpts from *The New Science*, ibid., I, 35–41, 46.

ordained." [20] He represented the universe "as a great city in which God by an eternal law" orders affairs. Those who break this law do so at their peril and wage war against themselves.

This discussion may cause the reader to suppose that the concept of providence was at the heart of Vico's philosophy of history. It was not. The emphasis here on Vico's concept of providence is due to the thrust of this essay. Vico's real contribution to the development of historiography must for that same reason be bypassed.

IV

Moreover, Vico's influence on his own times was not great nor was he responsible for nullifying Bossuet's elaborations of the workings of providence. The responsibility for that rests on Voltaire (d. 1778). Voltaire was a historian as well as a philosopher and with Hume, as Collingwood remarks, inaugurated a new school of historical thought.[21] In his *Candide* Voltaire levied a devastating criticism against the concept of providence. He found no empirical evidence of any kind in the course of history for a belief in divine governance. Voltaire saw the reliance on providence being replaced by a faith in man's ability to care for his own well-being and tranquility.[22] Like Montesquieu, his contemporary, Voltaire had no brief for providence, design, or meaning in history and final causes.

Voltaire's contemporaries, especially those in England, were generally of one mind with him. David Hume (d. 1776) in *The History of England from the Invasion of Julius Caesar to the Revolution of 1688* showed his contempt for the Puritans because of his skepticism. He did not entertain the Puritan idea of providence nor did he operate with that concept in writing his *History*.[23]

---

[20] Max Harold Fisch and Thomas G. Bergin, trans., *The Autobiography of Giambattista Vico* (Ithaca, N. Y.: Cornell University Press, Great Seal Books, 1963), p. 169. Vico wrote the *Autobiography* in 1725.

[21] Collingwood, p. 76. E. Fueter, *Geschichte der neueren Historiographie* (Munich and Berlin: Oldenbourg, 1911), p. 350, claims that the historiography of the *Aufklärung* was founded by Voltaire. Fritz Stern, "Introduction," *The Varieties of History from Voltaire to the Present* (New York: World Publishing Co., Meridian Books, 1956), p. 14, says that Voltaire "was a very self-conscious pioneer of a new type of philosophical and cultural historian."

[22] Löwith, pp. 108–11.

[23] Fueter, pp. 364–67.

And there was Gibbon. Edward Gibbon (d. 1794) owed much to Tillemont (d. 1698) for the historical information he needed to produce his *History of the Decline and Fall of the Roman Empire*. He did not use Tillemont's metaphysical or theological presuppositions. The Frenchman belonged to a school of historians who believed that "their task was to restore to primitive purity the palpable proof of God's Divine Providence." Gibbon disregarded Tillemont's pious phrases by which he interpreted his sources. He would not grant that a miracle happened at the Milvian Bridge in 312, nor would he date the conversion of Constantine until late in the emperor's life. It meant that in his interpretation of Constantine, Gibbon was deliberately denying providence in history. It was not that Gibbon would make so bold a statement. His inuendoes, witticisms, irony, and sarcasm, now one, now the other, alert the reader that Gibbon is not in sympathy with the providential approach to history. For example, in telling about the administration of justice among the Germanic tribes, Gibbon remarks:

> In every religion, the Deity has been invoked to confirm the truth, or to punish the falsehood, of human testimony; but this powerful instrument was misapplied and abused by the simplicity of the German legislators. . . . The sin and scandal of manifest and frequent perjuries engaged the magistrates to remove these dangerous temptations; and to supply the defects of human testimony by the famous experiments of fire and water. These extraordinary trials were so capriciously contrived that in some cases guilt, and innocence in others, could not be proved without the interposition of a miracle. Such miracles were readily provided by fraud and credulity; the most intricate causes were determined by this easy and infallible method; and the turbulent Barbarians, who might have distained the sentence of the magistrate, submissively acquiesced in the judgment of God.[24]

The repudiation of the idea of providence left a vacuum in the diagnosis of the meaning of history. Eighteenth-century philosophers and historians generally held that history had meaning and therefore had to find a substitute for the traditional belief in providence. That substitute was the idea of progress.

---

[24] Edward Gibbon, *The End of the Roman Empire in the West: The Barbarian Conquests and the Transition to the Middle Ages: A. D. 439–565*, ed. J. B. Bury (New York: Harper & Bros., Harper Torchbooks, 1958), pp. 136–37; footnotes omitted.

Turgot (d. 1781), paying "prudent lip-service" to the idea of providence in planning a universal history, made the idea of progress his hermeneutical principle. Condorcet (d. 1794), too, looked to the idea of progress as the organizing principle which gives history purpose. "He had acknowledged Providence," writes Bury, "and . . . the place which he assigned to Providence was that of a sort of honorary President of the development of civilization who might disappear without affecting the proceedings . . . ." [25]

Condorcet's disciple, Auguste Comte (d. 1857), is the outstanding 19th-century proponent of positivism. In the development of civilization Comte saw three stages: "the Theological, or fictitious; the Metaphysical, or abstract; and the Scientific, or positive." These three stages correspond to childhood, youth, and manhood. Within each of the three stages there are substages; for example, the theological has fetishism, polytheism, and monotheism. Comte wrote:

> The Theological system arrived at the highest perfection of which it is capable when it substituted the providential action of a single Being for the varied operations of the numerous divinities which had been before imagined. [26]

Hence, in his theory of progressive evolution Comte discarded the function of providence, replacing it with a *prevision ration rationelle*. Comte's theory was not far from Jouffrey's hypothesis of the fatality of intellectual development, which also was meant to replace the belief in providence. However, the most incisive critic of the idea of providence in this period was Pierre Proudhon (d. 1865).

Proudhon wanted man "to chase the idea of God out of his mind incessantly," so that man can become equal to God. "Take away this providence," he wrote, "and God ceases to be human." The attributes of God as Providence, according to Proudhon, are refuted by the happenings of history. Nevertheless, as one writer states: "It is the faith in a coming Kingdom of God which inspired Proudhon's fight against God and providence for the sake of human progress."

---

[25] Bury, p. 207. On Condorcet and Turgot see Bury, pp. 154—58, 202—16; Löwith, pp. 91—103. Patrick Gardiner, *Theories of History* (Glencoe, Ill.: The Free Press, 1959), pp. 51—58, reprints a selection from Condorcet's *Sketch for the Progress of the Human Mind* from June Barraclough's translation.

[26] Gardiner, pp. 75—76, from Conte's *Cours de philosophie positive* in Harriet Martineau's translation; Nash, II, 9.

V

Thus, between the middle of the 18th century and the middle of the 19th the idea of progress had almost supplanted the idea of providence as an explanation of the pattern in history. The idea of progress seemed to dominate the thinking of the historians of the 19th century, as the idea of providence had dominated the thinking of historians from Augustine to Bossuet. Yet there were other theories and explanations of history besides progress in the thought patterns of philosophers and historians of the 19th century. Among these were the theories of Herder, Hegel, Marx, and others.

Johann Gottfried von Herder (d. 1803), "the 'gate-keeper' of the nineteenth century," belonged to the Romantic movement. He wrote a 4-volume *Ideas for the Philosophy of the History of Mankind.* His main propositions have been summarized by Robert Flint:

> I. The end of human nature is humanity; and that they may realize that end, God has put into the hands of men their own fates.
>
> II. All the destructive powers in nature must not only yield in time to the preservative powers, but must ultimately be subservient to the perfection of the whole.
>
> III. The human race is destined to proceed through various degrees of civilization, in various revolutions, but its abiding welfare rests solely and essentially on reason and justice.
>
> IV. From the very nature of the human mind, reason and justice must gain more footing among men in the course of time, and promote the extension of humanity.
>
> V. A wise goodness disposes the fate of mankind, and therefore there is no nobler merit, no purer or more abiding happiness, than to cooperate in its designs.[27]

What does Herder mean by "God" and "a wise goodness"? The question must be answered somewhat categorically by saying that Herder's theology borders on pantheism. Herder rejected the supernatural in history. He wrote:

> The God I look for in history must be the same as the God of nature; for man is but a tiny particle of the whole, and the history of mankind resembles that of the worm closely connected with the

---

[27] *The Philosophy of History in France and Germany* (New York: Scribner, 1874), p. 386, quoted by Barnes, p. 193.

tissue it inhabits; therefore, the natural laws by which the Deity reveals itself must reign in man likewise.[28]

Georg Wilhelm Friedrich Hegel (d. 1831) developed an elaborate metaphysical system in his *Philosophy of History*, published posthumously. He presupposed that "Reason is the law of the world" and that it is "the True, the Eternal, the Absolute Power."[29] Yet he said, "The world is not abandoned to chance and external accident [external contingent causes] but controlled by *Providence*."[30] He wrote:

> The truth that a Providence, that is to say, a divine Providence, presides over the events of the world corresponds to our principle; for divine Providence is wisdom endowed with infinite power which realizes its own aim, that is the absolute, rational, final purpose of the world.[31]

Hegel criticized those who were not ready to apply faith in providence "to the whole, the comprehensive course of world history." He was not satisfied with a narrow, individual application of faith in providence, or with those who would deny that it is impossible to know God. "The divine wisdom, or Reason, is the same in the large as in the small." Hegel called his method "a theodicy, a justification of God."

This compelled Hegel to face the question, What is the ultimate

---

[28] Quoted by Thompson, *A History of Historical Writing* (New York: Macmillan Co., 1942), II, 137. See Thompson, II, 133—38; Fueter, pp. 407—11; H. E. Barnes, *A History of Historical Writing* (Norman, Okla.: University of Oklahoma Press, 1937), pp. 193—94; G. P. Gooch, *History and Historians in the Nineteenth Century* (Boston: Beacon Press, 1959; first published in 1913); Peter Meinhold, *Geschichte der kirchlichen Historiographie* (Freiburg and Munich: Verlag Karl Alber, 1967), II, 93—97; Tillinghast, pp. 147—81. Nash, I, 68—84, has a treatment of Herder and an excerpt from his *Ideas.* See p. 79 for the citation given by Thompson. Herder uses the term "Providence." He says, for instance, to refute the idea of providence: "Nothing has tended more to obstruct this impartial view, than the attempt to consider even the bloody history of Rome as subservient to some secret limited design of Providence." Nash, I, 78. See also ibid., I, 79, where again he makes it evident that he does not believe in the idea of providence.

[29] G. W. F. Hegel, *Reason in History: A General Introduction to the Philosophy of History*, trans. Robert S. Hartman (New York: The Liberal Arts Press, 1953), p. 11. See also Nash, I, 86—107, and Gardiner, pp. 60—73; both of them bring excerpts from Hegel in J. Sibtree's translation; Tillinghast, pp. 182—220.

[30] Hegel, trans. Hartman, p. 14. The bracketed phrase is Sibtree's translation.

[31] Hegel, trans. Hartman, p. 15.

purpose of the world? He argued that this ultimate purpose is that which is willed in the world itself. This brought him to conclude that the Idea, God, and the nature of His will are one and the same. Its manifestation as the human spirit is freedom; in its purest form it is Spirit. We cannot here follow Hegel's arguments on the idea of freedom, the means the Spirit utilizes to realize the Idea, his discussion on the individual both as subject and object of history, and the state as the realization of the Idea. He spoke about the legal and religious foundations of the state. In his discussion of the individual as the object of history Hegel advanced the concept of "the cunning of Reason." [32] The general Idea does not come forward; it uses the passions of men as its agents. Providence is as wholly immanent in world order as reason is in man.

> Man is an end in himself only by virtue of the divine in him — that which we designated at the outset as *Reason*, or, insofar as it has activity and power of self-determination, as *Freedom*.[33]

Hegel climaxed this section of his discussion with the conclusion:

> This good, this Reason, in its most concrete representation, is God. God governs the world. The actual working of His government, the carrying out of His plan is the history of the world.[34]

Hegel argued that the course of world history is from the east to the west. The dialectical movements of history in which its interest is detached from the individual and attached to the state make the German people the bearer of the Christian principle. Ultimately the synthesis results in the realization of the Idea and of Freedom as "the ultimate result which the process of history is to accomplish." It is the absolute idealization of the Prussian State as the embodiment of God's will.

---

[32] Ibid., p. 14. See also pp. 15–22. Hegel's concept of the "cunning of reason" may well be compared to Immanuel Kant's thought that "the very thing then that makes history appear meaningless turns out to be the instrument used by Nature to bring about the development of man's potentialities." Nash, I, 50. Kant wrote: "Such a justification of nature—or rather, let us say, of Providence—is no insignificant motive for choosing a particular point of view in contemplating the course of the world." Nash, I, 65.

[33] Hegel, trans. Hartman, p. 44.

[34] Ibid., p. 47.

Analysts of Hegel's thought, such as Collingwood, Bury, and Eduard Fueter, have bypassed the emphasis which Hegel gave to his concept of providence. Löwith looked at it carefully, compared it with Augustine's concept, and concluded that Hegel saw Christianity in terms of speculative philosophy and secularized the Christian faith. The religious and irreligious in Hegel's thought Hegel himself summed up in his famous dictum, *Die Weltgeshichte ist das Weltgericht.*[35]

Karl Marx (d. 1883), who had no idea of providence and dismisses the existence of God, used Hegelian dialectics in fashioning his dialectical materialism. The emphasis which Marx and his collaborator Friedrich Engels (d. 1895) put on technical and economic factors, the process of production and the ultimate victory of the proletariat, need no elaboration at this point. In the production, exchange, and distribution of wealth "the final causes of all social changes and political revolutions are to be sought, not in man's brain, but in man's insight into eternal truth and justice," Engels said.[36] This is in reality a materialistic form of the doctrine of providence. The secularization of providence yielded in Marx's thought to the inevitability of the development toward communism.

VI

The outstanding historian of Germany in the 19th century was not Engels but Leopold von Ranke (d. 1886). To assay his contributions to historiography is not our task at this time. Known for his objectivity and his devotion to history as a science *per se*, he nevertheless had a well-formulated and distinctive belief regarding providence. His delight in studying history, according to Peter Geyl, was "the getting a view of God's government," or as Ranke also called them, "God's vicissitudes in the world." Geyl quoted a sentence from a letter which Ranke wrote to his brother Heinrich in 1820:

> God lives and is observable in the whole of history. Every deed bears witness of him, every moment proclaims his name, but espe-

---

[35] Löwith, pp. 54

[36] Nash, I, 126. Excerpts from Marx and Engels are given in Nash, I, 108–30; Gardiner, pp. 126–38; Stern, pp. 142–58.

cially do we find it in the connecting line that runs through history." [37]

From that Geyl concluded: "Ranke's soul is flooded with reverence at the spectacle afforded by history, for it is all God." Gooch quoted Ranke as saying: "No history can be written but universal history. I am enchanted by the loftiness and logic of the development and, if I may say so, by the ways of God." Ranke thought of states as intellectual entities, creations of the human spirit, thoughts of God.

There is somewhat of Augustine in this view and somewhat of Luther. There is even a bit of the mystical. We note another aspect of Ranke's belief in God in history—that every epoch is *coram Deo*. Every epoch is immediately responsible to God and should be so studied. The 15th century should not be studied, in the first instance, for the sake of the 16th; it should be studied for its own sake. Why? "All the appearances of history equally belonged to God's plan." [38] Meinecke recognized the reverence which Ranke had "for God's action in history, his happiness in being allowed to contemplate it." Ranke, he pointed out, gave us the example that "history must teach us to see historic periods and phenomena *sub specie aeternitatis*, each directly related, or immediately, to God." It is difficult to overemphasize this concept in Ranke's approach to the idea of providence.

If Ranke was preeminent among the German historians of the 19th century, Thomas Babington Macaulay (d. 1859) may be acclaimed as the foremost English historian of the century. His *History of England from the Accession of James II* has been acclaimed as "the greatest historical work in the English language since Gibbon," [39] or as Thompson said, "No other history in English countries has ever approached Macaulay's *History* in popularity." [40] For all that,

---

[37] Peter Geyl, "Ranke in the Light of the Catastrophe," *Debates with Historians* (Groningen: J. B. Wolters; The Hague, Holland: Martinus Nijhoff, 1955), p. 7. The substance of the sentence is quoted also by Gooch, p. 73. See also p. 6. The literature on Ranke is too extensive to be given in any detail here. See Gooch, pp. 72–119; Fueter, pp. 472–91; Barnes, pp. 245–49; Thompson, II, 168–86.

[38] Geyl, p. 8; Stern, p. 288, in an excerpt from Meinecke. See also Geyl, pp. 14 and 16.

[39] Gooch, p. 283.

[40] Thompson, II, 296. The literature on Macaulay is extensive. See Gooch, pp. 276–85; Barnes, p. 219; Thompson, II, 294–300; Fueter, pp. 513–16.

Macaulay has contributed to literature to a greater extent than to history, valuable as his work is and particularly valuable as his *Essays* on history are. Macaulay quoted the dictum that "history is philosophy teaching by example." However, in his discussions of the functions or role of the historian he did not suggest that the historian might indicate an awareness of providence.

Thomas Carlyle (d. 1881) did. Carlyle, like Macaulay, wrote an essay "On History" and in it made direct reference to the saying that history is "Philosophy teaching by Experience." With that he compared a belief in providence. Carlyle wrote:

> Truly, if History is Philosophy teaching by Experience, the writer fitted to compose History is hitherto an unknown man. The Experience itself would require All-knowledge to record it, — were All-wisdom needful for such Philosophy as would interpret it, to be had for asking. Better were it that mere earthly Historians should lower such pretensions, more suitable for Omniscience than for human science; and aiming only at some picture of the thing acted, which picture itself will be at best a poor approximation, leave the inscrutable support of them an acknowledged secret; or at most, *in reverent Faith,* far different from that teaching of Philosophy, *pause over the mysterious vestiges of Him, whose path is in the great deep of Time,* whom History indeed reveals, but only all History, and in Eternity, will clearly reveal.[41]

But Carlyle's name is coupled with the great-man theory of history. This does not mean that he ruled out God. When the great man does not appear, no matter how loudly the times call for him, it is because "Providence had not sent him." Carlyle found it altogether suitable that Martin Luther was born of poor parents, "doubtless to that end by the Providence presiding over him and us and all things." Yet it was almost a side remark when Carlyle referred to providence, deep as was his sense of the guiding hand of God in the affairs of men.

VII

Realistically, because he was living in the 19th century, one does not expect Carlyle or any one of his contemporary historians to be another Bossuet or Mather. God's sovereignty was no longer being

---

[41] Stern, pp. 95–96; emphases added.

affirmed in works purporting to be scientific history, even though the author might hold that belief. The impact of the natural sciences was one of the factors in diminishing the traditional belief in God's sovereignty. Charles Darwin's *Origin of Species* (1859) established the evolutionary theory. Men accepted the evolutionary process as a substitute for creation, and this process pointed out aspects of the natural world which men found difficult to reconcile with providence.[42] Though Darwin did not pose the question, the post-Darwinian question became: Do natural selection and the survival of the fittest set aside not only the Creator but also God's continued creation?

Darwin's theories were embraced by Herbert Spencer (d. 1903) and made part of the theory of progress. Spencer assumed a final cause, a divine force which set in motion factors and forces, the Unknowable existing behind all phenomena. Spencer wrote:

> In the moral as well as in the material world accumulated evidence is gradually generating the conviction that events are not at the bottom fortuitous, but that they are wrought out in a certain inevitable way by unchanging forces.[43]

Yet such a dictum, feeble as it is, did not reintroduce in any respect the idea of a ruling providence.

The idea was weakened, too, by the misusers of Biblical criticism and by many of those who went on the "quest of the historical Jesus." We need not detail them nor give them "equal time" with the proponents of the doctrine of providence. Suffice it to say that the doctrine of providence was corroded by various theories and hypotheses during the last half of the 19th and the first half of the 20th century.

William James in the Gifford Lectures of 1902, *The Varieties of Religious Experience*, was negative on this belief; he was corrected by C. C. J. Webb, who spoke of "the presence of a Power behind appearances, a Disposer of events," as Wood points out.[44] Surveying

---

[42] See John C. Gienapp, "Providentialism and Evolutionary Biology," pp. 217 to 240 below

[43] Quoted by Bury, p. 339.

[44] H. G. Wood, *Belief and Unbelief since 1850* (Cambridge: University Press, 1955), p. 85, with reference to C. C. J. Webb's *Religious Experience*, pp. 37–38.

the claims of the mystical experiences of the religious, Wood comes to the conclusion that both quests, looking for God within nature and looking for God outside nature, are proper. He concluded:

> Certainly God cannot be exhaustibly revealed in history, in spite of Bernedetto Croce, but as certainly, if history has any real meaning or significance, God must be in it, and he will be the disposer of events and judge of conduct.[45]

Joining the ethical question with the interpretive brings us face to face with the criticism of Thomas Buckle (d. 1862) in his *Principles of History*. He found that the historian is confronted with an insurmountable problem if he believes that "in the affairs of men there is something mysterious and providential, which makes them impervious to our investigation."[46] He saw an intimate connection between physical laws and human behavior, the organization of society, and the character of individuals.

The scientific school of historians of the 19th century put an emphasis on history as a science. Critical historical scholarship put an emphasis on objectivity and the gathering of "cold, hard facts." The stress on history as a science ruled out theological presuppositions of history based on preconceived notions of providence. The French historian Fustel de Coulanges, insisting that "history is and should be a science," nevertheless could hint that man has "a divine guardian watching over his descendants."[47] However, the English historian E. H. Bradley in *The Presuppositions of Christian History* (1874) would not go even that one-quarter step, but thought of the need of critical history as the starting point of historical knowledge.[48] His successors, for instance, Cook Wilson, Bertrand Russell, and J. B. Bury, ruled out any idea of providence in history. In the conclusion to *The Idea of Progress* Bury wrote:

> Does not Progress itself suggest that its value as a doctrine is only relative, corresponding to a certain not very advanced stage of civilization; just as Providence, in its day, was an idea of relative value, corresponding to a stage somewhat less advanced?

[45] Wood, p. 97.

[46] Stern, p. 128; see pp. 128–31.

[47] Ibid., p. 171; see also p. 106.

[48] Collingwood, pp. 134–41.

Or will it be said that this argument is merely a disconcerting trick of dialectic played under cover of the darkness in which the issue of the future is safely hidden by Horace's prudent god?[49]

The haunting question persisted even with Bertrand Russell about the use, value, and meaning of history. When he argued for the value of free thought, he acknowledged that humility was needed in the pursuit of truth, "a kind of humility which has some affinity to submission to the will of God."[50]

VIII

Looking away from the philosophers of history and the historians of the 19th century, what can we say about the church historians? Roman Catholic historians maintained the doctrine of providence. Thompson says of Johann Adam Möhler (d. 1838):

> Möhler did not believe that history should be a mere catalogue of facts; he demanded an organic development and was the first [Roman] Catholic writer to adopt the Hegelian principles in history, substituting for the impersonal Idea the Catholic God.[51]

Johann von Döllinger (d. 1890), Karl von Hefele (1893), Johannes Janssen (d. 1891), Heinrich Denifle (d. 1905), and Ludwig von Pastor (d. 1928) are counted among the foremost Catholic historians of the late 19th and early 20th centuries. They do not flaunt their belief in providence, but this is not a denial on their part that God rules in history. For Roman Catholic historiography guidelines were given in Leo XIII's instruction *Saepenumero* (1883). He said that the "first law of history is to presume to say nothing false," affirming thereby the validity of objective history. He held that "all history shouts out" that God is the supreme governor of mortal events. He plugged for a theology of history rather than for a philosophy of history and exhorted Roman Catholic historians to turn to St. Augustine, the author of *De civitate Dei*.[52]

---

[49] Bury, p. 352.

[50] *Understanding History and Other Essays* (Wisdom Library; New York: Philosophical Library, 1957), p. 102.

[51] Thompson, II, 537; see also pp. 537—49.

[52] See the references given in Sister M. Claudia, *Dictionary of Papal Pronouncements*, Leo XIII to Pius XII [1878—1957] (New York: P. J. Kenedy & Sons, 1958), No. 650.

Protestant church historians of the 19th century were not unaffected by Augustine. Whatever other factors influenced these historians: Romanticism, German philosophy, the revival movements, or Pietism, the influence of St. Augustine cannot be discounted. August Neander (d. 1850) was not explicit in stating his Augustinianism, but his piety endorsed it. "It is the heart that makes the theologian" *(Pectus est, quod theologum facit)* was his watchword. Biography became for him the realization of the activities of providence.[53]

Already during Neander's liftime Leopold von Ranke produced his *History of the Popes* (1834 — 36) and his *History of the Reformation Period* (1839 — 47). Ranke's critical examination of primary sources gave example and encouragement to the Protestant church historians of the century. Ferdinand Christian Baur (d. 1860) played an important role in this development. His contributions have received a reassessment in recent years, resulting in a new appreciation of his scholarship and philosophical thought. His accomplishment cannot be recited at this point. For us it is important to note his concept of providence. Hodgson has summarized Baur's position by saying: "God 'lives' historically; history is God's triune life." And again: "History always points to God, and God to history." Hodgson, with references to sermons Baur preached on the occasion of marriages and deaths, documents Baur's conviction that "all events in objective and personal history are clearly and mysteriously ordered by the guiding hand of God."[54]

In *Die Epochen der kirchlichen Geschichtsschreibung* Baur, surveying the historians of the earlier periods, pointed out that Eusebius had a pragmatic historiography which found in history examples of rewards and punishments given by God; he documented his contention by a long quotation from the *Vita Constantini.* The church historians Socrates, Sozomenus, and Theodoret, who came after Eusebius, portrayed the ruling hand of God as one which dispensed rewards and punishments. Baur referred to Gregory of Tours and

---

[53] Thompson, II, 560 — 61; Meinhold, II, 151 — 61.

[54] Peter C. Hodgson, ed., *Ferdinand Christian Baur on the Writing of Church History,* in *A Library of Protestant Thought* (New York: Oxford University Press, 1968), pp. 63 — 64.

the Venerable Bede as historians "who gladly make use of whatever opportunity presents itself to draw attention to the Providence visible in so many phenomena of life, both rewarding and punishing." The Magdeburg Centuriators, Baur said, proceeded from the same point of view.

Baur pointed out, too, that Johann Lorentz von Mosheim (d. 1755) of the University of Göttingen made some major contributions to history. Mosheim defined church history

> as the clear narration of what has happened in the society of Christians, outwardly and within, in such a fashion that from the continuity of cause and effect we can recognize divine Providence as it establishes and sustains, and thus becomes wiser and more pious.[55]

Moreover, according to Baur, Ludwig Timotheus Spittler (d. 1810) found chance or providence of importance in the study of the history of the church. However, for Spittler there seemed to be no distinction between chance and providence. Baur also pointed out that Gottlieb Jakob Planck (d. 1833) emphasized that God worked through men. Baur was critical of the pragmatic view of history, which makes providence dependent on the favor of the moment.

But the greatest and one of the most prolific Protestant hisorians of the scientific school, Adolf von Harnack (d. 1930), needs to be singled out. Harnack belongs more to the 19th than to the 20th century. His outstanding historical works were written by 1904: *Lehrbuch der Dogmengeschichte* (1886—90); *Geschichte der altchristlichen Literatur bis Eusebius* (1893—1904); *Die Mission und Ausbreitung des Christentums in den ersten drei Jahrhunderten* (1902). Thompson said of him: "Wherever one reads him, in Harnack Protestant historiography has attained objectivity, perfected its method, and accepted the requirements of scientific work." [56] This objectivity and

---

[55] Ibid., p. 143; see also pp. 68, 77, 103—4, 113—24, 142—52, 180, 188, 197—98; Meinhold, II, 113—24.

[56] Thompson, II, 568. Other outstanding historians, for example, Ernst Troeltsch (d. 1923), cannot be treated because of space limitations. Adolf Harnack, *Christianity and History*, trans. Thomas B. Saunders, 2d rev. ed. (London: Adam & Charles Black, 1900), p. 59, wrote: "I am well aware of the gravity of this assertion [that God Himself governs the course of history and is leading it to its goal], and I am far from disputing anyone's right to make it if he chooses." He himself does not choose to make the assertion. Faith, he says, cannot rest on demonstrated details of fact. "Testimonies, documents assertions—when all is said, to what do they amount?" Ibid., p. 61.

scientific spirit required that Harnack not explain any of the phenomena in the history of the church by referring to the doings of providence. The question is not whether Harnack did or did not believe in providence. The question is whether he used or did not use the idea as a key for explaining history. The answer to that question is in the negative.

Harnack, it is true, made references to the belief in providence. In his *History of Dogma* he traces the development of the doctrine of God during the first five centuries of the church's existence. Regarding providence he writes:

> The justification of divine providence and the production of Theodicies were called for by Manichaeism and fatalism on the one hand, and the great political catastrophies and calamities on the other. It was taught that God constantly remained close to his creation, preserving and governing it. With this, rational beings were looked upon in their numerical sum total as the peculiar objects of divine providence. Providence was also defended in opposition to the loose and unstable form in which earlier and contemporary monotheistic philosophers had avowed it; it was recognized in principle to be a power protecting also the individual creature.[57]

Harnack continues by showing some of the problems and uncertainties which the Christian theologians encountered. They regarded the doctrine of providence as part of natural theology and did not connect it with the doctrines of Christ, redemption, or the church. Generally they distinguished degrees of providence and some of the theologians, according to Harnack, "recognized that faith in providence was first made certain through Christ, and that Christians were under the particular providence of God." [58]

Again, Harnack treats the doctrine of providence as held by the Scholastics. He points out that under the topic of God's governance (*De gubernatio rerum*) Thomas Aquinas has the subdivisions: the goal of governance (*finis gubernationis*), upholding (*conservatio*), and the changing of things (*mutatio rerum*).[59] Harnack does not thereby

---

[57] Adolf von Harnack, *History of Dogma*, trans. Neil Buchanan from the 3d German ed. (New York: Russell & Russell, 1958), III, 249–50.

[58] Ibid., III, 250.

[59] Ibid., VI, 185–86, and 186, n. 2. Harnack, in *What Is Christianity?* pp. 32–33,

commit himself to the Thomistic formulations, nor does he attempt to refute them. He merely states them.

IX

Turning to the American historians of the 19th century, we find movements parallel to those in Europe. Francis Parkman, the gentleman-scholar writing in the best literary tradition of the English historians, saw France in the New World as "an agent of Divine Providence." [60] Other historians of his generation would not deny the concept of providence. None of them, however, made the idea of the guiding hand of God in history a factor in their interpretation of America's past, though the idea of a "manifest destiny" had a strong grip on the popular fancy. The third quarter of the 19th century saw the advent of scientific history on the American scene. John Highman includes in scientific history the critical approach to evidence and an "impersonal, collaborative, secular" spirit, "impatient of mystery, and relentlessly concerned with the relation of things to one another instead of their relation to a realm of ultimate meaning." [61] In that "realm of ultimate meaning" we may include the will and workings of God. Scientific history cannot demonstrate empirically that God is active in history. It was coupled with a belief in evolution and a faith in progress.

The rise of "the new history" in American historiography produced a book by that title from the pen of James Harvey Robinson (1912), although Edward Eggleston had used the term already in 1900. The "new history" emphasized relevance, pragmatism, comprehensiveness, evolution, a distrust of literature and philosophy,

---

asserted that God rules and governs and man can move His power by prayer and make it a part of his experience. See Floyd V. Filson, "Adolf von Harnack and His 'What is Christianity?'", *Interpretation,* VI (January 1952), 54. Wilhelm Pauck, "The Significance of Adolf von Harnack's Interpretation of Church History," *Union Seminary Quarterly Review,* XIII, 3 (March 1958), 31—43, has a valuable evaluation of Harnack. See also Meinhold, II, 263—87.

[60] Page Smith, *The Historian and History* (New York: Alfred A. Knopf, 1964), p. 48. On Francis Parkman see Jameson, *History of Historical Writing,* pp. 125—32.

[61] John Highman with Leonard Krieger and Felix Gilbert, *History,* in *The Princeton Studies: Humanistic Scholarship in America* (Englewood Cliffs, N. J.: Prentice-Hall, 1965), p. 94. The change from a general belief in providence is told by Martin E. Marty, "From Providence to Progress, A New Theology," *Righteous Empire: The Protestant Experience in America* (New York: The Dial Press, 1970), pp. 188—98.

and objectivity. It did not reintroduce the notion of providence.

Two names stand out among those enrolled among these historians: Carl L. Becker and Charles A. Beard. In 1910 Carl L. Becker wrote to Frederick Jackson Turner: "To me nothing can be duller than historical facts, and nothing more interesting than the service they can be made to render in the effort to solve the everlasting riddle of human existence." [62] He is counted among the relativists. For instance, in his essay "What Is Historiography?" he sees the gods fading away into "pale replicas of their former selves" and pining "alone in an indifferent universe." [63] Becker maintained that the notion of "facts speaking for themselves" was preposterous. He was uncertain that scientific history had an appreciable influence on social life, even though historians acclaimed what he with some irony called "that wonderful idea of Progress." [64]

Becker operated with the notion that "every normal person does know some history, a good deal in fact." In his celebrated presidential address to the American Historical Association in 1931, Becker defined history as "the memory of things said and done." He continued:

> If the essence of history is the memory of things said and done, then it is obvious that every normal person, Mr. Everyman, knows some history. . . . Without this historical knowledge, this memory of things said and done, his to-day would be aimless and his to-morrow without significance.[65]

He was conscious of the fact that Mr. Everyman and the professional historian were groping for "the definitive and impregnable meaning of human experience . . . final answers to life's riddle." [66] He does suggest that for some the concept of providence can furnish an answer.

---

[62] Quoted in Highman, p. 120, from B. T. Wilkins' *Carl L. Becker*, p. 32.

[63] *American Historical Review*, XLIV, 1 (October 1938), 28.

[64] "What Are Historical Facts," a paper first printed in *The Western Political Quarterly*, VIII, 3 (September 1955), 349–50; Bobbs-Merrill Reprint Series in European History, E-17. Also found in Nash, II, 177–93.

[65] "Everyman His Own Historian," *American Historical Review*, XXXVII, 2 (January 1932), 223.

[66] Ibid., p. 233. Highman, *History*, p. 120, notes Becker's "preoccupation with 'the everlasting riddle of human existence.'"

The second of the historians we singled out, Charles A. Beard, spoke about "Written History As An Act of Faith" in his 1933 presidential address before the American Historical Association. He sought a pattern in history and found that there were "only three broad conceptions of history as actuality." He stated the three and concluded:

> History is chaos and every attempt to interpret it otherwise is an illusion. History moves around in a kind of cycle. History moves in a line, straight or spiral, and in some direction. The historian may seek to escape these issues by silence or by a confession of avoidance or he may face them boldly, aware of the intellectual and moral perils in any decision — his act of faith.[67]

Beard made a plea for "the wider and deeper philosophic questions involved in the interpretation of history," believing that by an exploration of the right questions "the noble dream of the search for truth may be brought nearer to realization."[68]

X

Both Beard and Becker were influenced by Benedetto Croce. Croce belonged to the idealists among whom the German, Wilhelm Dilthey (d. 1911), was the most important.

Dilthey held that there is meaning in history. There are interactions of society, he said, and "throughout history a living, active, creative and responsive soul is present at all times and places."[69] For him the individual processes of history fit together in a systematic fashion, and it remained for the historian to discover and understand these processes and their relationships. This meant, as Dilthey's editor pointed out, that "all the meaning of human life is linked to its temporal structure."[70] Dilthey himself wrote:

> The significance which a fact receives as a fixed link in the making of the whole is a relation in life and not an intellectual one, not

---

[67] *American Historical Review*, XXXIX, 2 (January 1934), 228 – 29.

[68] "That Noble Dream," *American Historical Review*, XLI, 1 (October 1935), 86, 87.

[69] Wilhelm Dilthey, *Pattern and Meaning in History*, ed. H. P. Richman (Harper & Bros., 1962), p. 67, from his *Gesammelte Werke*, VII, iii, 254.

[70] Richman's "General Introduction" in *Pattern and Meaning*, p. 32. Dilthey wrote, ibid., p. 163, from *Werke*, VII, iii, 255 – 56: "Life is fulness, variety, and inter-

an insertion of reason or thought into a part of the event. The significance emerges from life itself.[71]

History, according to Dilthey, taught "the existence of a large variety of 'expressions of life,' determined by the passing conditions of historic times." Dilthey spoke of "the relativity of every metaphysical or religious doctrine which appeared in the course of time" and the "ruins of religious traditions." With Dilthey you have the complete secularization of the idea of history, only without a materialistic bias.

R. G. Collingwood (d. 1943), as critic, blamed Dilthey for permitting history to disappear altogether and replacing it with psychology. Dilthey's approach was entirely anthropocentric and permitted no activity of God in history, particularly when seen from Augustine's, Calvin's, or Bossuet's point of view. Collingwood also criticized the providential view of history. Of the medieval historians he wrote:

> In their anxiety to detect the general plan of history, and their belief that this plan was God's and not man's, they tended to look for the essence of history outside of history itself, by looking away from man's actions in order to detect the plan of God; and consequently the actual detail of human actions became for them relatively unimportant, and they neglected the prime duty of the historian, a willingness to bestow infinite pains on discovering what actually happened.[72]

One might note that while this may be true, and hence providence may be a distraction from the "facts" of history, it is not so *necessarily*, and a distraction from the facts is not inherently a *perversion* of the facts. Collingwood praised Immanuel Kant for not even mentioning the Christian view of history. He allowed that there is a his-

action—within something continuous—experienced by individuals. Its subject matter is identical with history. At every point of history there is life. And history consists of life of every kind in the most varied circumstances. History is merely life viewed in terms of continuity of mankind." See also Gardiner, pp. 213—25, for another excerpt from Dilthey dealing with "The Understanding of Other Persons and Their Life-Experiences."

[71] Dilthey, *Pattern and Meaning*, p. 75, from *Werke*, VII, iii, 240.

[72] Collingwood, p. 255; see pp. 171—76.

tory of religion, but thereby he did not make any concessions to the validity of the providential view of history.[73]

Another idealist already mentioned, Benedetto Croce (d. 1952), also rejected out of hand the idea of providence in history. In his discussion of "Historical Determinism and the 'Philosophy of History'" he dubbed each "a void and a nothing."[74] Progress, liberty, science, for instance, were to him myths. "They are myths not less than God and the Devil, Mars and Venus, Jove and Baal, or any other cruder form of divinity."

Of more significance for our inquiry into the idea of providence as employed by historians, particularly church historians, is Isaiah Berlin's discussion of "Historical Inevitability." The presuppositions of any theory of inevitability are that there are laws which govern the world and that it (inevitability) has a direction. The larger "wholes," Berlin said, govern the lives and actions of individuals. Scientific or philosophical history, according to Berlin, deals with forces, which are not identified in the same way by different theorists. Determinism eliminates individual responsibility. Berlin writes:

> If the history of the world is due to the operation of identifiable forces other than, and as little affected by human wills and free choices (whether these occur or not), then the proper explanation of what happens must be given in terms of the evolution of such forces.[75]

Berlin asked: Is it true that "whatever is, is necessary and inevitable?" His answer is that "determinism is not and need not be a serious issue."

Agreeing with Berlin, Ernest Nagel says that the doctrine of historical inevitability is untenable. He examines the major arguments for determinism and proposes that the value of a factor in

---

[73] Ibid., pp. 314–15. Louis O. Mink, "Collingwood's Dialectic of History," *History and Theory*, VII, 1 (1968), 3–37, does not discuss Collingwood's approach to the problem of providence. This is true also of Leon J. Goldstein, "Collingwood's Theory of Historical Knowing," ibid. IX, i (1969), 3–36.

[74] Gardiner, pp. 233–41.

[75] Nash, II, 313, from *Four Essays on Liberty* (London and New York: Oxford University Press, 1954), pp. 22–23. See Hans Meyerhoff, ed., *The Philosophy of History in Our Time: An Anthology* (Garden City, N. Y.: Doubleday & Co., Anchor Books, 1959), pp. 249–69.

history is "determined" by the value of other factors occurring at the same time. Although he disagrees with Berlin because "determinism does not entail any doctrine of historical inevitability," he concludes:

> I do not believe that determinism is a demonstrable thesis, and I think that if it is construed as a statement about a categorical feature of everything whatsoever it may even be false.[76]

The discussion is of importance for our topic because a belief in providence is sometimes equated with a belief in determinism. We cannot agree with this equation. There remains the inscrutable in the ways of God that may appear as inevitable, predetermined by the Ruler of the universe, but only for those who demand an explanation that rules out faith, or those whose judgment may be faulty.

Nevertheless the nature of historical explanation is a problem not easily solved. The positivists and the idealists and the relativists came forward with solutions. In the years around 1960 the discussion reached its height. Valuable as these discussions were, they brought no argumentations about the idea of providence in history. Providence was ignored. Philosophers of history, except those who espoused an avowed Christian understanding of history, dismissed considerations of the providential view. Also the cultural historians found no place for providence, if they reckoned with the concept at all, in their explanation of historical phenomena.

XI

With the upsurge of the concern for philosophies of history after World War II, the exponents of a Christian understanding of history also asked to be heard.[77] The question was not posed in terms of the aphorism of classical theologians: "God is the co-operative cause of all that occurs." For example, this cooperation has been detailed by Quenstedt:

> God not only gives and preserves to second causes the power to act, but immediately influences the action and effect of the creature, so that the same effect is produced not by God alone, nor by

---

[76] Ibid., II, 349; see also pp. 319−22, 343.

[77] "The 'Meaning of History' and the Writing of History," E. Harris Harbison, *Christianity and History* (Princeton, N. J.: Princeton University Press, 1964), pp. 35−52.

the creature alone, nor partly by God and partly by the creature, but *at the same time by God and the Creature,* as one and the same total efficiency, viz., by God as the universal and first cause, and by the creature as the particular and second cause.[78]

The scholastic distinctions between *necessitas consequentiae* and *necessitas consequentis* and the problems of contingency and chance are not treated by contemporary Christian philosophers of history. Change obviously is another basic question in a consideration of causation. Patterns of history may reveal meaning in history; however, that meaning may be involved or concealed in the question of causation. Ultimately interrelationships complicate the considerations given to change, causation, and meaning. Yet in some of the most representative discussions in the 20th century about the problem of causes the question of providence is not raised.

In the van among those who raised the question, for his forum was the inner sanctum of the professional historians, was Kenneth Scott Latourette.[79] He addressed the American Historical Association as its president in 1948 on "The Christian Understanding of History." In his address he affirmed:

Christians believe that God is the creator of the universe and rules throughout all its vast reaches, whether, to man, the unimaginable distances and uncounted suns or the inconceivably minute world of the atom, whether in what men call matter or in what they call spirit. This means that man lives and history takes place in a universe, that all of reality is one and under the control of God, and that the human drama is part and parcel of the larger unity of God's creation. Ultimately in His own way, so the Christian view maintains, God is sovereign in the affairs of men.[80]

Latourette reiterated Calvin's concept of God's sovereignty and

---

[78] Heinrich Schmid, *The Doctrinal Theology of the Evangelical Lutheran Church,* trans. Charles A. Hay and Henry E. Jacobs, 4th ed., rev.; reprint of 1899 ed. (Minneapolis: Augsburg Publishing House, n. d. [1961], p. 180, quoted from *Theologia Didactico-Polemica,* I, 531.

[79] Latourette is the only man who has served as president of the American Historical Association and of the American Society of Church History. See also Meinhold, II, 409—20. An important survey of the resurgence of the belief in providence by church history is found in Nelson R. Burr's article "The American Church Historian and the Biblical View of History," *Historical Magazine of the Protestant Episcopal Church,* XXXIX, 4 (December 1970), 348—59.

[80] Nash, I, 229; for the article see *American Historical Review,* LIII, 3 (April 1949), 259—76; reprinted in Nash, I, 223—45.

Calvin's theological view of history. In his address Latourette did not use the word "providence." However, he spoke of God's continued activity in history. Moreover, he faced the question of the presence of evil. He asked: "Has God failed? Is His sovereignty compromised?" His answer presupposed a degree of freedom for man's will. "Yet," he said in faith's victory over reason, "if God is love and is sovereign, His judgments must be a way to the triumph of His love."

The problem of evil, the triumph of tyranny and oppression, the tragedies of inhumanity in all generations, these and kindred questions confront the philosopher of history, the theologian, the historian, and every person engaged in some measure of reflection. How can the demonic be reconciled with the omnipotence of God and His goodness? The contentions that God brings good out of evil (Gen. 45:5-8) and that in everything God works for good with those who love Him (Rom. 8:28) must be accepted in faith. These are the assumptions with which the individual Christian operates who disclaims pure pessimism or cruel fate.

Pessimism was one of the hallmarks of Oswald Spengler's (d. 1936) philosophy of history. Others were relativism, determinism, and the cyclical approach. He writes:

> Countless shapes that emerge and vanish, pile up, and melt again, a thousand-hued glittering tumult, it seems, of perfectly willful chance — such is the picture of world history when first it deploys before our inner eye. But through the seeming anarchy, the keener glance can detect those pure forms which underlie all human becoming, penetrate their cloud mantle, and bring them unwillingly to unveil.[81]

Cultures arise and decay and world history is the collective biography of these cultures, recurring in regular forms and movements in their morphological relations which permits them to be labelled organisms.

Spengler's English counterpoint, but a historian of greater stature than Spengler, is Arnold Toynbee (b. 1881). His 12-volume *A Study of History* poses problematics for every historian of the century. One of the problems so raised is Toynbee's concept of prov-

---

[81] Nash, I, 151.

idence (a term he avoids).[82] Nevertheless, in his *Study of History* he embarked on "the quest for a meaning behind the fact of history" and the exposition of this quest assumed mystical, even rhapsodic, proportions. Toynbee has scorn for the providence-minded Bossuet and "the Medieval-minded Early Modern Western historians." The "antinomian" historians who reject "laws of nature" are guilty of hybris. They ought to admit "that it might, after all, at least be an open question whether 'laws of nature' were or were not found governing the affairs of Man in Process of Civilization." Toynbee embraces the cyclical approach to history, finding, for example, the war and peace cycle.

In his grand effort to establish the relation between law and freedom in history, Toynbee comes to the conclusion: "Law and Freedom in History prove to be identical, in the sense that Man's Freedom proves to be the law of a God who is identical with Love." Toynbee refers to "God's outstretched hand reaching down to meet the upstretched hand of the struggling human climber" and to "the inevitable consequence of hybris," namely, "the nemesis which a Modern Western Society invited by succumbing to a Gibbonian Weltanschauung."

The elusiveness of Toynbee's idea of providence is compounded by his espousal of Absolute Reality as "the spiritual presence behind the phenomena."[83] This Reality is revealed only partially; it is a mystery to which there is more than one approach, the object of worship of all the higher religions. "It is of the essence of Absolute Reality that it is omnipresent," says Toynbee. It manifests itself in the social milieu according to Toynbee.[84] However, the Absolute Reality is neither Alpha nor Omega. He says flatly: "The thesis that God is Alpha and Omega does not merely involve a conception of the

[82] Arnold J. Toynbee, *A Study of History* (New York: Oxford University Press, Galaxy Book, 1963), X, 126−44. See also ibid., IX, 173−80, 234−87.

[83] Toynbee, *An Historian's Approach to Religion* (London: Oxford University Press, 1956), p. 273; see also pp. 257−58, 295−97.

[84] Ibid., p. 278: "An historian's first approach to the higher religions will be by way of the social milieu in which they make their epiphany. They are not the product of their social milieu; the events that produce them are encounters between human beings and the Absolute Reality that is in, and at the same time, beyond, all the phenomena of Existence, Life and History; and any soul may meet God at any time and place in any historical circumstances."

Universe that is incredible; the thesis itself is unverifiable." Nevertheless, to Toynbee history has meaning.

> To believe that history has some significance and some purpose may be an unverifiable act of faith, but at any rate this is, for the participant, less difficult to believe than it is to believe that history is senseless.[85]

Love and righteousness, to him as he defines them, give validity to life and to the universe. And with all that, "God's omnipotence is vindicated by acknowledging him openly to be the author of evil."

A more positive approach to the idea of providence than Toynbee's is that of his fellow countryman, Herbert Butterfield. God to him is the God of history. Therefore academic history and the problems it discusses have value, "if only to learn through their interconnections the ways of Providence."[86] In weighing "Providence and the Historical Process," he posited "a Providence that we must regard as lying in the very constitution of things."

> Whether we are Christian or not, whether we believe in a Divine Providence or not, we are liable to serious technical errors if we do not regard ourselves as born into a providential order.[87]

Butterfield did not discard the idea of progress, but found it part of the providential order, the work of providence, although providence does not guarantee progress. A second kind of providence in Butterfield's thought "moves over history with the function of making good out of evil." The forces of evil are overcome by the Suffering Servant, the power of love. However, to find the hand of God in history a person must first of all find it in his personal experience. He must recognize, too, that God acts in judgment in the affairs of men, particularly when men themselves want to play providence.[88]

According to Butterfield, to do technical history does not mean

---

[85] Toynbee, *Experiences* (New York and London: Oxford University Press, 1969), p. 163; see pp. 154—67.

[86] Herbert Butterfield, *Christianity and History* (New York: Charles Scribner's Sons, 1950), p. 22.

[87] Ibid., pp. 95—96; see also idem, *History and Human Relations* (London: Collins, 1951), p. 71.

[88] Butterfield, *Christianity and History*, pp. 96—98, 59—60; idem, *History and Human Relations*, pp. 52-55.

for the believer in providence that he is not under some kind of discipline.[89] He is not denying the hand of God in history, if he cannot demonstrate providence. Yet the historian will be prepared for surprises and will judge each generation, as Ranke said, equidistant from eternity.[90]

A more ambivalent stance was presented by Karl Löwith, who found it impossible to impose on history or to draw out of history a reasoned order or the working of God. "The problem of history is unanswerable within its own perspective," he said. Neither faith nor reason can per se establish a meaningful plan of history, for chance or fate, not reason or providence, seems to govern history. However, by faith one can "know" that all things converge on and are represented in Jesus Christ as Savior.[91]

A whole host of theologians, some operating with the concept of *Heilsgeschichte,* others with some variant of this concept, focused on the centrality of the Christ-event in history. To them this is the key to history, gives meaning to it, and demonstrates the activity of God in history. It provides the solution to the problems of freedom, purpose, and even of suffering and evil.[92]

One practicing historian will be singled out to show how his concept of providence is evident in his interpretation of history.

---

[89] Butterfield, *History and Human Relations,* pp. 103, 136, pp. 147–48: "If in life a man has accepted the Christian view of things, he will run these values throughout the whole story of the past, and, taking the very basis of narrative which historical scholarship has provided, he may see every event with an added dimension. He will have used historical evidence in order to become a closer and a better student of Providence." E. Harris Harbison in his essay on "The Christian Understanding of History" in *Christianity and History,* pp. 3–78, has followed Butterfield, yet deserves a fuller treatment than a passing mention in a footnote. Meinhold, II, 566–69.

[90] Butterfield, *Christianity and History,* pp. 65–66. Ibid., p. 67: "We envisage our history in the proper light, therefore, if we say that each generation—indeed each individual—exists for the glory of God; but one of the most dangerous things in life is to subordinate human personality to production, to the state, even to civilization itself, to anything but the glory of God."

[91] Löwith, *Meaning in History,* pp. 184–99; see p. 184: "The Christian interpretation of history stands or falls with the acceptance of Jesus as Christ, i. e., with the doctrine of the Incarnation."

[92] Reinhold Niebuhr, H. Richard Niebuhr, J. V. Langmead Casserley, Albert C. Outler, Joseph Cambon, Hendrik Berkhof, Hans Urs von Balthasar, Alan Richardson, John McIntyre, Roger L. Schinn, Eric Rust, George A. Buttrick, Donald C. Masters, Paul Tillich, John Warwick Montgomery are among the theologian-historians who could be discussed in this connection.

Kurt Dietrich Schmidt (d. 1964), the eminent church historian and historian of dogma, complained that history and the church alike had not taken earnestly the concept of *sola gratia*.[93] Historians have become anthropocentric and history has become the account of what man does. If the historian truly conceives of God as the director of history *(Lenker der Geschichte)*, he does not think of Him as a *deus ex machina*, but as ordainer of all history.[94] Of course, God uses people to carry out His purposes in history, but history is totally God's work. Schmidt writes:

> In the twentieth century we have learned anew that behind all history we must see God at work, as certainly as it is man's doing. To interpret history from this new, regained insight, that is the great task that stands before us.[95]

To Schmidt the history of the church is the history of Christ's continuous activity in the world. Christ is hidden in this history, but He is the agent and mover of the forces and people through whom He works. Admittedly this view calls for faith and raises difficulties, but it is the view to which church historians should be committed, Schmidt believes.[96]

Much more could be said about the wrestlings of historians, church historians, theologians, and philosophers with the idea of

---

[93] Kurt Dietrich Schmidt, "Gott und Mensch in Geschichte und Kirchengeschichte," *Gesammelte Aufsätze,* ed. Manfred Jacobs (Göttingen; Vandenhoeck & Ruprecht, 1967), p. 306.

[94] Ibid., p. 312: "Selbstverständlich, theozentrische Schau heisst *nicht,* dass Gott hier und da einmal in die Geschichte eingreift; ein *deus ex machina* wäre theologisch und historiographisch gleich unmöglich. Es heisst vielmehr, dass Gott *alle* Geschichte setzt, den *ganzen* Ablauf. Alleinwirksamkeit Gottes! Die Sinngebung, die Deutung, das Gottesvertrauen hängt total davon ab, dass mit *diesem* biblischen Satz ernst gemacht wird." Italics in the original.

[95] Schmidt, "Zur Grundlegung der Kirchengeschichte," ibid., p. 325; see pages 314—25 for the entire essay, esp. pp. 323—25.

[96] Schmidt, *Grundriss der Kirchengeschichte* (Göttingen: Vandenhoeck & Ruprecht, 1954), pp. 4 and 9 f. See p. 9: "Die *Schwierigkeit* solcher Darstellung der Kirchengeschichte ist freilich unübersehbar. Denn die klare Schau des göttlichen Tuns in der Geschichte ist uns verwehrt; die Geschichte des Reiches Gottes kann niemand schildern. Es ist vielmehr schon ausgesprochen worden, dass die Geschichte Christi in der *Verhüllung* ist. Das heisst, dass Gottes Wille zwar, weil Christus gekommen ist, schon jetzt auf Erden geschiet, dass er aber doch nicht evident ist." Italics in the original. See also Meinhold, II, 490—92.

providence in their writings. Jestingly, A. E. Housman wrote in
A Shropshire Lad:

> Walt does more than Milton can
> To justify God's ways to man.

In a pessimistic mood, the poet William Butler Yeats concluded in
The Countess Kathleen:

> The years like great black oxen tread the road,
> And God the herdsman goads them on behind,
> And I am broken by their passing feet.

Far better it is to say with this same poet in the *Ballad of Father
Gilligan:*

> He Who is wrapped in purple robes
> With planets in His care,
> Had pity on the least of things
> Asleep upon a chair.

Voices of Change:
The Arts and Divine Providence

Warren Rubel

We see that we are all artists, suggested the late Francois Mauriac, by the way we treat the human corpse at death. Despite our painful awareness of the meaning of death, of the disintegration of body processes, of irretrievable loss, we arrange the limbs, we dress the naked body. We give to the dead body a final dignified human form: order for chaos, repose for disintegration, the sign of revitalizing sleep, hands folded in expectation.

We see that we are interpreters and critics by the way we probe the meaning of these illusions or "tricks" played on the body. Do we compassionately arrange the lifeless limbs because we seek to conceal from ourselves the terrible truth of death? Do we shape the body to reveal somehow the essence of our deepest beliefs about the issues of life and death? Or before death's presence, do our fears and hopes merge into a disturbing crisis of belief? We know that responses to these questions run a wide emotional and conceptual spectrum. Nevertheless, the shape we give to the body, like the shape the artist gives to his medium, may disclose pertinent relationships between the mystery of God's providential care for us, the inexplicable qualities of our life experience, and the available explanations we seize on to give meaning to our faith.

If we probe the arts to catch a glimpse of the light they throw on our contemporary understanding of God's providence, we are faced at the outset with difficulties. What kinds of questions shall we ask? Most discussions about the arts in the modern world tend to stress one of four interrelated contact points: the artist and the creative process, the artifact as aesthetic object, the "world" to which the artifact is tied, and the audience. Even a rapid glance at each of these genuinely complex points reveals obvious shifts in the ways in which we may respond to the question of God's providential care for the world and for us. Here we place primary stress on our task as interpreters from within the Christian faith.

The arts for the Christian have served primarily a preparatory or propaedeutic purpose. They prepare us for receiving the Gospel and for appropriately responding to the Gospel in a variety of ways. They confront us with the past, with our needs for responding to the past in the present, and for shaping the future in the present. Close familiarity with the arts forces us to face both the delight and the intractability of artistic media, alerting us to the basic stuff our world is made of as well as to the complications of the human sensorium. They intensify in us our awareness of our own humanity. And through the consciousness of the artist who is a Christian we may participate with redeemed humanity in conscious praise of God. In interpreting the arts, however, it may prove helpful to distinguish between a consensus and a conflict propaedeutic.

By far the preponderant attitude within the church has been to view the arts with a consensus propaedeutic. Dennis De Rogemont said:

> Art is an exercise of the whole being of man, not to compete with God, but to coincide better with the order of Creation, to love it better and to reestablish ourselves in it. Thus art would appear to be like an invocation (more often than not unconscious) to the lost harmony, like a prayer (more often than not confused) corresponding to the second petition of the Lord's prayer—'Thy Kingdom come.' [1]

De Rogemont's statement is charitable, particularly when one considers the actual distant relationship between the arts and the church since Reformation times. And the humility and severity of De Rogemont's position are reflected in his unwillingness to speak of the artist as "creator." De Rogemont's position, happily applied, deepens the Christian's response to his faith and his culture. Mistakenly applied, it may lead to an indulgent patronizing of the arts. Because we may tend to be imperial rather than collegial with the artist or his work, there is need for a conflict propaedeutic. Northrop

---

[1] "Religion and the Mission of the Artist," *Spiritual Problems in Contemporary Literature*, ed. Stanley R. Hopper (New York: Harper & Row, 1957), p. 177.

Frye's argument for the autonomy of culture provides the basis for such a position:

> Culture's essential service to religion is to destroy intellectual idolatry, the recurrent tendency in religion to replace the object of its worship with its present understanding and forms of approach to that object. . . . Just as no argument in favor of a religious or political doctrine is of any value unless it is an intellectually honest argument, and so guarantees the autonomy of logic, so no religious or political myth is either valuable or valid unless it assumes the autonomy of culture, which may be provisionally defined as the total body of imaginative hypothesis in a society and its tradition. To defend the autonomy of culture in this sense seems to me the social task of the intellectual in the modern world: if so, to defend its subordination to a total synthesis of any kind, religious or political, would be the authentic form of the *trahison des clercs*.[2]

To be open to the autonomy of culture is to be open not only to deepening our insights but also to altering them. These positions necessarily collide with one another. Because the world is God's world, however, these conflicts realistically describe the actual tension we live through in our relationships to the arts.

Keeping these assumptions in mind, I begin with brief descriptive sketches of key themes associated with the loss of the sense of divine providence in the modern arts, particularly the verbal arts because they involve us with language about providence. There is much that is unhappy and repetitive about such a diagnosis, but it is necessary to the larger task of the essay, namely, to show how the interpreter may respond to notions of transcendent order and purpose in the arts. Second, I should like to focus more narrowly and more rapidly on shifts in our attitudes to the artist and the work of art which are also related to our interpretative task. Finally, I should like to suggest how some recent accents in our understanding of providence may help us deepen, even alter, some of our perspectives on divine providence in our common life.

I

Each literary work in the contemporary period takes us on a journey to awareness. That journey may include a shock of recog-

---

[2] *The Anatomy of Criticism* (Princeton: Princeton University Press, 1957), p. 127.

nition when we see the comic or tragic dimensions of human life. "Man is the only animal that laughs or weeps," wrote William Hazlitt, "for he is the only animal that is struck with the difference between what things are and what they ought to be." Our consciousness of that difference ties us tightly to the arts. We may discover through the arts that we stand on a slippery surface between illusion and reality. Because to see is to interpret, we may chance on beauty or ugliness where we had not seen it before. Or we may suddenly recognize how we have learned with the artist to separate truth from the public view of truth. At the heart of the matter today lies most often the search for human identity.

Eric Bentley has suggested that the sense of anticlimax, of disenchantment with man's image of himself, is "*the* idea of modern literature." Accompanying this idea is its emotional counterpoint — the feeling of desolation. Alfred Kazin sized up the modern situation when he claimed of Joe Christmas, the victim in William Faulkner's *Light in August:*

> More and more, not merely the American novel, but all serious contemporary novels, are concerned with men who are not real enough to themselves to be seriously in conflict with other men. Their conflicts, as we say, are "internal"; for they are seeking to become someone. Joe Christmas lives a life that is not only solitary but detached . . . actually he is concerned only with the process of self-discovery, or self-naming.[3]

From one literary perspective, we find man in a dislocated and disconnected world. In this world man's search for identity and for self-naming is a desperate one. God seems to have become an exile. Man remains a creative and estranged symbol-maker in a mute natural world. Civilized, urban, industrial man remains both attracted to and repulsed by the threat and promise of technology. And each of the disconnections we respond to in the literature — man from God, man from nature, man from technology, man from man — feeds the essential disconnection man feels within himself. The result is the alienated man. Unable to establish meaningful relationships with a reality beyond himself, he turns from the past,

---

[3] "The Stillness of *Light in August*," *William Faulkner: Three Decades of Criticism,* ed. Frederick J. Hoffman and Olga Vickery (New York: Harcourt, Brace and World, 1960), p. 264.

which no longer seems usable. He turns away from human community, for the lives of those around him often seem as remote and inauthentic as his own. When he searches within himself, he finds no center upon which the passions, desires, and intent of his life may converge in a meaningful way. And at the end, in fiction as well as in our personal histories, there is death.

The overall impression leads one to a sharp sense of the diminution of man's understanding of himself. The more we know, the less we understand. This particular theme of man's lost, blurred, or attenuated image of himself, beaten fine and thin in the literature and the now ponderous criticism overlaying it, has led to a number of reactions. Some choose not to read. Roger Shinn writes of intelligent and sensitive men who, caught in the overt pressures of decision-making in the establishment, turn from imaginative literature.[4] These men cannot afford the bitter-sweet luxury of interior meditation offered by the alienated artist. There is too much else to worry about: continuous wars, racial tension, pollution, disturbed ecological balances, shrinking natural resources, overcrowding, displaced peoples, poverty, crime, famine, noise, loss of privacy, student unrest, and disintegrating familial, social, and political structures.

Some take a carrion attitude. Jan Myrdal claimed that the writer is "a small, subversive white animal letting out words that like termites eat away the foundations of Western culture."[5] Some light candles in the dark. Saul Bellow said, "Even if we live in a Waste Land . . . or if we do not live in an age of gold, we have choices: We can either shut up because the times are too bad, or continue because we have an instinct to enjoy, which even these disfigured times cannot obliterate."[6] And some picture for us a new emerging culture "beyond alienation," a new hopeful "consciousness," like the one proferred by Charles Reich in *The Greening of America.*

The writers of many original works and their critics suggest norms for man. These norms, mirroring our plight, light up the

---

[4] *New Directions in Theology Today. Volume VI — Man: The New Humanism* (Philadelphia: The Westminster Press, 1968), p. 112.

[5] *Saturday Review*, Aug. 13, 1966, p. 43.

[6] *Saturday Review*, April 3, 1965, p. 20.

exigencies of our human situation. The norms are partially related to man's potential for heroic encounter, even if the encounter means naming man's despair. Man's potential for heroic encounter seems to depend on the worth man places on himself in a field of value relationships. Although C. S. Lewis once remarked wryly that man's worth aside from God is zero, one irony in our Western tradition is that man has been seldom discussed apart from that God-man relationship. That is true even when man claims that God is dead. The key norm seems to cluster about a number of major literary types. Each is related to a loose generic norm very much alive in both popular and sophisticated imagination: the norm of the heroic type.

Perhaps because he lacks a heroic self-concept, man in much modern drama, fiction, and poetry seldom seems to struggle against fate, to shape his destiny, to defy the gods, much less to feel that his life participates in the meaningful ordering of divine providence. He lives in a border situation where the question can be asked about the meaning of life. But the question of being is raised within the context of a world view where man is thrown back on himself to create his own meaning. He must shape the meaning of his life from within, or find some shape or form within which he can act as if his life were meaningful. Writer after writer has woven into the contemporary literary carpet a design offering a different vantage point for observing this worn and diminished figure of man in the present.

The typical hero in our popular literature has generally been the common man, the careful craftsman, the honest homesteader and farmer, the dedicated soldier, the stolid and solid man in the gray flannel suit. In our earliest American literature he is a Chingachgook or Hawkeye or Deerslayer of Cooper's Leatherstocking series. In later writers he may be a Eugene Gant or a Moses Herzog or a Willy Loman. Sometimes he is capable of reforming the evils imposed upon him by uncommon men or uncommon conditions. When he is no longer able to fight or comprehend the conditions, he is unwilling to compromise his hopes or aspirations. Often he holds on to hope and trust despite his limited knowledge of the ambiguity of good and evil in men's hearts and in the institutions men serve.

If these common heroes are not offsprings of the gods, or even Adams in or out of Eden, they are Adam's children who, cast out of Paradise, learn to face what they fear. Ultimately they say yes to the universe and to man's place in it. Even our folk heroes in their bright comic absurdity—Paul Bunyan, Pecos Pete, John Henry—point us to men's work in a place. And we trust some of the incongruities of the folk imagination.

A second major type is the metaphysical or social rebel-hero. Two mythic examples are Captain Ahab of Herman Melville's *Moby Dick* and Thomas Sutpen of William Faulkner's *Absolom, Absolom.* Consider Ahab. The importance of the rebel-hero rests on Ahab's complaint. What Ahab cannot abide is the inscrutability of the gods, the riddling ambiguity of the natural world, and especially the burden of uncertainty that both perceptions leave with him, particularly since he seems to be an unjust sufferer in a world he never made. He did not name Ahab Ahab.

The white whale becomes nature's hieroglyph, the accessible embodiment of inscrutable and malignant evil in the universe. Ahab mourns to the reader as he reaches compassionately for Pip, the demented cabin boy: "Ye believers in gods all goodness, and in man all ill, lo you! see the omniscient gods oblivious of suffering man." Ahab finally strikes the whale. If he could have, he would have struck the sun. In his dying breaths, having heaved his harpoon at Moby Dick, Ahab turns his face from the sun, the life-giving force in nature. Why he turns seems apparent. Once watching the living whale's jetting as a vain attempt to intercede with the sun, Ahab thought, "In vain, Oh Whale, dost thou seek intercedings with yon all-quickening sun, that only calls forth life, but gives it not again." All nature while living turns toward the sun, and like the dying whale, dying, turns to the old, dark chaos.

Ahab, the human rebel in nature, turns from the sun *before* death, for nature and the whole universe cheat man in his deepest hopes. Ahab, like the social rebel generally, is placed in a Job-like situation. And his answer to that situation is not accommodation, acceptance, or trust. He uses his mysterious freedom to create his own kind of world. He is a hero of a sort. He faces what he fears with hate. And there is understandable if perverse justice in his hatred.

August Strindberg suggested in his preface to *Miss Julie* that drama is the bible of the common man, the picture book of consensus. If so, then drama reveals a disturbing though interesting picture, for most of us have been reared in our own generation on the anti-hero. Often diminished in physical, intellectual, and imaginative stature, resilient and compromising, sensitive to the relativity of human truth, admirably self-compensating in his search for surrogates — sex, drugs, intellectual mysticism — he seeks to make life bearable if not joyful. The "epic theatre" of Bertolt Brecht, which has been gaining wider audiences in America in the past few years, disturbingly and effectively presents the new anti-hero, like Anna Fierling of *Mother Courage and Her Children*. Mother Courage lives and argues as one of the desperately poor that traditional virtues — like bravery, courage, loyalty, or heroism — are unnecessary in a well-regulated country. She contends that whenever great virtues are present something is wrong; that is, one human being is really using other human beings for his own self-interest. Mother Courage's acid remarks reflect her attitude of capitulation to all those forces in life that wear men down so that rather than seeking justice, men seek primarily to exist. As one of the poor of the earth, Mother Courage's accommodation to the destructive forces opposing her supports a new kind of heroism.

More popular has been Samuel Beckett's *Waiting for Godot*. A tragic comedy once billed as the laugh-hit of two continents, this strangely moving and delicately wrought play presents the dilemma of two men, Estragon and Vladimir, who, with nothing to do but wait in a universe where nothing happens, still wait. They inhabit a universe where everything changes and everything remains the same — except for man. Man moves in a straight declining line from birth to death. Both men are anti-heroes. No matter how debilitated, how apparent their shriveling mental, physical, and moral powers, they still support one another in a forced interdependence that is a heroism of a sort. They keep their appointment. They wait in a universe where reason, dialog, action appear absurd. Even plays about old religious heroes, like Robert Bolt's *A Man for All Seasons* or John Osborne's *Luther*, offer Sir Thomas More against a background of nearly overwhelming court chicanery and Martin Luther as a kind of scatological hero. Our sense of the heroic diminishes.

The more recent theatre of the absurd tries to communicate to the audience a sense of the senselessness of the human condition and man's incapacity for dealing with his condition. When dealing with individual character, this kind of theatre radically devaluates recognizable character rather than using the theatre for depicting subtle revelation of character in a play. Even in the "theatre of cruelty" the focus of the playwright like Jean Genet or Peter Weis, acting on Antonin Artaud's earlier revolutionary work, is to lead man communally through a purging ritual experience. Each of these movements in the theatre is in part a reaction to the realistic conception of character in drama—to the ready acceptance of both playwright and audience that man, both within the limits of the play and beyond, has the mysterious freedom to choose his fate, that he can be, in the highest or meanest sense of the words, responsible or irresponsible. That man is accountable, answerable to God for his thoughts, words, and deeds—as most Christians speak in the confessional portions of their Sunday morning services—is the very notion that seems strange amidst the mass movements of our time.

Two other kinds of heroes in our present consciousness complete one kind of spectrum about man. If the literary artist tries to give us the partial truth about man in the form of an illusion, some hucksters of the American imagination give us lies under the guise of truth. Their verbal instruments are the communication media. Their character is the pseudo-hero. Randall Jarrell characterized the plot: success, celebrity, periodicity. The product largely of a youth-oriented and journalistic culture, the pseudo-hero awaits his apotheosis, and then quickly his demise and often unsavory and anonymous burial.

A final kind of hero is the sick hero. Some of the darkly absurd heroes in Thomas Pynchon's work, Joseph Heller's *Catch-22*, and Philip Roth's Portnoy of *Portnoy's Complaint*, are recent examples. Comically pitiful, Portnoy, who has his own notions of man's image —somewhat unrelated to his complaint—serves primarily as a therapeutic scapegoat for our image of man. This self-lacerating picture of man suggests even to the impious and detached the Hasidic saying, "If you rake muck back and forth, it is still muck." That Roth captured with ringing authenticity the hero of his confession seems true enough. But aesthetic authenticity radically disconnected from whatever of common virtue remains in the world around it is like a beautiful woman without integrity, a gold ring in a swine's snout. The rhetoric of the sick-hero is grotesque indeed. Perhaps there lies a saving note in this kind of fiction and this kind of hero. He illuminates the dark, comic negatives of inverted and spiritually diseased man.

By the early 1970s the sharp outlines of this particular image of man became blurred. By earlier conventional standards, the stature of man has rapidly diminished — so much so that the very qualities we admire in a man may have changed with the times, with shifting values, and with our highly tempered sense of the severe limits of individual human potential in the modern period. Man appears in much contemporary literature as a victim, a passive victim more acted upon than acting, more shaped by than shaping the larger forces outside of himself.

II

The dislocations in our image of man are reflected in man's relationship to nature also. Interpreting his curious allegory of Pan, Francis Bacon (d. 1626) wrote:

> His crook, also, contains a fine representation of the ways of nature, which are partly straight and partly crooked; thus the staff, having an extraordinary bend towards the top, denotes that the works of Divine Providence are generally brought about by remote means, or in a circuit, as if somewhat else were intended rather than the effect produced, as in the sending of Joseph into Egypt.[7]

What is perhaps most remarkable to us is Bacon's easy interpretive movement from nature to history. There is no break in the crook. Like some great surging tidal wave moving through time, the question of whether the natural universe is friendly to us or not receives increasingly complicated replies. Perched on what seems to be a crest of this wave, we can see how Bacon's early 17th-century distinction between revealed and natural knowledge of God and the universe led to two important results: the distinction released the natural world from Satan's dominion; and it gave to human reason a principal role for organizing knowledge gained from investigation. It separated that knowledge from the controlling authority of an ecclesiastical and intellectual tradition, thus leading to the increasing

---

[7] *Bacon's Essays and Wisdom of the Ancients* (Boston: Little, Brown, and Co., 1895), p. 338.

development of natural science as an autonomous and amoral realm of study.[8]

Bacon's enthusiasm, never in his own writing severed from its religious roots, blossoms in the language of the 18th-century poets of reason and the enlightenment and in the inherited and continued metaphor of the "great chain of being." Alexander Pope's intended epitaph for Sir Isaac Newton captures the optimism man must have felt in a universe accessible to human reason:

> Nature and Nature's laws lay hid in night:
> God said, "Let Newton be!" and all was light.

James Thomson, another poet of the same period, wrote on a rainbow and Newton's prisms of light in his address to "Spring":

> Meantime, refracted from yon eastern cloud,
> Bestriding earth, the grand ethereal bow
> Shoots up immense; and every hue unfolds
> In fair proportion, running from the red
> To where the violet fades into the sky.
> Here, awful Newton, the dissolving clouds
> Form, fronting on the sun, thy showery prism;
> And to the sage-instructed eye unfold
> The various twine of light, by thee disclos'd
> From the white mingling maze.

These links between nature's laws and man's mind in Pope and Thomson become eventual arguments for rationalist and romantic alike of man's precarious but hopeful life in this world. Whether one thinks or feels with the mind, in a universe where God moves through general laws one need study only nature to learn how to be beneficent. For instance, having "demolished" the need for revelation as another form of unnecessary secondary authority, Thomas Paine argued in *The Age of Reason:* "The creation we behold is the real and ever-existing Word of God, in which we cannot be deceived.

---

[8] See Basil Willey, "Bacon and the Rehabilitation of Nature," *The Seventeenth Century Background* (Garden City, N. Y.: Doubleday and Co., 1953), pp. 32—48. See Paul Goodman's *New Reformation: Notes of a Neolithic Conservative* (New York: Random House, 1970) for a more recent discussion of the breaks between moral and natural philosophy stemming from Bacon's kind of separation.

It proclaims his power, it demonstrates his wisdom, it manifests his goodness and beneficence."[9]

William Wordsworth, apparently not drawing on a meaningful religious tradition in his early poetry and without the mythology that earlier classicist and Christian alike could call on, asserted in *The Recluse:*

> How exquisitely the individual mind
> (And the progressive powers perhaps no less
> Of the whole species) to the external World
> Is fitted: — and how exquisitely, too —
> Theme this but little heard of among men —
> The external world is fitted to the mind.

Ralph Waldo Emerson looked on the physical universe as a vast temple covered with hieroglyphs and he saw divine unity behind the puzzling masks nature wears. At least he did so affirm, certain that his experience of totality and relationship and wholeness in nature was a subjective state of being tying him to the vaster Being holding all life in perpetual creative process in a meaningful universe. The purpose of man, he once claimed, was that he should become a little "Providence," not a fop or fool. Common to the poetry and prose of deist and romantic is the confidence in the ultimate unity of the natural universe and man's eventual harmonious place in it. There seemed little doubt, as Hans Holbein had shown in his late medieval woodcuts from the *Danse Macabre,* that the sun wears a face — and that face of nature is graciously human.

But here too disconnections become disturbingly apparent. Not that man no longer recognized his own fragile and ambivalent dependence on nature as well as nature's indifference and eventual destruction of him. Rather, having turned to nature when there seemed nowhere else to go, he found the old questions of man's place in the natural world abrasively persistent.

The probing and cautioning had begun before the middle of the 19th century, of course. David Hume had shown how the very assumptions and arguments that Alexander Pope used in his *Essay on Man* about man's relationship to the natural world and the natural

---

[9] *The Age of Reason* (New Rochelle, N. Y.: Thomas Paine Historical Association, 1925), p. 101.

world's relationship to God were as easily denied as affirmed by human reason. And in 1799, a year after William Wordsworth published the first edition of his *Lyrical Ballads* announcing the poetry of the new romantic sensibility, Friedrich Schleiermacher anticipated the counter-romantics. To the sentimental romantic's unquestioning admiration for nature, he rejoined that this kind of joy in nature is not truly religious and apt to be ephemeral.[10]

Schleiermacher went on to extol the legitimate feelings either child or sage may have when contemplating nature in its wholeness — the very kind of feeling Wordsworth's poetry would subsequently arouse in many and which persists today.[11] Yet Schleiermacher persisted in attacking the glib identifying of a feeling one gets from natural beauty as a reliable religious experience, thus challenging the romantic view. Eventually others denied that there was any significant connection between God, nature, and man. Meanwhile the natural universe appeared more and more as a riddle, and the literary mind struggled with its ambiguities. This transition can be illustrated by several examples.

Emily Dickinson's poetry represents one of the better examples of the struggle with the meaning of nature in this transition period. Although she remained in her poetry nature's celebrant, she continued throughout her poetry to be its puzzled victim, too. Her sense of ambiguity is neatly portrayed in the use of the color white. The color, with its evocation of ambiguity and even inscrutability, leaped into literary prominence in Melville's chapter on "The Whiteness of the Whale" in *Moby Dick*. Newton's prism of "white mingling maze," as James Thomson had called it, refracted the beauty of the rainbow when exposed to the sun. It seemed to dissolve into meaninglessness when exposed to the analyzing mind. The same kind of question haunted Miss Dickinson in a brief poem that neatly evokes the perpetual human situation: what the human eye sees in nature, what the mind concludes, what the heart ironically hopes:

---

[10] *On Religion: Speeches to Its Cultured Despisers* (New York: Harper & Row, 1958), p. 65.

[11] So in Paul Goodman's recent *The New Reformation* one hears Goodman, both in his own arguments and in his moving tribute to his son, Matty, who was killed in a mountain climbing accident in 1967, urge the recurrent need for a primary relationship to nature and to the literary tradition that gives man his sense of wholeness and order.

Apparently with no surprise
To any happy flower,
The frost beheads it at its play
In accidental power.

The blond assassin passes on,
The sun proceeds unmoved
To measure off another day
For an approving God.

In this brief poem the inanimate sun and frost world, the vegetable world of the flower, and the Divine Power controlling all are jostled, even dislocated, by the ironic human voice in the poem. What from one point of view could be called the "pathetic fallacy" — the speaker's attributing human feelings to the inanimate objects in the poem — becomes from another vantage point the assumed unity of interrelationships among God, man, and nature. In the poem the obvious split between what happens in nature and what the speaker or hearer of the poem would ideally hope to happen provides the irony.

There is an inscrutable mystery to nature's apparent brutality as the frost, the "blond assassin," beheads beauty. On the surface level of the poem there is affirmation: All this takes place for an approving God. Below the surface meaning lies the ironic rack on which the human being is pulled two ways: The truly faithful heart has always said that God gives and God takes away. As part of nature, the faithful heart has a questioning, heart-sharing mutability with the decapitated flower. A hymn of the 19th century, William Cowper's "God Moves in a Mysterious Way," sharing its common short meter with Miss Dickinson's poem, sounds a different tone and attitude:

Judge not the Lord by feeble sense,
But trust Him for His grace;
Behind a frowning providence
He hides a smiling face.

His purposes will ripen fast,
Unfolding every hour;
The bud may have a bitter taste,
But sweet will be the flower.

Blind unbelief is sure to err
And scan His work in vain;

God is His own Interpreter,
And He will make it plain.

In either case the human being is left with the distressingly bitter taste of feeble sense, feeble mind, feeble faith. In Miss Dickinson's poem, moreover, "frost" and "blond" move neatly with one another to evoke the color white with its suggestion of blankness and meaninglessness.

Robert Frost in "Design," a sonnet carrying all the ominous innocence and malignant whiteness of Melville's meditation on the whiteness of Moby Dick, portrays a fat, white, dimpled spider carrying a dead moth on a blighted white, heal-all flower in a grizzly morning rite. The concluding sextet of the poem raises a question: What could bring these things together in the night to appear in the innocence and freshness of the morning but a design of darkness? And the sextet ends with a quick, ironic reservation: "If design govern in a thing so small."

To the Christian mystic, like the psalmist of old, or a poet like Henry Vaughan or Thomas Traherne, God moved in a dazzling darkness. To the modern observer, nature mirrors a bright abyss of meaninglessness. To Samuel T. Coleridge (a sensitive man agonized by his sense of dislocation between the external world and his inner sensibility in "Dejection: An Ode") the problem lay in his own sensibility and feeling, particularly in the dissecting cast of his mind. To Albert Camus it is precisely this sense of dislocation that leads to the honesty of the sense of absurdity in the modern human predicament: in the natural world, man is an outcast. And human reason is helpless.

What one seems to discover then in this modern theme is another disconnection. Man's relationship to nature moves from affirmation to the experience of ambiguity to questioning to denial. Nature, aside from offering man a precarious interdependent state and the promise of beauty, remains inscrutable, indifferent, even hostile, the more hostile as we get to understand the mysteries of what can be known about her. One appears to have the answer only to discover that the answer raises another question. Having sensed God's withdrawal from the world, man leaned upon nature, but as he scrutinized the nature he leaned upon, he was brought more and more to realize that nature both sustains and stuns man. Because it stuns man, and because he knows it, he cannot be reconciled to it — not completely.

Dislocation in literature is a sign not only of dislocation between nature and man. Behind the sense of dislocation is the loss of meaning, a disconnection from an old ordering of things. Albert Camus' evaluation of the European literary scene in "Helen's Exile" summarizes contemporary man's relationship to nature:

> "Only the modern city," Hegel dares write, "offers the mind a field in which it can become aware of itself." We are thus living in the period of big cities. Deliberately, the world has been amputated of all that constitutes its permanence: nature, the sea, hilltops, evening meditation. Consciousness is to be found only in the street, because history is to be found only in the streets — this is the edict . . . Landscapes are not to be found in great European literature since Dostoevsky. History explains neither the natural universe that existed before it nor the beauty that exists above it.[12]

Yet it was a sense of God moving in history that separated the people of Israel from their nature-worshiping neighbors. Perhaps that is why Dietrich Bonhoeffer in his explanation of the first three chapters of Genesis asks the question: What do the waters, the land, the earth, the lights, and the stars have to do with human existence? And Bonhoeffer replies: "Nothing — the stars go their way, whether man is suffering, guilty or happy. And in their fixedness, they praise the Creator. The stars do not look down upon man, they do not accuse, nor do they comfort. They are totally themselves in an unapproachable remoteness. They shine by day and by night, but they do it without concern for us. The stars do not take part in man's existence."[13] For Bonhoeffer the great temptation of man, who according to the Biblical account of creation was not even present when the world of the fixed and the numbered was created, is to seek comfort in it or to escape to it as a place concerned with his experience. Our intelligences may be powerful enough to penetrate deeply into the evolution of our strangely incredible universe. We may ponder its unbelievable majesty and question how its apparent

---

[12] *The Myth of Sisyphus and Other Essays* (New York: Random House, Vintage Books, 1955), p. 136.

[13] *Creation and Fall*, trans. John C. Fletcher, (London: SCM Press, 1959), p. 27.

design is a result of chance. But whether the result of chance or design, it does not offer us the smallest clues to our human fate or destiny.

III

The totem pole neatly points to primitive man's identification of the human with the animal world. The robot or mechanical man points to modern man's vacillating courtship of technology. And technology, strengthening our power over nature, seems to widen the breach between man and nature. This development is understandable, perhaps because technology represents an overwhelming amplification and extension of natural and human powers. What is frightening about this extension and amplification is that in their results these powers are often indeterminable. We sense a supreme irony in the way the loss of belief in a providential Deity has been replaced by belief in technology's future for man. Possibilities for technological death in our world are as ever-present as the demons of plague were in the medieval world.

Ambivalent attitudes toward science and technology contrast with men's hopes for a utopian community where applied scientific knowledge enhances the life of the civilized commonwealth. In fact, old hopes are greeted by contemporary fears. Granville Hicks has observed how predominant in science fiction remains man's suspicion of technology. And there are additional signs of the tension.

Richard Brautigan's neat poetic identification of man and nature isolates all the more expressionistic plays like *The Hairy Ape* and *Dynamo,* two of Eugene O'Neill's treatments of man's not "belonging" in the modern technological and industrial world. Yet the plays affirm the inevitability of this kind of world. In *Dynamo* O'Neill presented strongly the ideological conflicts between the past with its God of lightning, its personal God of vengeance and His ministers — like the Rev. Hutchins Light — and the new world of electricity. The dynamo paradoxically embodies impersonal power and gives off a maternal hum — a new god which men can worship. Reuben Light, the minister's son in the play, chooses to serve the dynamo, only to sacrifice himself and his possibilities for human love upon it.

195

The past is not dead because one is ignorant of it or even considers it dead. Rather the past appears discontinuous with the present. Conrad Richter caught this feeling in *The Waters of Kronos*. Old John Donner, returning to his hometown, Unionville, Pa., expresses the irretrievable way in which technology separates the present from the past. As he drives to Kronos Gap, the road suddenly discloses what he had feared: "The high concrete dam breast like the white end of a colossal burial vault whose lid was blue water running back for miles, shutting in forever his grandfather's Vale on Union, reaching high on the hill and clasping every hollow." Stopping his car, John Donner tries to convince himself that what he sees and his reaction to it are the price of progress. But he cannot. The narrator continues:

> He couldn't shake off the feeling that under his feet he had come upon something frightening. He had had a glimpse, small as it was, into an abyss whose unfathomable depths were shrouded in mist, a bottomless chasm that he had known existed, if only in the back of his mind and in the back of everyone else's mind, but which he had never seen face to face or looked down into before. Perhaps one had to be old as he to recognize what one saw, to understand first how man had struggled up so painfully and so long, and then with that sad knowledge to come upon one's own once living, breathing and thinking people swallowed up in the abyss, given back to primordial and diluvian chaos.[14]

Rip van Winkle's 20-year sleep, his discovering that a community had changed, had become more restless, more given to commerce, becomes the living myth of each generation.

The passing of frontier America, for example, with its accompanying need for individual ingenuity and its apparent high regard for the traditional virtues we still so often associate with the frontiersman — the love of the land, pride in owning land won often in difficulty from the wilderness, strong independence joined with willingness to help the neighbor in need (that special genius De Tocqueville observed in Americans), family loyalty — all these have nurtured in the 20th century a new individual protest to technological doom.

For the late Albert Schweitzer the threat to one child from

---

[14] *The Waters of Kronos* (New York: Alfred A. Knopf, 1960), p. 7.

atomic fallout was a catastrophe for humanity. For Edward Teller and Albert Latter the results from atomic fallout remained an indeterminate question among other questions of the kind of harm that may or may not come to future generations from fallout. For William Blake each man through the use of imaginative vision becomes God. For Albert Einstein contemporary man must rid himself of any conception of a personal God.

The struggle seems inevitable, and it promises to be perpetual, for to many technology represents a new kind of tyranny. The mass of knowledge we have about the natural world seems merely to expand in ratio to the number of men and instruments we develop for studying the world. The past, so argued Walter Ong, is synchronically present in the contemporary world.[15] As our knowledge of the past becomes more and more available, it may prove less and less useful.

Because of the apparent irrevocability of the technological uses of nature, man's freedom to determine his own life and that of his children seems much more limited than it was even before the turn of the century. If one must choose between nature and the machine, one may find that, like Mark Twain, he may choose to see man as machine, helplessly carried along like cosmic flotsam in an infinite universe. Chance is fate, and the individual man's comparatively puny physical and mental powers heighten the pathos of his predicament. Mark Twain developed this notion in his essay *What Is Man?* In his more effective *The Mysterious Stranger* he finally rejects the whole universe as a dream. In his rejection he affirms individual man's capacity, even his stature, by giving form to the protest, yet his essential thrust seems to be for getting man out of history.

What heightens the pitifulness of man's predicament and prompts some of the fantastically irrational protests of the early 1970s is that to some the comforts of the past are no longer pertinent. Statistical trends threaten to abrogate the meaning and stifle the cry of individual suffering. Perhaps one of the reasons so many readers were attracted to Saul Bellow's *Herzog* is that Herzog's incessant letter writing, his expressing his personal outrage to people of conse-

---

[15] "Synchronic Present: Modernity in Literary Study," *In the Human Grain* (New York: Macmillan Co., 1967), pp. 41–51.

quence, his vulnerability and his flawed humanity, even his acting *as if* his opinion were important — all these affirmed the significant dimension of an individual's response to life.

More threatening to the individual are the values increasingly attached to technology — orientation to the future, specifically future perfection, accompanying focus on efficiency, and obsession with the profit motive.

Suspicion of technology focuses, too, on the technologist. The observing and studying intellect outruns the sympathetic heart, knowledge outruns wisdom, and the technological elitist manipulates human beings as things rather than persons. Ivan Turgenev captured some of the pathos of the change between the old cultural sensibility and the new scientific sensibility in *Fathers and Sons* in the characters of Bazarov and Arcadii. Although Aldous Huxley's *Brave New World* and George Orwell's *1984* both captured the fears in fiction also, Rex Warner's reissued *The Aerodome* represents another allegory of this perpetual struggle and this distinctly modern disconnection between man and technology by placing an English village in opposition to an aerodome. Justice, pity, love, and forgiveness — the values of the village and of a struggling and sinful humanity — stand in sharp contrast to the values of the aerodome — efficiency, perfection, power, wealth, and invulnerability. Each place, the village and the aerodome, reveals partial truths about man, about his rootedness in nature and his need for transcending nature with powers of mind and imagination by mechanizing it. Yet mechanized nature may dehumanize man at the same time that it offers him fantastic possibilities for providentially ordering his world.

IV

So far we have traced some of the major outlines in modern man's disenchantment with his own experience of the world. Perhaps this movement culminates in the poetry, drama, and fiction about God. Whether the God of a particular past culture is dead, whether God has in fact withdrawn, whether there has developed a growing consciousness of God's apparent withdrawal from our technological world, to these questions the answers vary. A single impression seems clear: one major literary theme in the modern period focuses on the sense of a disconnection between God and the world.

Belief in the objective reality of "the great chain of being" extended from the middle ages through baroque pessimism and Milton's *Paradise Lost* into the 18th century as part of a common classical and Christian heritage. And the idea received one of its fuller literary expressions in Alexander Pope's lines from the first epistle of the *Essay on Man:*

> See, through this air, this ocean, and this earth,
> All matter quick, and bursting into birth.
> Above, how high, progressive life may go!
> Around, how wide! How deep extend below!
> Vast chain of being! which from God began,
> Natures ethereal, human, angel, man,
> Beast, bird, fish, insect, what no eye can see,
> No glass can reach; from Infinite to thee,
> From thee to Nothing.

More important perhaps was Pope's assertion in the third epistle that this chain of being was also a chain of love. Arguing in terms of the scientific language of his day, he used the smooth-rolling couplet to reinforce the sense of order in a poem about order.

But this kind of confidence diminished rapidly. The dominant shattering experience is the growing consciousness of the apparent withdrawal of God from this world, the encroachment of chaos on the world of order, and the development of systems of explanation satisfactory in themselves. Many sensitive people do not experience God in the same personal way that men earlier could claim His presence. Whether we look long at history or stare at the cinema-scope screen of man's contemporary struggle with the problem, the witness to God's absence is present.

The changes in religious sensibility that swept across Europe in 17th-century orthodoxy, 18th-century rationalism, and 19th-century romanticism issued in the modern period, where God seems to have been removed from the world. This particular historical thread has been traced in recent literature.[16] We can point to the apex of the idea in 19th-century poems like "Rugby Chapel," Matthew Arnold's poignantly restrained and moving elegy for his clergyman-

---

[16] Nathan A. Scott Jr., *The Broken Center: Studies in the Theological Horizon of Modern Literature* (New Haven: Yale University Press, 1966). Scott's recent *The Wild Prayer of Longing* (New Haven: Yale University Press, 1971) carries the analysis to the loss of figural interpretation.

father Thomas, in his "Dover Beach," and especially his lines from "The Grand Chartreuse," where he sees himself between the old classical-Christian and the modern worlds:

> Wandering between two worlds, one dead,
> The other powerless to be born,
> With nowhere to rest my head,
> Like these, on earth I wait forlorn.

The sense of the withdrawal of God is not only a part of the historical record but is also important for our understanding of the modern situation. Perhaps nothing better illustrates this predicament than the interest in the Book of Job, a Biblical book in which the modern reader finds a mirror of his problem. Ostensibly the book concerns a man patient under suffering. But today's reader sees something else in the rugged poetic structure of the book. Job's patience and obedience in the prolog and epilog are pertinent but frail bindings for Job's mounting outrage with the God whom he feels certain has abandoned him and whom he feels will not even condescend to argue with him. Crushed by the useless words of his "comforters," Job feels that God is distant.

Archibald MacLeish's *J. B.*, picking up the Job story, summarily testifies to the modern consciousness of God's withdrawal from the world scene and to man's rejection of traditional religious answers to man's contemporary sense of injustice and evil in the world. We need not be familiar with the details of the play to realize that many in the audience mistakenly assumed that because the play used the Book of Job as a basis for its characters, plot, and theme, it was a deeply religious play. To anyone viewing the play in terms of the modern spirit, it was obvious that one of the main thrusts of the play was to point out that if God does exist, God does not care about man in the 20th century.

One stage effect in the play is the voice of God, the voice speaking in prolog and in the final scenes of the play. This God, J. B. politely but directly rejects, because He is the God who has permitted such horrifying injustices as the death of the innocents in the bombing of Hiroshima and Dresden as well as the senseless deaths of J. B. and Sarah's children in the play. Such outrageous injustice and such absurd mass suffering cannot be explained away by false contemporary comforters. One, like Bildad, argues that individual injustice simply does not and cannot matter because the process of history finally bears man along to a meaningful purpose. Another, like Eliphaz, takes man's high sense of personal responsibility and its accompanying guilt and explains it away or throws it back on the irresponsible universe. A third, like Zophar, answers to man's present suffering with a theological jingle.

Throughout the early episodes in the play, Nickles, wearing the mask of self-conscious awareness and speaking with the voice of cynicism and near despair, recites his doubting jingle:

> If God is God He is not good,
> If God is good He is not God:
> Take the even, take the odd,
> I would not sleep here if I could. . . .
> Except for the little green leaves in the wood
> And the wind on the water.[17]

Although there are peculiar nuances in the last two lines of the stanza, as if beauty were a coquette both calming and deceiving man, an old issue is raised in the first two lines. Traditionally the presence of evil in the world called for a theodicy or defense of God's ways toward man, particularly an explanation of the presence of radical evil in man's experience.[18] MacLeish's play *turns* from this problem to the more immediate question of how man can live in a universe where, if God does exist, He does not seem to care.

Toward the end of the play Nickles, wearing the mask of Satan, hovers over J. B., whose children have died in senseless accidents, whose body is covered with atomic burns, and whose wife has left him. Nickles asks J. B., "What's the worst thing you can think of?" J. B. replies, "I have asked for death. Begged for it. Prayed for it." Nickles counters, "Then the worst thing can't be death." If God is absent, if He does not seem to care, if the old ties between the eternal and temporal order have been broken, then meaningless life becomes a greater threat than death itself.

Both the Book of Job and *J. B.* are testaments to man's experience of a universe in which God seems absent. Each in his own way

---

[17] *J. B.* (Boston: Houghton Mifflin Co., 1958), pp. 14—15.

[18] See Regin Prenter, *Creation and Redemption,* trans. Theodor I. Jensen (Philadelphia: Fortress Press, 1967), for an excursus on the limitations on theodicies, pages 208—9, note.

rebels against the distant God—Job repents and receives his world and returns to worship God. J. B., when Sarah returns with the sprig of forsythia, accepts his human world again. And J. B. offers Sarah the comfort of human love in a universe filled with distant, cold, still stars. Neither acts like a renegade outside the human race. Both Job and J. B. are victim and rebel and both yea-say even though God and the universe stun them.

Perhaps the most radical stance for those who feel that God has withdrawn emerges in what has been called "religious atheism." In its baldest form the position of the religious atheist appears to run something like this: Because the shape of life for most people is from beginning to end cruciform, often filled with unjustifiable and unreasonable suffering and the final certainty of death, and because these people in the midst of their suffering need hope so that they will not despair, one should act as if God did exist, even if one knows that there is no God.

In *The Martyred,* a book dedicated to Albert Camus and his "strange form of love," Richard Kim developed this strange love in a story of the martyrdom of 12 Korean ministers. The narrative focuses on Mr. Shin, one of two ministers released mysteriously by the communists. Along with a young captain who tells the story, the reader follows the enigma of Mr. Shin, a man who may have been a betrayer but who gives himself in uncommon devotion to his people as an encouraging pastor and preacher. In a revelatory scene toward the end of the book Mr. Shin and the captain argue almost deliriously why Mr. Shin should deceive his people by glorifying a god who understands human suffering when no such god exists. As the young captain verbally attacks the old minister, Mr. Shin clutches the young man's arms and whispers to him compassionately that he understands how the captain must have suffered. The utterly astonished captain then hears Mr. Shin's agonized confession of how in life he has found "only man with all his sufferings . . . and death, inexorable death!"; how after death he was sure there was nothing and how he needs to give to his people assurance that they will triumph in the kingdom of God. To the captain's rhetorical questions, "To give them the illusion of hope? The illusion of life beyond the grave?" Mr. Shin replies: "Yes, yes! Because they are men. Despair is the disease of those weary of life, life here and now full of meaningless sufferings. We must fight despair, we must destroy it and not let the sickness of despair corrupt the life of man and reduce him to a mere scarecrow." [19]

Mr. Shin's despair is his cross. This final scene is especially moving, particularly when one remembers that Mr. Shin had earlier revealed the truth to his dying wife. Her look of despair helped make him a proclaimer of illusion. Although he believes that there is no god, he acts as if God exists; he prays, he preaches, he comforts with hope. He is a kind of saint without God. Courage becomes a strange form of love — not just to face the truth but to live for other men as if it were the truth when it is not. Man lives, moves, and has his being in a closed horizon.

V

As suggested earlier, most critical theories about the arts in the modern world tend to stress one of four interrelated contact points: the artist and the creative process, the artifact as an aesthetic object, the "world" to which the artifact is tied, and the audience. So far we have diagnosed some themes suggesting the essential breakup of our traditional world view. It may be helpful to turn attention briefly to a number of other questions of a more theoretical nature to get a larger vision of our task of relating the arts to our understanding of divine providence.

Consider the artist. Aristotle, observing fundamental actions in men, distinguished the artist as maker from the philosopher as knower and from the politician as doer. Each man acts within a hierarchy of conceptual precision. Because the world the artist makes is a probable rather than an actual world, the knowledge of the truth the artist shapes is less exact than the knowledge of the truth of the philosopher or the statesman's knowledge of the doing of the good. Yet the artist remains indispensable to the human community. The immense power of art, which the Greeks called *psychogogia* (a leading or persuading of the soul), was its capacity to develop human feelings and motivations toward moral, social, and religious values which were assumed to be true and good for their own sakes. In tragedy, Aristotle's primary example, the artist by shaping action,

---

[19] *The Martyred* (New York: George Braziller, Inc., 1964), p. 256.

thought, character, diction, music, and spectacle into an appropriately moving form leads his viewers through a therapeutically enlarging experience. The poet as playwright is the "sayer." He celebrates common values in the community and through mimic delight leads the community to wisdom. The communal experience is possible because the public view of truth is common to all.

It is a commonplace of literary history that Aristotle's classical notion of the artist as shaper of the truth, however provisional the form of that truth and however minimal the reading of Aristotle, dominated classical and Christian understanding of the arts.

The key classical notion is that the artist is not so much the discoverer of truth or the doer of the truth. He shapes the truth. He keeps alive the feel of truth. In Alexander Pope's words, he gives a fresh rendering to what "oft was thought but ne'er so well expressed." This accent on the artist as shaper, the poet as "sayer," continues in our own time, but with a major difference. There is no longer a general or public view of truth. There remains a mainstream in the classical-Hebraic-Christian tradition, but that mainstream is continually fed by strongly disruptive currents, some of which we have already noted. More of them will flow into that mainstream in Darwinism, Marxism, Freudianism—all of which will shrink our traditional approaches to the role of God's providential care for the world, for each pictures modern man in a kind of closed system in which the struggles and conflicts of men may be explained without recourse to God's general or special providence.[20]

We note the subsequent alteration in the understanding of the poet. As sayer the poet was always a man speaking to men. Even William Wordsworth's essentially empirical approach to poetry depended on his seeing the poet as a man differing from other men

---

[20] Freud, for example attacked the religion of the common man for his belief in divine providence in *Religion as an Illusion*. He offers a "naturalistic" explanation for human feelings of transcendence in *Civilization and Its Discontents*. His insights have been carried into the political realm by Harold Lasswell, *Psychopathology of Politics,* and by Erich Fromm, *Escape from Freedom.* John Gardner writes in *The Recovery of Confidence* (New York: W. W. Norton and Co., 1970), p. 27: "At the same time people were less and less inclined to explain their daily lives and institutions in terms of God's will. And that trend has continued to this day. Less and less do men suppose, even those who believe devoutly in a supreme being, that God busies himself with detailed, day-to-day administration of the world."

only in the degree of his sensibilities, his knowledge of the human soul, his rejoicing in "the spirit of life that is in him," and in his ability to communicate in words "emotions recollected in tranquillity." Like John Keats, the poet as sayer might well agree that an eagle is not so fine a thing as truth. But then our idea of truth without our felt experience of the eagle might not be so fine a thing either. Hence the poet makes for us the "little world" of the poem.[21] Although we may call him shaper, man of sensibility, living seismograph, antennae of the race, human radar in the cultural fog, we see the artist increasingly as "seer" as well as "sayer."

Not yet fully explored is a direction literature has taken in the form of the novel itself. We are perhaps so close to its development that it will be left to the cultural historians of another generation to evaluate the relationship of form to belief in the novel. But even now one runs across side comments like Amos Wilder's: "The novel as it has evolved in the modern period is a form which is only possible in a world whose view of man and society has been shaped by Christian presuppositions."[22] J. Hillis Miller hints that the spectacular rise of the novel as a literary genre in the 19th century parallels the emphasis during the same period on God's transcendence and the simultaneous loss of the sense of God's immanence in the affairs of men.[23] God has been "pushed out" of man's affairs through the rise of science and technology, and the rise of industry and commerce threatens a burgeoning population with new economic and balance-of-power questions. The novelist offers to the confused reader a surrogate form of order. Like the New Testament gospel writers, who interpreted Christ's life, death, and resurrection as events restoring order and meaning in the cosmos, the panoramic novelist of the 19th century — men like William Thackeray or Charles Dickens or Thomas Hardy in England, like Leo Tolstoy and Fyodor Dostoevski in Russia, like Honore de Balzac, Emile Zola, and recent

---

[21] For a historical and critical treatment of the development of the poem as a bearer of its own fact and value system, see Robert Langbaum, *The Poetry of Experience* (New York: W. W. Norton and Co., 1957).

[22] *The Language of the Gospel: Early Christian Rhetoric* (New York: Harper & Row, 1964), p. 20.

[23] *The Disappearance of God: Five Nineteenth-Century Writers* (Cambridge, Mass.: Harvard University Press, 1963).

authors like Jules Romains in France, like William Faulkner in America—offer men a vision of life, giving through the novels hope for a new world or reflecting in the novels the despair of the present world. Frank Kermode, asserting that books are "fictive models of the temporal world," has elaborated a theory of fiction based on man's perpetual "sense of an ending." He sees in fiction, both in its origins and its present directions, an attempt to "repeat the performance of the New Testament" by providing "secular concords of past and present and future." The difference between Christian and post-Christian man is that the Christian believes in an ending, the post-Christian man accepts the need for fictional concords to give sense and order to this life.[24] Either they find God in man or they see the universe freed for man.

Perhaps offering a rebuttal to Plato's sometimes harsh treatment of the artist, Aristotle claimed that poetry, because it dealt with the probable and universal, was more important than history, which dealt with the particular and the past. In the modern world the writer, originally a craftsman or worker with words, becomes more and more a "creator," or in Nicholas Berdyaev's terms, a "microtheos."[25] Goethe developed a formula for the artist's embodying the transcendent in his work.[26] Samuel T. Coleridge spoke of the artist as the one who participates in the great "I am" of God Himself. Northrop Frye treats the poet as agent of "human apocalypse." And

---

[24] *The Sense of an Ending: Studies in the Theory of Fiction* (New York: Oxford University Press, 1966), p. 59.

[25] David B. Harned, *Theology and the Arts* (Philadelphia: The Westminster Press, 1966), p. 97.

[26] Walter Sorell, *The Duality of Vision: Genius and Versatility in the Arts* (Indianapolis: The Bobbs-Merrill Co.), pp. 241—42: "In May 1815 Goethe sent what he called a 'general confession of faith' to the young son of the Mayor of Frankfurt, Christian Heinrich Schlosser, a little-known statement which is not even included in the most complete editions of Goethe's work of 140 volumes. In this confession he formulates a theory on the arts:
    a. Everything is found in nature that is in the subject matter.
    y. and a bit more of it.
    b. Everything is found in the subject matter that is in nature
    z. and a bit more of it.
    b can recognize a, but y can only be surmised through z. Out of it emerges the balance of the world and the balance of the circle of life in which we are caught. That human being able to embrace all four in utmost clarity has always been called GOD by all people."

gradually in our poetry, drama, and fiction the artist becomes the subject of his own work.

Increasingly one gets the impression, then, that the artist is not just the man different in degree, nor only the anguished, alienated man. He is different in kind. Alexander Pushkin spoke of him in the "The Prophet" as the poet-prophet Isaiah, God-seized. Ralph Waldo Emerson described the poet in "Uriel," John Milton's archangel of the sun in *Paradise Lost*, as a speaker with piercing eye shuddering the sky and shaking the gods. Even the cautious Yankee poet, Robert Frost, considered "Uriel" Emerson's finest poem.

Is the artist creator in divine frenzy exploding his private vision on the heavy-lidded eye and fat-laden year of the common world around him? Is he a creature in discipline composing, as craftsmanlike as he can, an expression in vital form of old ideas and new feelings? From our present vantage point the artist in the modern world still plays a precariously double role as "sayer" and "seer."

Blending skill with sensibility and imaginative insight, the effective artist has a special gift for what John Keats referred to as "negative capability" when he spoke of Shakespeare's work. In its broad sense the term refers to a double movement in the elusive process the artist goes through from raw experience to finished work. On the one hand, the artist seems to have peculiar gifts for responding to life with what William Butler Yeats called, "blood, imagination, and intellect running together." Immersion, engagement, participation in real or imaginary experience, perception of what is important amidst all the flux and flow of life describe his response to the world without and within him. He also has the ability to shape his experiences so that his work represents an imaginative distillation of his insights.

As our image of man seems to be weakened in the poetry, drama, and fiction of our time, our image of the artist is strengthened — primarily because the artist increasingly fulfills both prophetic and priestly roles in our culture. As prophet he continually reminds us through imaginative art that we are capable of the perverse, the vile, the bestial — of almost unimaginable chaos, thus maintaining in us our own sense of corruptibility and sinful creatureliness. Without these reminders we would be frighteningly vain and insensitive to our own limitations and to what R. G. Collingwood saw as the corruption of consciousness which the artist continually wishes to tear from us.[27] As priest the artist offers to us the counterpoise of man's essential dignity; of the tragic dimensions and quality of human life; of our potential for order, grace, productivity, joy; of our response to a world shot through with divine resonance and with that spirit of transcendence which Lionel Trilling has suggested is present in all great art.[28]

VI

We see the dimensions of this "spiritual" ascendancy in changing critical attitudes to the work of art also. Within his poetry Dante presented a strong case for the workings of Divine Providence, as he did in *The Divine Comedy*.[29] Geoffrey Chaucer in *Troilus and Cressida* pondered the problem of divine providence, with strong leanings on Beothius's *Consolation of Philosophy*. Shakespeare may puzzle our intellect and will as he puzzles Hamlet with questions of readiness to believe and to act before the mysteries of divine providence and human freedom.[30]

Gradually other forms of spiritual transcendence replace explicit concern with divine providence. We cross lines once again, as Bonhoeffer suggested, from the Holy Spirit *(geistlich)* to the human spirit *(seelisch)*. But that human spirit remains restless in its quest and its disclosures.

In a world of prose, as Stephen Spender has called our world, the arts fulfill more and more the role of vital religion because the prose world is "a world of weakened traditions, almost devoid of ritual, ceremony, and symbols within life which play more than an ornamental role in the community." [31] Alfred Kazin claimed that for the young "literature is much more than a subject of study . . . it is

---

[27] *Principles of Art* (New York: Oxford University, 1938), p. 336.

[28] "Hawthorne in Our Time," *Beyond Culture* (New York: The Viking Press, 1968), p. 201.

[29] Cantos XVI-XVIII of *The Purgatorio,* or Canto VI of the same on prayer.

[30] William Hamilton, "Hamlet and Providence," *The Christian Scholar* (Fall 1964), pp. 193—207.

[31] *The Creative Element* (New York: British Book Center, 1954), p. 20.

nothing less than a form of personal salvation."[32] Lionel Trilling summarized his experiences as a teacher more or less "forced" to offer courses at Columbia University in modern literature:

> No literature has ever been so shockingly personal as that of our time—it asks every question that is forbidden in polite society. It asks if we are content with our marriages, with our family lives, with our professional lives, with our friends. . . . The questions asked by our literature are not about our culture but about ourselves. It asks us if we are content with ourselves, if we are saved or damned—more than anything else, our literature is concerned with salvation. No literature has ever been so intensely spiritual as ours.[33]

Luigi Pirandello caught this religious intensity in *Six Characters in Search of an Author*, a pivotal play in the modern theatre. In this drama of ideas Pirandello poses a question that seemingly has an obvious answer: Which is more powerful in its hold on human consciousness, life itself or dramatic art? The entire play suggests that author, director, actors, words, audience expectations—all these place impossible limitations on any author's communicating through his characters the anguish and poignancy of human suffering. The characters seeking an author will never find an adequate matrix for full realization of what life is as it is experienced. Then why not just live, immersing oneself in the pain and pleasure of the conscious moment? Above all, why try to give form to that which cannot be caught by form? Because, so Pirandello indicates through his play, life as it is experienced is a perpetually present torrent of sensations and reflections rushing swiftly into the past. Literature arrests the torrent of time that carries all men to death and out of human memory. Literature—the letter rather than the spoken word or the visual image—is the refined human answer to Job's despondent cry: "Oh that my words were written! Oh that they were inscribed in a book! Oh that with an iron pen and lead they were graven in rock forever!" Literature gives permanence and dignity, transcendence in time, to the fleeting quality of human life. It offers

---

[32] Quoted by Douglas M. Davis, "The Literary Critic: He Determines the Shape of Our Literature," *The National Observer*, Oct. 25, 1965, p. 22.

[33] *Beyond Culture*, pp. 8—9.

to the reader a momentary flight from time, a sacred space in which he can hear characters ask him who he is.

Accents on the poem as a "divine stasis" reflect a similar emphasis.[34] Literary criticism in the 19th and early 20th centuries was primarily historical criticism. If a poem were compared to a red balloon, it would have been tied to the earth in time and space by a hundred historical and biographical strings. Criticism often attacked or approved the poem or the poet for being moral or immoral. It often ignored the poetry as an objective art form. The "new criticism," building on romantic conceptions of the poet's creating like nature itself, or like a catalyst bringing about a chemical change, detached the poet from the poem. Northrop Frye has given us a classical definition:

> The discursive writer writes as an act of conscious will, and that conscious will, along with the symbolic system he employs with it, is set over against the body of things he is describing. But the poet, who writes creatively rather than deliberately, is not the father of his poem; he is at best a midwife, or more accurately still, the Womb of Mother Nature herself. . . . The fact that revision is possible, that a poet can make changes in a poem not because he likes them better but because they are better, shows clearly that the poet has to give birth to the poem as it passes through his mind. He is responsible for delivering it in an as uninjured state as possible, and if the poem is alive, it is equally anxious to be rid of him and screams to be cut loose from all the navel-strings and feeding-tubes of his ego.[35]

Consequently the poem becomes for the reader an experience or speech-event, a revelatory process in which the poem reads the reader, an imaginative apocalypse.[36]

---

[34] This accent has been attacked increasingly. See D. G. James, *Skepticism and Faith.* More recently Walter Ong argues for the contemporary poet's need to shift his informing metaphor from the eternal and the permanent to the evolutionary and historical: "Evolution, Myth, and Poetic Vision," *In the Human Grain,* pp. 99–126.

[35] *Anatomy of Criticism,* p. 98.

[36] In painting one thinks of the work of Wassily Kandinsky with color, Piet Mondrian with color and design, and Paul Klee, who paints out of his personal history, as attempts to reaffirm the transcendent in the visual arts.

VII

In broad strokes we have outlined in the arts a twofold response to the question of the meaning of divine providence for modern man. One movement in the verbal arts reveals nearly overriding concern with the malaise of our Western culture, a malaise described in terms of a breakup of tradition, a loss of coherence. Another movement reveals the artist and the work of art assuming increasing importance for modern man as bearers of transcendence, hope, and order. A final question remains: Are there significant relationships between these movements and our Christian understanding of divine providence?

First, our understanding of the idea of divine providence in the arts is roughly analogous to the life of the word "wit" in Renaissance and Neoclassical periods. The word "wit" lost its force and fullness. Yet ideas of wit modulated into key ideas and images associated with words like imagination or ideas of great intellectual energy, words and ideas with which we feel fairly comfortable. Insofar as the words "divine providence" are tied to ways we think and feel about God's ultimate purposes for the world (general providence) and individual experience of that design (special providence), we sense a deep need for construing our understanding in terms more appropriate to our modern experience. Seldom does one notice specific reference to these words in the modern arts. This does not mean that language about God's providence is irrelevant to modern man. Rather, change in emphasis is apparent. The emphasis stresses God's activity and our response to grace in the details of human existence, in the structures of human awareness, in the mystery of our freedom to choose among alternatives.

Nathan Scott suggests this by asserting that Dietrich Bonhoeffer's contributions provide the fulcrum for new modes of theological activity in exploring nerve-endings between theology and literature.[37] The God of explanation is dead. The imaginative writer's "blik" dances out for us in appropriate form some of the questions and answers to the pressures of adversity and the freedoms of grace. In imaginative literature we find a peculiar paradox—full secularity

---

[37] "Theology and the Literary Imagination," *Adversity and Grace: Studies in Recent American Literature* (Chicago: University of Chicago Press, 1968), pp. 1—25.

resonating to the "beyond." That is, the meeting point between our Christian belief in divine providence and the modern arts is in living out the drama of personal history and in giving personal history expressive form in language. In the modern period, moreover, the relationship between the historic Christian community and the arts depends on a continuing dialectic.

If our ultimate struggle as men is the struggle with chaos and disorder, then language is the tough, pliable, and expressive form with which we seek to order the chaos. Holy Scriptures provide us with an authoritative norm. The narrative modes of Scripture with their story movements from first to last things, their sense of total history, and their special concrete historical realism lead us into the special awareness of man in the Old Testament. In that awareness of man, captured in the ancient forms of Hebrew recital with their subtle variations in form and theme, we find, according to Amos Wilder, a special characteristic, "holism." For Wilder holism is "the scope of awareness, the multidimensional reality and realism, the inclusion of the private and the public, of the inner life and the social-historical, of somatic and visionary, of ethical and metaphysical." [38] In other words, Scripture provides us with a narrative ground plan of responsible and irresponsible man in motion, both shaped by his covenantal relationship to his Creator God and shaping his future out of that relationship. Scripture presents us with a "map of existence" for contemplating the structures of order against chaos, meaningfulness against unreason, life against death, being against nonbeing.

This movement culminates in the death and resurrection of Jesus Christ. Through faith in Christ we become the battleground for the struggle between life and death. This struggle, shaped and experienced on all levels of our human existence, ties us in our dying and living with Christ to all of creation in its dying and living, including those works of the human spirit we ordinarily assign to the arts.

More specifically, we are brought back once again to the arts as explanatory, or propaedeutic, in the Christian life, that is, in our living out our Christian faith in the here and now. As we suggested

---

[38] *The New Voice: Religion, Literature, Hermeneutics* (New York: Herder and Herder, 1969), p. 57.

in our introduction, this propaedeutic moves in two directions, that of consensus and that of conflict.

As a consensus propaedeutic it deepens our understanding and our expressive response to our faith. The arts deepen our understanding of our faith because Biblical norms and Biblical study, though authoritative for faith and practice, do not give us the grasp and feel of our contemporary world. Sally McFague Te Selle argues:

> The New Testament, though an ample guide in terms of motives for discipleship, paradigms for action, and forms of instruction, does not provide us with a concrete, intricate, contemporary knowledge of the powers of the world and the hearts of men that we need if our love is to be truly appropriate and imaginative. It does not investigate the negativities of life as a preliminary to a realistic, profound trust in God, nor does it enter into the labyrinths of the hearts of men in preparation for an appropriate response to their deepest needs. Literature, however, does both of these.[39]

Not that literature preempts the central concern of the Christian life. Te Selle concludes that although "literature is not at the heart of the Christian life, not at the secret moment between God and man when the man is constrained to put total trust in God's love . . . it is relevant to the working out of that moment in the man's attempt to know his world and man more fully that he might trust God and love man more appropriately."[40] That is the realm of providential care and providential trust.

Effective literature can intensify our understanding of what it means to be human and, accordingly, intensify our understanding of what it means to be a redeemed human being. Effective literature, as one of the arts, disrupts flat stereotypes in our perceptions and responses to the world, and it carries us beyond the ordinary continuum of human experience. It arrests our concentration in moments of wonder. It carries us through the nooks and crannies of the limits and possibilities of human destiny, leads us through the pressures and complexities and ambiguities of self-definition, and through its imaginative ordering points us to a higher reality by serving the

---

[39] *Literature and the Christian Life* (New Haven: Yale University Press, 1967), p. 161.

[40] Ibid., p. 163.

special role in culture of awakening our faculties of perception and revising our ways of looking at things.

The genuine test of the effectiveness of the arts depends on our determination to carry insight into action by turning back to the "everyday," to the common life we share as Christians with all men. We may flee from time to the work of art as a "calculated trap for meditation," only to return to the risk of faith we encounter in the decision-making processes of our daily life.

The arts also deepen our expressive response by alerting us to the significance of the life of forms in the public and private devotional life of the church. If we live in a world of a confusion of tongues, and if Western man's voice is changing, the pilgrim church needs a new speech and new art forms to move along with our growing consciousness of ever-expanding reality. Poets and sculptors reconcile man and technology. Artists like Robert Motherwell and dancers like Merce Cunningham paint and dance on principles of indeterminacy, thus marrying insights in science with artistic form and execution. Musicians like Benjamin Britten draw on medieval miracle plays, Japanese No Drama, contemporary literature, and modern musical idioms. Other musicians, learning a new language, experiment with computers and electronic synthesizers. Poets improvise with the vitality of colloquial speech. We can do no less as men, taking from our heritages treasures both old and new.

A conflict propaedeutic helps us also. Sympathetic response to the arts opens us to the contingent nature both of our personal value systems and the larger formal and informal value structures which have shaped us in our families and the institutions we serve. The specific community may thus be preserved from the reactionary, that is, from one that has lost its capacity for flexibility of spirit. In our preaching and pastoral care we may carry into practice Regin Prenter's wise exhortation, aptly drawn from the arts, that "Christian preaching and pastoral ministry must in their reference to the creation and earthly life shun all cheap rationalizations of life's painful contradictions; they must refrain from anticipating the outcome of the drama at the opening of the first act." [41] At the same time a conflict propaedeutic brings the imaginative and the religious into

---

[41] *Creation and Redemption,* p. 211.

a healthy polemic relationship. We need to study the doctrines of modern man, his myths (speed, change, novelty), his heroes (epic, anti-hero, pseudo-hero, rebel, sick-hero), his rhetorics.

Through the arts there remains for mortal man the resonance of promised transcendence. Man still longs for a homeland, yearns for peace. This homeland he seeks to repossess. Our Christian faith becomes pertinent when we face the old and the new Adam in ourselves and in other men, still yearning for and still needing salvation.

Providentialism and Evolutionary Biology

John C. Gienapp

Modern evolutionary biology has very little explicit connection with any doctrine of providence. One can read the works of many contemporary biologists, even those who deal with issues far wider than biology itself, without finding any direct reference to providence.[1] This has not always been the case, however. Before the mid-19th century many naturalists understood biology in the direct light of their own belief in divine providence. Darwin's theory of evolution by natural selection challenged the widely held belief in divine providence over the world of living creatures. Eventually it led to the present situation in which nearly all forms of providentialism have been banished from biology. This article describes the connection between providentialism and biology as it was established in the 17th century and shows the way in which this connection was broken by the development of the biological theory of evolution by natural selection.

The providentialism[2] that held sway among naturalists drew directly on the development of science during the 17th century. The science of the 17th century resulted from a fusion of Greek and

---

[1] For example, Sir Gavin de Beer, *Streams of Culture* (Philadelphia: J. B. Lippincott Co., 1969); Julian Huxley, *Essays of a Humanist* (New York and Evanston: Harper & Row, 1964); George Gaylord Simpson, *This View of Life* (New York: Harcourt, Brace & World, 1964); Theodosius Dobzhansky, *The Biology of Ultimate Concern* (New York: The New American Library, 1967).

[2] I have tried to talk of providentialism rather than about a doctrine of providence, since no naturalist or biologist to my knowledge ever worked out a full-scale doctrine of providence which they explicitly integrated into their biological work. One can only find hints of providential views, including views of creation, that are used in biological contexts. Ultimately they rest on widely held views of creation and providence that were taken for granted by the scientists who used them. Full elaboration of these concepts is beyond the scope of this essay.

Christian ideas, which reacted together to produce a new view of nature.[3] Essential to this new view was the recognition that nature could be reduced to mathematical-mechanical principles. Galileo described nature by saying that "the book of nature was written in the language of mathematics" and that the task of science was to penetrate the veil of phenomena to find the principles that lay beneath. Numerous examples of success in finding the principles occurred. Galileo established the kinematics of projectile motion and falling bodies. Descartes established the law of refraction and used it to explain the optics of the rainbow. Newton axiomaticized the laws of motion and established the theory of gravitation. On the basis of these he could deduce almost all of celestial and terrestrial mechanics as a matter of course. What emerged then from the Scientific Revolution was a world in which many features, such as the motion of the planets, that had formerly been explained by invoking angels or celestial intelligences, were now simply explained by the laws of mechanics and gravity, which God (in Newton's view) had established in the beginning. Since the exponents of the new view of nature were almost without exception steeped in the Christian tradition, they had little trouble linking their views of nature with the concept of the Creator God. From this resulted the prevailing view that John Greene has called "static creationism." [4]

In the static view of creation many of the ongoing features of the cosmos were explained as the result of the laws of matter and motion, but these explanations did not extend to origins because, it was argued, all the basic structures of the universe came directly from the hand of the Creator. Consequently these structures showed evidences of the Creator's design and were preserved by the Creator from change. In astronomy, for example, Newton thought the planets were held in their orbital motion indefinitely by the operation of the law of gravitation, but he could not imagine how their particular order and motion could have arisen without the direct intervention of divine power. He argued:

---

[3] This view is described in almost any history of science or monograph on 17th-century science. E. Dijksterhuis, *The Mechanization of the World Picture* (Oxford: Clarendon Press, 1961).

[4] John Greene, *The Death of Adam* (Ames, Iowa: State Univ. Press, 1959), Preface.

The motions which the planets now have could not spring from any natural cause alone, but were impressed by an intelligent Agent. For since comets descend into the region of our planets and here move all manners of ways . . . it is plain that there is no natural cause which could determine all the planets, both primary and secondary, to move the same way and in the same plane, without any considerable variation; this must have been the effect of counsel.[5]

Likewise, Newton argued, the basic units of matter were directly created by God in the beginning, were given their particular properties by design, and were indestructible.

It seems probable to me that God in the beginning formed matter in solid, massy, hard, impenetrable, movable particles, of such sizes and figures, and with such other properties and in such proportion to space as most conduced to the end for which he formed them; and that these primitive particles being solids are incomparably harder than any porous bodies compounded of them, even so very hard as never to wear or break in pieces, no ordinary power being able to divide what God himself made one in the first creation.[6]

In geology, too, features such as mountains and oceans were assumed to be permanent. The 17th-century English clergyman and naturalist John Ray summed up this position when he said that the works of creation were "the Works created by God at first, and by Him conserved to this day in the same state and Condition in which they were first made."[7]

Furthermore, Ray extended the view of static creation into natural history. He conceived of biological species as the stable units or the created structures of natural history.[8] Ray defined species on the basis of reproductive physiology — all those animals that could interbreed and produce fertile offspring belonged to the same

---

[5] Isaac Newton, *Newton's Philosophy of Nature,* ed. H. S. Thayer (New York: Hafner Publishing House, 1953), pp. 47-48.

[6] Ibid., p. 175 – 76.

[7] Greene, p. 5.

[8] The novelty of Ray's position needs to be stressed, since it is often assumed today that naturalists almost always believed that species were fixed. Naturalists before Ray had little grasp of the species concept. Conway Zirkle, "Species before Darwin," *Proceedings of the American Philosophical Society,* CIII (1959), 636 – 44.

species. The regular processes of nature could account for the continual replenishment of a species through reproduction, but if one traced the history of a species backward through time the breeding population eventually reached the smallest possible number—a single pair. No law of reproduction could account for this pair, Ray thought; it must have been created by God in the beginning. Thus natural history, too, was interpreted as part of a static creation. The Creator in the beginning had established permanent units of nature; they persisted without essential change, except perhaps on a few extraordinary occasions.[9] To them it was unthinkable that God would not preserve all His creatures in the light of the static view of creation. Ray and others denied that animals could become extinct.

The idea of static creation led easily to a view that may loosely be called providential.[10] If the Creator had designed all the permanent units of nature, then they were good. In addition, they were all created to serve His purposes. Thus Thomas Burnet argued that the Biblical deluge was a natural result of the drying of the earth's crust, which then cracked open and allowed underground water to escape. But at the same time it was synchronized with the events of human history, so that it served God's purposes in relation to men. It also accounted for the deserts, mountains, caverns, and general disorder now found on the surface of the earth. It was "the great Art of divine Providence, to adjust the two worlds, human and natural . . . to . . . correspond and fit one another, and especially in their great Crises and Periods." [11] With regard to animals a kind of providentialism also obtained. In his book *The Wisdom of God Manifested in the Works of the Creation* Ray attempted to show how well the structure of animals was adapted to their functions. It seemed clear to Ray that the Creator had foreseen all the contingencies of life and all the purposes that animals were to serve, wisely designing the animals to meet these ends. Each system or structure of an animal contributed to its overall harmony. Thus adaptation of structure to function was evidence of God's wisdom and benevolence, indicating the goodness

---

[9] Ray admitted a few transformations of species. John Ray, *Historia Plantarum,* I, 42.

[10] The view cannot be called a doctrine of providence in any Biblical sense. It draws heavily on Stoic concepts.

[11] Quoted in Greene, p. 41.

of His creation. The correct way to study and understand animals was to interpret their structures and physiological processes in the light of the ends for which they had been designed. In *The Wisdom of God* Ray argued that every species had been given means to defend itself against enemies, "and these Means are so effectual, that notwithstanding all the endeavors of Man and Beast to destroy them, there is not to this day one Species lost of such as are mentioned in Histories, and consequently and undoubtedly neither such as were at first created." [12]

The providentialism expressed by Thomas Burnet in his *Sacred Theory of the Earth* and by John Ray in *The Wisdom of God Manifested in the Works of the Creation* was assimilated into natural theology, especially the kind known as physico-theology, which received its best-known expression in the work of William Paley, archdeacon of Carlisle. Paley's main argument was that the works of nature could not have come into existence except by the hand of a wise, powerful, and benevolent Creator. To buttress his assertion, Paley referred to many cases of adaptation in nature. He described the eye, showing how the clear cornea, the lens, the aqueous humor, the iris, and above all the great flexibility of the eye in adapting itself to changing light intensity and distance made the eye infinitely superior to any man-made optical instrument. Its very existence must therefore presuppose a designer who is greatly superior to the designer of a man-made instrument.[13] Paley adduced other instances of adaptations: some from anatomy, such as the working of various bones, tendons, or muscles; some from the life history and behavior of animals, such as the cooperation of the social insects; some from the particular adaptations of animals to their habitats, such as the proboscis of the elephant or the venom of the rattlesnake. Paley argued that all these had to be wisely designed by the Creator. They could not have resulted from chance any more than a watch could result from chance. In his argumentation Paley supported what I have here called providentialism, since it required divine contrivance and

---

[12] John Ray, *The Wisdom of God as Manifested in the Works of the Creation*, 2d ed. (London: S. Smith, 1692), p. 129.

[13] William Paley, *Natural Theology* (New York: American Tract Society, n. d.), pp. 20 ff.

in some cases supervision for living organisms to fulfill the plans of the Creator.

Paley's *Natural Theology* was widely read, even by Charles Darwin; as student he admired it greatly. Paley's view of the relationship of the Creator to the creation was generally accepted, implying as it did that in creation God took great pains to design all parts of nature wisely, to foresee all possible conditions of life, and to make living creatures capable of fulfilling His plans.

Once accepted, Paley's view and its corollaries about God's foresight and planning in nature became principles for explaining various phenomena in natural history. As more and more became known about living creatures and the history of the earth, puzzling evidence of change in nature cropped up. Naturalists often resorted to the principle of providentialism to explain these aspects of change in nature. For example, John Ray thought that extinction of created species was impossible. During the 18th and early 19th centuries, however, it became clear that extinction had indeed occurred. The task of naturalists was to reconcile this with the idea of the wisdom and goodness of God's plan for the world. James Parkinson in England and Georges Cuvier in France developed similar explanations for the extinction of animals. These naturalists said that extinctions were due to great and sudden catastrophes which enveloped the earth from time to time — catastrophes similar to the flood described in Genesis. But how could such catastrophes be reconciled to God's providence? it was asked. James Parkinson answered with the argument that although the catastrophes extinguished great numbers of plants and animals, they were beneficial because they led to the formation of great beds of coal. Perhaps God's plan was to provide these beds of coal for men, yet not in such a form that men would have them immediately at hand. Perhaps God intended man to search for them to develop thereby his innate powers. Perhaps they were intended "to urge him to change from the savage to the civilized state." [14]

Similarly naturalists were called upon to explain the fossil record. It began to appear that the earth had a long history before the

---

[14] Quoted in Greene, p. 121. See also C. Gillispie, *Genesis and Geology* (New York: Harper & Bros., 1959).

advent of man. Furthermore, the fossil record seemed to show a progression from simple to complex animals. Parkinson and Cuvier invoked a "law of progress." They maintained that God intended the progress that the fossil record revealed. God, they argued, arranged each series of animals as way stations on the road to perfection. The animals were successive variations on a theme that led ultimately to the crown of creation — man himself. Louis Agassiz, the great American naturalist, a pupil of Cuvier, held this view even after Darwin published the *Origin of Species*. Throughout his writings Agassiz talked of the great plan of creation in which the Creator produced successive variations on the main types of animals. Among the vertebrates there was a special kind of progressive plan. From the first appearance of vertebrates in the fossil record to the present there was a gradual, progressive elaboration of the vertebrate plan, leading to ever more flexible and complicated sense organs and body structure. This plan culminated in man, who was "not only the temporal end but also the goal of all development." [15] These examples are perhaps sufficient to show how some naturalists attempted to interpret both extinction and the fossil record in the light of doctrines of creation and providence.

A similar situation obtained with regard to the "species question," that is, the question of the nature and stability of species. Ray had assumed that species never changed substantially. The minor variations between animals of the same type could be ignored, since they were strictly limited in their extent. However, naturalists found during the 18th and 19th centuries more and more evidence that animal species had indeed changed. While Ray had assumed that distinct species of animals could not hybridize and produce fertile offspring, other naturalists showed that the dog, the wolf, and the jackal could interbreed. Either they were all the same species and descended from an original pair, or species were not completely distinct. Each of these alternatives presented difficulties. With the former it was necessary to explain the mechanism by which the original type diverged to produce dog, wolf, and jackal; with the latter taxonomy was thrown into hopeless confusion with no sure criterion by which to distinguish species.

[15] Louis Agassiz, "Notice sur la succession des Poissons," *Annales des sciences naturelles*, Zoologie, 3e série, XLIV (1844), 253.

However, even the facts of hybridization could be reconciled with the idea that God designed and superintended all of creation. The great Swedish taxonomist Carl Linnaeus suggested that perhaps God had not created each species of plants in the beginning after all. Perhaps He had only created one species in each genus and had then allowed them to hybridize with one another, thus eventually producing all the species now known.[16] Several English naturalists suggested that interspecific hybridization in animals occurred in a few species because God foresaw that they would be useful to man and provided a way in which new breeds of domestic animals could be established. Thus the isolated incidents of fertile interspecific hybrids were providential, just as much as the usual sterility between species providentially prevented the mixing of species. The clergyman-naturalist George Herbert allowed more change in species while still assuming a providential design. It accorded with the highest conception of the power of God, he argued, to assume that God had created as few species of plants and animals as possible and wisely designed nature so that all the rest would be produced during the course of time.[17] These examples again are typical of the way in which naturalists reconciled their understanding of nature with a belief in creation and providence, using the latter belief to overcome explanatory difficulties in the former.

Reconciliation of this sort became difficult after the publication of Charles Darwin's *On the Origin of Species* in 1859. The idea of evolution was not new, but Darwin's mastery of the evidence for change raised the idea that species evolve. Darwin advanced evolution from its previous state of ridiculed speculation to the status of an acceptable scientific theory. In so doing he greatly diminished the importance of the concept of static creation that was the framework for much previous biological thinking. More important, Darwin proposed a new explanation for adaptation, an explanation that was at odds with the widely held "providential" view. According to Darwin's theory of natural selection, all animals were in some measure subject to alteration, especially when exposed to altered environ-

[16] Carl von Linné, *A Dissertation on the Sexes of Plants*, trans. James E. Smith (London: George Nicol, 1786), p. 55.

[17] William Herbert, "On Hybridization amongst Vegetables," *Journal of the (Royal) Horticultural Society of London*, s. 1, II (1847), pp. 6 ff.

ments. Offspring produced under these conditions varied in a purely random manner, but the variations were in turn heritable. Some of these variations might improve the animal's adaptation to the environment, while most of them were harmful. The best adapted animals would be able to survive and produce more offspring than those that varied in a less adaptive fashion. Thus the entire population would gradually become better adapted to the environment.

Darwin's theory challenged belief in a providential arrangement of nature because adaptations were seen not as the result of design and foresight on the part of the Creator but as the result of chance processes in nature. Darwin labored hard to show that even such complex features as the eye could have developed by a slow increment of favorable variations. He turned Paley's argument on its head, for Paley had compared the eye to a telescope, showing that both were instruments for the reception of light rays. If the telescope indicated the contrivance and skill of a telescope maker in the designing and arranging of the lenses and aperture to get the best results, the eye by its greater complexity must all the more indicate a designer. Darwin countered:

> It is scarcely possible to avoid comparing the eye to a telescope. We know that this instrument has been perfected by the long continued efforts of the highest human intellects; and we naturally infer that the eye has been formed by a somewhat analogous process. But may not this inference be presumptuous? Have we any right to assume that the Creator works by intellectual powers like those of man? If we must compare the eye to an optical instrument, we ought in imagination to take a thick layer of transparent tissue, with a nerve sensitive to light beneath, and then suppose every part of this layer to be continually changing slowly in density, so as to separate into layers of different densities and thicknesses, placed at different distances from each other, and with the surfaces of each layer slowly changing in form. Then a power watching and selecting the variation which produces a distinct image. Then this be multiplied a million times ... and may we not believe that a living optical instrument might thus be formed as superior to one of glass as the works of the Creator are to those of man? [18]

Furthermore, Darwin argued that in animals of various sorts all

[18] Charles Darwin, *On the Origin of Species,* facsimile of the first edition (Cambridge: Belknap Press, 1959), 188–89.

kinds of different eyes were found, some considerably better than others. Also every part of the eye had variations. He believed it was possible to produce even an eye by the process of random variation and selection. He concluded this was the only way in which it could be produced.

To those who attempted to minimize natural selection and to assume that some directive agency or wise designer lay behind the evolutionary process, Darwin insisted that natural selection was based on a chance process. If God provided the variations that were selected, what about those that were destroyed? It seemed so wasteful and inefficient a way to proceed that Darwin could not see a providential hand behind it. How could God produce millions of individuals and allow only a few to survive? How could there be so much suffering? "What a book a devil's chaplain might write on the clumsy, wasteful, blundering, low, and horribly cruel works of nature!" Darwin wrote.

> There seems to me too much misery in the world. I cannot persuade myself that a beneficent and omnipotent God would have designedly created the Ichneumonidae with the express intention of their feeding within the living bodies of caterpillars, or that a cat should play with mice. Not believing this, I see no necessity in the belief that the eye was expressly designed. On the other hand, I cannot anyhow be contented to view this wonderful universe, and especially the nature of man, and to conclude that everything is the result of brute force. I am inclined to look at everything as resulting from designed laws, with the details, whether good or bad, left to the working out of what we may call chance. Not that this notion *at all* satisfies me. I feel most deeply that the whole subject is too profound for the human intellect. A dog might as well speculate on the mind of Newton. Let each man hope and believe what he can.[19]

Elsewhere Darwin wrote:

> The old argument of design in nature, as given by Paley, which formerly seemed to me so conclusive, fails, now that the law of natural selection has been discovered. There seems to be no more design in the variability of organic beings and in the action of natural selection than in the course which the wind blows.[20]

---

[19] Quoted in John Greene, "Darwin and Religion," *European Intellectual History Since Darwin and Marx*, ed. W. W. Wagar (New York: Harper, 1966), p. 22.

[20] Darwin, *Autobiography*, p. 87.

Thus Darwin could see no design in adaptation; whether some larger design lay behind the random action of natural selection, he could only confess ignorance.

In Darwin's work, then, designed adaptation was banished. There was only the operation of inexorable laws. Slowly environments changed. Conditions became dryer or wetter. Continents rose and sank. Slowly animals changed with the environments, but in the process the vast majority perished. Only a few of the species alive today, Darwin predicted, would survive to reproduce offspring a million years hence. Yet there was still something more. Deep in his heart Darwin believed that there was a direction in which evolution was leading. There was progress. Behind natural selection, as Darwin sometimes pictured it, there stood Nature, almost personalized Nature that never faltered or made a mistake, Nature that unerringly picked out the favorable variations. The history of a species was therefore a history of continual improvement.

> We can so far take a prophetic glance into futurity as to foretell that it will be the common and widely spread species, belonging to the larger and dominant groups, which will ultimately prevail and procreate new and dominant species. As all the living forms of life are the lineal descendants of those which lived long before the Silurian epoch, we may feel certain that the ordinary succession by generation has never once been broken, and that no cataclysm has desolated the whole world. Hence we may look with some confidence to a secure future of equally inappreciable length. And as natural selection worked solely by and for the good of each being, all corporeal and mental endowment will tend to progress towards perfection.[21]

Although Darwin denied purpose in nature when he talked about adaptation, he could not banish progress entirely. The view that all endowments would tend toward perfection gave him support when he came to talk about the evolution of man.

In the *Origin of Species* Darwin resolved to avoid the whole subject of the origin of man, since it was "so surrounded with prejudices."[22] He merely said that by means of the evolutionary

---

[21] Darwin, *Origin*, p. 489.

[22] Darwin, *Life and Letters of Charles Darwin*, I, 487.

theory "light would be shed on the origin of man and his history." [23] Yet in 1871 Darwin's *Descent of Man* appeared. In this work Darwin applied his theory of natural selection to the question of the origin of the human race. Although he gave considerable weight to sexual selection as a mechanism of change in man, Darwin argued that natural selection was still the dominant mechanism by which a brutelike ancestor had become man:

> Our early semi-human progenitors would not have practiced infanticide or polyandry. . . . There would have been no prudential restraint from marriage . . . . Hence the progenitors of man would have tended to increase rapidly; but checks of some kind, either periodical or constant, must have kept down their numbers, even more severely than with existing savages . . . . Beneficial variations of all kinds will thus, either occasionally or habitually, have been preserved, and injurious [sic] eliminated. [24]

The same kind of random process that had produced new species of animals was responsible for the origin of man. There were no higher purposes at work. This was antiprovidentialism with a vengeance; it countered the dominant patterns of Western thought about man and his society. If Darwinism were true, one could hardly speak of man as a creature of God, much less speak of God's providential care of him.

Yet there was a contradiction in Darwin's thought. On the one hand, he seemed to believe that human life was meant to be a struggle in which the strong survived and the weak perished. He argued that no lessening of the severity of the struggle should be allowed, for improvement could not occur unless natural selection operated. On the other hand, Darwin said that the progressive improvement in the human race included refinement in morality, an ethic of cooperation, and sympathy for all men instead of ruthless competition. He believed that this "higher morality" developed as a matter of course in the process of evolution. Such a morality would have selective value, Darwin believed, and groups in which it flourished would survive, leading to further progress in moral and cultural sensibilities.

---

[23] Darwin, *Origin*, p. 488.

[24] Quoted in Greene, *Death of Adam*, p. 323.

A tribe including many members who, from possessing a high degree of the spirit of patriotism, fidelity, obedience, courage, and sympathy, were always ready to aid one another, and to sacrifice themselves for the common good, would be victorious over most other tribes; and this would be natural selection. At all times throughout the world tribes have supplanted other tribes; and as morality is one important element in their success, the standard of morality and the number of well-endowed men will thus everywhere tend to rise and increase.[25]

Yet Darwin did not bring evidence for this. Indeed as an explanation of actual events it seems very naive.[26] Belief in the inevitable progress of man's moral and spiritual values could hardly be derived from the principles of evolution by natural selection, try as Darwin might. He accepted it without realizing the difficulties. For him it was a sort of providentialism, though he would not have admitted it. Darwin doubted the powers of man to answer the deepest questions of mankind because of his lowly origin.

With me the horrid doubt always arises whether the convictions of man's mind, which has been developed from the mind of the lower animals, are of any value or at all trustworthy. Would any one trust the convictions of a monkey's mind, if there are any convictions in such a mind?[27]

He continued in his conviction of inevitable progress. At some future date man would be far advanced over his present condition. Darwin was still steeped in the larger Christian view that he had known from his youth. Behind the flux of secondary causes there must be some first principle, which insured that the world progressed and above all that man progressed.

Between the two contradictory principles exemplified in Darwin's work later biological work has oscillated. Either nature is blind, without design and subject only to stochastic laws, or some law of progress lies behind it, giving at least the possibility of a transcendent reality.

---

[25] Darwin, *Descent of Man*, p. 132.

[26] One would hardly argue that the Europeans displaced the North American Indians because of their high degree of patriotism, etc.

[27] Darwin, *Life and Letters*, I, 285.

Darwin's work posed a serious challenge to those biologists who wished to interpret nature as revealing God's design and providential care of organisms. Some naturalists rejected evolution by natural selection because it was simply incompatible with all they believed about nature.[28] The well-known American botanist Asa Gray, on the other hand, attempted to reconcile evolution by natural selection with a belief in traditional natural theology—a belief that included providentialism. Gray himself was not immediately ready to grant that Darwin's evolutionary theory was fully correct, but he was willing to grant it at least a provisional status as a plausible scientific theory. He was therefore concerned to show that evolution, if it were demonstrated, did not contradict natural theology. Everything ultimately remained the same, he argued.

> The whole argument in natural theology proceeds upon the ground that the inference for a final cause of the structure of the hand and of the valves in the veins is just as valid now, in individuals produced through natural generation, as it would have been in the case of the first man, supernaturally created. Why not, then, just as good even on the supposition of the descent of man from chimpanzees and gorillas, since those animals possess these same contrivances? [29]

Darwinism required chance to operate, it was argued; thus it was incompatible with design. Not so, replied Gray. Of course, there were accidental aspects of nature, but this did not negate God's design that underlay nature. What is more accidental, he asked, than the accumulation of vegetable matter in a peat bog and its transformation into coal? Yet this does not prove that the coal beds were not stored up for man's benefit.[30] Furthermore, Gray argued, though selection of the best adapted animals was scientifically explicable, variation was not. The immediate cause of variations might well be God's activity. Even if the origin of variations could

---

[28] Louis Agassiz is perhaps the best-known example of this. E. Lurie, *Louis Agassiz: A Life in Science* (Chicago: University of Chicago Press, 1960), pp. 252 ff. Another example is Richard Owen. Roy Macleod, "Evolutionism and Richard Owen," *Isis*, LVI (1965), 259–80.

[29] Asa Gray, *Darwiniana*, ed. A. Hunter Dupree (Cambridge: Belknap Press, 1963), p. 123.

[30] Ibid., p. 127.

someday be explained in a scientific way, the ultimate origin of things was still unanswered.

> So the real question we come to is as to the way in which we are to conceive intelligent and efficient cause to be exerted, and upon what exerted. Are we bound to suppose efficient cause in all cases exerted upon nothing to evoke something into existence — and this thousands of times repeated, when a slight change in details would make all the difference between successive species? Why may not the new species, or some of them, be designed diversifications of the old? [31]

Gray further argued that the absence of intermediate forms between species was difficult to explain. Perhaps that too indicated providential design in the diversification of species. [32]

Gray's general argument was plausible, but its effect was small. Darwin and Thomas Henry Huxley refused to accept it, and their view for the most part carried the day. For one thing, Gray's subsidiary arguments about designed variation and the absence of intermediate forms were seriously challenged as the mechanism of variation became known. At the end of the century Robert Cecil, the Marquis of Salisbury, complained in a presidential address before the British Association for the Advancement of Science that many naturalists accepted natural selection as the means of explaining adaptation simply because without it they would have no other theory except design, which was repugnant to them.

> Professor Weismann adds another reason for his belief in natural selection which is certainly characteristic of the time in which we live. 'It is inconceivable,' he says, 'that there should be another principle capable of explaining the adaptation of organisms without assuming the help of a principle of design.' The whirligig of time assuredly brings its revenges. Time was, not very long ago, when the belief in creative design was supreme. Even those who were sapping its authority were wont to pay it formal homage, fearing to shock public conscience by denying it. Now the revolution is so complete that a great philosopher uses it as a *reductio ad absurdum*, and prefers to believe that which can neither be demonstrated in detail, or imagined, rather than run the slightest risk of such a heresy. [33]

---

[31] Ibid., pp. 130–31.

[32] Ibid., p. 121.

[33] Robert Arthur Talbot Gascoyne-Cecil, Marquis of Salisbury, "Presidential Address," *Victorian Science* (New York: Doubleday & Co., Anchor Books, 1970), p. 367.

Cecil himself preferred to take a position similar to Asa Gray's, but he found the tide of opinion running strongly against him.

As Loren Eiseley says: "Darwin did not destroy the argument from design. He destroyed only the watchmaker and the watch. . . . Only a *certain type of design argument* had been eliminated by Darwin, namely, the finalistic one." [34] Gray and Salisbury were correct in pointing this out. Yet their voices went largely unheeded. It was psychologically difficult for Darwin and Huxley to slough off Paley without concluding that there was no design in nature. The majority of biologists followed them rather than Gray or Salisbury.[35]

Huxley followed Darwin in asserting that the world of biology gave no evidences of divine providence. Like Darwin, Huxley felt no need to invoke a nonmaterial cause to account for the evolution of human mental facilities; natural selection was sufficient. Nor could it be asserted that a benevolent deity cared for his creatures. Evolution involved too much imperfection, too much extinction, and too much suffering for that. It was not enough to argue that there was some good in all suffering and evil in nature, for this did "not help us see why the immense multitude of irresponsible sentient beings which cannot profit by such discipline should suffer." [36] However, Huxley hastened to absolve Darwin from the charge that the universe ran simply by chance. Rather it was the result of causal laws that held without exception.

> We have come to look upon the present as the child of the past and as the parent of the future; and, as we have excluded chance from a place in the universe, so we ignore, even as a possibility the notion of any interference with the order of Nature.[37]

In a way, there was a sense in which a plan remained. Everything followed from the original conditions of the universe.

---

[34] Loren Eiseley, *Darwin's Century* (Garden City: Doubleday & Co., Anchor Books, 1961), p. 197.

[35] While few biologists have attempted to retain Gray's view, there have been several who have attempted to restate the argument from design using new biological information, esp. W. H. Thorpe, *Science, Man and Morals* (Ithaca: Cornell University Press, 1966).

[36] T. H. Huxley, *Collected Essays*, IX, 142.

[37] Ibid., IV, 47—48.

The whole world, living and not living, is the result of the mutual interaction, according to definite laws, of the forces possessed by the molecules of which the primitive nebulosity of the universe was composed. If this be true, it is no less certain that the existing world lay potentially in the cosmic vapour, and that a sufficient intelligence could, from a knowledge of the properties of the molecules of that vapour, have predicted, say the state of the fauna of Britain in 1869, with as much certainty as one can say what will happen to the vapour of the breath on a cold winter's day . . . .[38]

But who could know what the original conditions were, or what they implied about ultimate questions? Man who sees the order which pervades the seeming disorder of the world, who sees the drama of evolution unfolding before his eyes, learns in his heart of hearts "the lesson that the foundation of morality is to have done, once and for all, with lying; to give up pretending to believe that for which there is no evidence, and repeating unintelligible propositions about things beyond the possibility of knowledge." [39] Religious questions, Huxley concluded, could not be answered by the study of nature. He was content to let them rest unanswered.

Turning from biologists of the 19th century to those of the 20th, we see that Darwin and T. H. Huxley's general position has been widely followed. Julian Huxley argues that the development of science has rendered obsolete traditional theistic religions such as Christianity. The evolutionary theory explains the nature of the world without recourse to a personal God who has designed or who preserves the world.

Evolutionary man can no longer take refuge from his loneliness by creeping for shelter into the arms of a divinized father figure — a figure whom he has himself created, nor escape from the responsibility of making decisions by sheltering under the umbrella of Divine Authority, nor absolve himself from the hard task of meeting his present problems and planning his future by relying on the will of an omniscient but unfortunately inscrutable Providence.[40]

---

[38] T. H. Huxley, *Life and Letters,* I, 544 — 45.

[39] T. H. Huxley, *Collected Essays,* IX, 146.

[40] Julian Huxley, *Essays of a Humanist,* p. 79.

Huxley further says:

> In the evolutionary pattern of thought there is no longer either need or room for the supernatural. The earth was not created; it evolved. So did all the animals and plants that inhabit it, including our human selves, mind and soul as well as brain and body.[41]

For Huxley, there is no general purpose in nature. "The purpose that many philosophers and theologians like to think that they can discern in nature, and that Archdeacon Paley believed he had conclusively demonstrated, turns out to be merely an apparent purpose, the result of the wholly non-purposive working of natural selection." [42]

Yet if Huxley does not see purpose in nature, he does see a direction and progress. The history of life has been a history of the improvement of living substance, its ever-increasing variety and efficiency, its acquiring new properties, and organizing new forms. For Huxley life is constantly improving as it meets the challenge of the environment.

> Each new deployment, after steadily advancing over its new terrain, comes to an impasse. There is sometimes a path out of the impasse, but it is generally a devious one; it is through its twists and turns that life finds its way into a new field of maneuver; and this marks the beginning of another distinct step in progress.[43]

The most recent step in this progress has been the appearance of man himself. With this stage mere biological evolution has come to an end. Life has become self-conscious, and in so doing it has moved into the realm of psycho-social evolution. Since man is conscious of the whole evolutionary process, he can supply the purpose that has been lacking in evolution heretofore. The direction of the world that once rested in God's hands, Huxley now places squarely in the hand of man. Man is the one who will determine what the future of evolution will be.

> The broad outlines of the new evolutionary picture of ultimates are beginning to be clearly visible. Man's destiny is to be the sole

[41] Ibid., p. 78.

[42] Ibid., p. 50—51.

[43] J. Huxley, *Evolution in Action*, p. 101.

agent for the future evolution of this planet. He is the highest dominant type to be produced by over two and a half billion years of the slow biological improvement effected by the blind opportunistic workings of natural selection; if he does not destroy himself, he has at least an equal stretch of evolutionary time before him to exercise his agency.[44]

As in the thought of Charles Darwin, so in Julian Huxley's thought there is a fundamental contradiction. Nature is blind, opportunistic, and devoid of purpose. Not only does the scientific understanding of the world give no evidence for any transcendent God who directs the world process, in reality it tends to refute such a view. Yet at the same time Huxley continues to use words like progress, improvement, evolutionary advance. How can there be progress if there is no plan or goal? Perhaps these are meaningless metaphors that Huxley can do without, but the very fact that these or similar words are also used by others seems to indicate that they are important, indeed essential, to Huxley's larger outlook, regardless of the fact that they are at odds with his strictly biological outlook.

Most significant is Huxley's view of man. While the evolutionary theory strictly interpreted apparently does not demonstrate that man is the species on whom the evolutionary future depends, Huxley and most other evolutionary biologists assert that he is. "Man's destiny is to become the sole agent of evolution on this planet."[45] Huxley is not alone in this view of man. Theodosius Dobzhansky writes: "Judged by any reasonable criteria, man represents the highest, most progressible, and most successful product of organic evolution . . . . Most remarkable of all, he is now in the process of acquiring knowledge which may permit him, if he so chooses, to control his own evolution."[46] George Gaylord Simpson also expresses the attitude that future evolution is in the hands of man, although like Dobzhansky he recognizes that man may choose not to advance.

> Man has risen, not fallen. He can choose to develop his capacities as the highest animal and to try to rise still farther, or he can

---

[44] J. Huxley, *Essays of a Humanist,* p. 77.

[45] Ibid., p. 32.

[46] T. Dobzhansky, *The Biological Basis of Human Freedom* (New York: Columbia Univ. Press, 1960), p. 87–88.

choose otherwise. The choice is his responsibility, and his alone . . . . Evolution has no purpose; man must supply this for himself . . . .[47]

Huxley, Dobzhansky, and Simpson all agree that evolution is blind; yet somehow it produces men who are the highest types of living creature, who have purposes, and who can control the future of evolution. This seems to be a paradox. It appears that a transfer has taken place in biological thought similar to one that occurred in the 17th century in the physical realm. During the 17th century the attributes of God such as eternity, immutability, and infinity were successively transferred from God to the cosmos. So in the biological realm have the elements of design and purpose insofar as they still exist been transferred from God to the biological process and above all to man. According to many biologists man is both the goal and the director of biological evolution.

The distinguished Jesuit paleontologist Pierre Teilhard de Chardin addressed himself to the widely held idea that the course of evolution does indeed exhibit some sort of progress or direction with man as its goal. Chardin viewed evolution as an ascent of matter toward consciousness. The line of advance is evident in the increasing "complexification" of the nervous system. Human evolution is the latest phase of this general development; it will culminate in the union of all consciousness in the "Omega point," which is both the directing principle and the goal of the world process.[48]

Chardin's work is important for several reasons, not the least of which is that it is an attempt to reconcile Catholic doctrine with the evolutionary theory. How well it will fare in this regard remains to be seen.[49] Will it provide philosophical or theological justification for the use of metaphors such as *progress* and *improvement*, together with the assertion that man's destiny is to carry forward evolution in

---

[47] G. G. Simpson, *Biology and Man* (New York: Harcourt, Brace & World, 1969), p. 148.

[48] Teilhard's views are expressed chiefly in *The Phenomenon of Man.*

[49] It has been both praised and condemned in Catholic circles. Bruno de Solages, "Christianity and Evolution," *Cross Currents,* I (Summer 1951), 35 ff., is favorable; R. Nogar, "The Paradox of the Phenomenon," *Dominicana,* XLV (Fall 1960), 248–49, dismisses it.

the psycho-social or psycho-biological realm? The answer seems to be that it will not. While refraining from much traditional theological terminology, Teilhard clearly does have theological bases that determine his exposition of evolutionary history and direction. Evolutionary biologists generally have not found this palatable. They see his work as primarily theological and not biological. Julian Huxley speaks approvingly of many of Chardin's ideas in the introduction to *The Phenomenon of Man*, trying in several cases to show how they parallel his own, but he is baffled and confused by Chardin's attempt to introduce any specifically theological content into his vision.[50] But one may still ask Huxley to provide a justification for his own view of progress. Simpson is critical of Teilhard on slightly different grounds. He returns to the stricter interpretation of biological evolution as blind, opportunistic, and purposeless, then criticizes Teilhard for espousing orthogenesis and failing to show exactly how it works. In the end Simpson dismisses Teilhard's work as sheer mysticism.[51] Of course, resorting to this stance is a convenient way for Simpson to dismiss Teilhard, but it throws into sharper focus his own belief that man, if he wills, can control his own destiny. This still remains unsupported by the data of biological evolution.

It appears that Teilhard's attempt to reconcile evolution and theology, however useful it may be to theologians or to Christians generally, will not convince evolutionary biologists that the facts of their discipline imply the working of God, much less of His providence over life. Nor is there any other work by a biologist, it seems, that promises to do this.[52]

What meaning does all this have for a modern man who looks for some evidence of God's providence? Understanding the history of providentialism in biology may prevent him from looking for God's providence in the wrong place. The 17th- and 18th-century

---

[50] J. Huxley, *Essays of a Humanist*, pp. 208–9

[51] G. G. Simpson, *This View of Life*, (New York: Harcourt, Brace & World, 1964), pp. 231 f.

[52] Various theologians have developed useful ways of reconciling theology and the evolutionary theory. Jürgen Hübner, *Theologie und biologische Entwicklungslehre* (Munich: Verlag C. H. Beck, 1966), describes several. These attempts have not restored the "providential" element to biology, however.

naturalists used the idea of providence to explain adaptation in animals without examining the idea thoroughly. This is not surprising, for the idea was sufficient for the biological information that they knew. The characteristic idea that they used, namely, that God foresaw all the conditions of life, directly designed animals to meet them, and then so regulated the processes of nature as to preserve the animals, drew partly on the Biblical accounts of creation, literally interpreted, but equally or perhaps more so on Stoic concepts of providence that had been assimilated into the world view of the 17th century. The difficulty with the "providential" view in biology was that it could be used to explain everything and therefore nothing. In the instance of the species question, for example, some scientists could explain why interspecific hybrids were sterile by referring it to the providential design of the Creator that prevented the mixing of species. But other naturalists could explain why some interspecific hybrids were fertile by referring it to God's providential design for the good of man.

With its explanation of adaptation as the result of natural selection the evolutionary theory made considerable advance as a scientific theory and ultimately replaced the providential explanation of adaptation. The result was that the argument found in physico-theology—the argument that went from adaptation to a design to a designer—was challenged and shown to be inadequate.

Evolutionary biology, however, has not been able to find complete justification for the idea of progress in evolution or the idea that man is either the goal or is destined to be the director of evolution. These widely held ideas remain unintegrated with specifically biological concepts.

The fact that adaptation in animals can no longer be used as a direct argument for the providence of God is good, since it forces a reexamination of the doctrine that can once again emphasize Biblical and theological concerns and sweep away a doctrine of providence that rests on Stoic philosophy or scientific assertions. It calls for Christians to be reminded that knowledge of the way God deals with man and with the world must be derived from the ways He reveals Himself in the Word, not in nature itself. It may then be possible to turn away from an implicit assumption in most scientists' thinking about God and nature since the 17th century, namely, that nature is to reveal the goodness or benevolence of God. If nature does not reveal this, the argument has gone; it demonstrates the opposite— that there is no God. Perhaps reexamination of the Biblical data will suggest that nature reveals only the *Deus absconditus*, not the God who so loved the world that He sent His Son.

A further implication of contemporary evolutionary biology for the doctrine of providence lies in the continued use of the metaphors of progress, improvement, and similar words, together with the assertion that evolution culminates in man, who alone is capable of directing evolution to a higher level. These ideas are difficult, if not impossible, to derive directly from the theory of evolution by natural selection. Christians are justified in asking the questions: What if man destroys himself? What of evolutionary progress then? What in the evolutionary theory indicates that man is not merely an aberrant species with an overspecialized brain whose destiny is to disappear as other dominant forms have disappeared in the past? These are not idle questions, for more and more biologists today are reckoning seriously with the real possibility that man may not be able to control himself and his society and may in fact destroy himself in the relatively near future. But evolutionary biology, taken strictly, cannot produce humanly satisfying answers to these questions. Its principles permit the conclusion that man is only another species, subject to extinction. All his hopes and aspirations will have been no more than a cruel hoax of nature. The answers to the questions of man's future are not grounded in the study of nature, however much that may tell us about our world and ourselves. As Paul Holmer points out, these answers are grounded in religious concepts, which are radically different from scientific ones; the two can be mixed to gain a superficial synthesis only at the cost of a deeper confusion.[53] Evolutionary biology need not shake the modern Christian's conviction that God is at work in every aspect of the world's operation any more than understanding of reproductive physiology will shake his confession, "I believe that God made me and all creatures."

Evolutionary biologists have correctly pointed out that man has come to know far more about himself and his world than many

---

[53] Paul Holmer, "Evolution and Being Faithful," *Changing Man: The Threat and the Promise,* ed. Kyle Haselden and Philip Hefner (New York: Doubleday and Co., 1969), pp. 156–67.

previous generations ever thought possible. With that knowledge has inevitably come power—power to change and direct the course of human history and in a sense even human nature. To the question, How shall this power be used? the Christian also makes a response. On the one hand, his belief in providence, that God ultimately directs the world and human history, gives him the confidence that men should use what God has permitted them to learn in order to improve the quality of human life. At the same time he recognizes that God has given into man's hand the power to know and do evil as well as good. Power does corrupt; on this Biblical revelation and human history agree. If the past is any guide to the future, the possibilities are real that men may use their knowledge to enslave themselves rather than to free themselves. Rather than depressing the modern Christian man, however, this real possibility only spurs him on to the highest human actions as he participates in the "mystery of God's purpose, the hidden plan He so kindly made in Christ from the beginning . . . that He would bring everything together under Christ as Head." (Eph. 1:9-10)